Origami Book For Kids

*70 Amazing Paper Folding Projects
With Simple Step-By-Step
Video Instructions*

InterWorld Entertainment

© Copyright - All rights reserved.

The content contained within this book may not be reproduced, duplicated or transmitted without direct written permission from the author or the publisher. Under no circumstances will any blame or legal responsibility be held against the publisher, or author, for any damages, reparation, or monetary loss due to the information contained within this book, either directly or indirectly.

Legal Notice:

This book is copyright protected. It is only for personal use. You cannot amend, distribute, sell, use, quote or paraphrase any part, or the content within this book, without the consent of the author or publisher.

Disclaimer Notice:

Please note the information contained within this document is for educational and entertainment purposes only. All effort has been executed to present accurate, up to date, reliable, complete information. No warranties of any kind are declared or implied. Readers acknowledge that the author is not engaged in the rendering of legal, financial, medical or professional advice. The content within this book has been derived from various sources. Please consult a licensed professional before attempting any techniques outlined in this book.

By reading this document, the reader agrees that under no circumstances is the author responsible for any losses, direct or indirect, that are incurred as a result of the use of the information contained within this document, including, but not limited to, errors, omissions, or inaccuracies.

Symbols

Lines

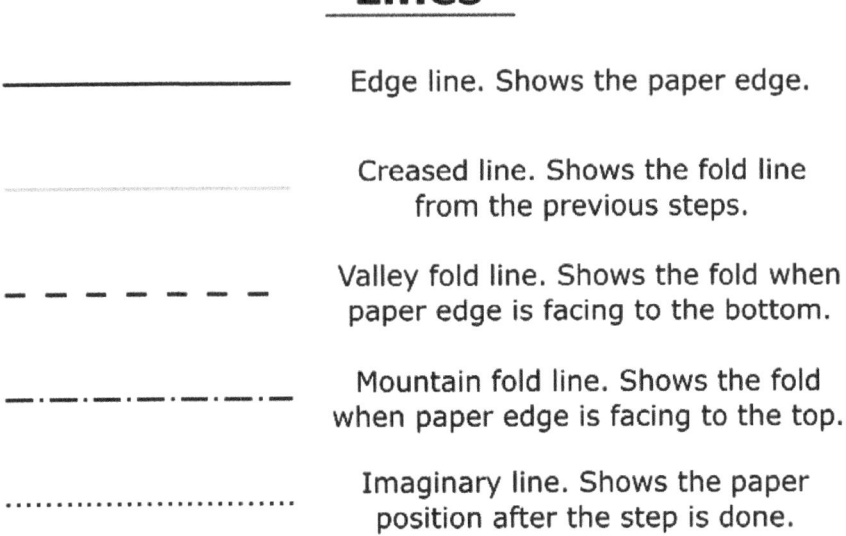

———————————— Edge line. Shows the paper edge.

———————————— Creased line. Shows the fold line from the previous steps.

— — — — — — — Valley fold line. Shows the fold when paper edge is facing to the bottom.

—·—·—·—·—·—·— Mountain fold line. Shows the fold when paper edge is facing to the top.

·························· Imaginary line. Shows the paper position after the step is done.

Arrows

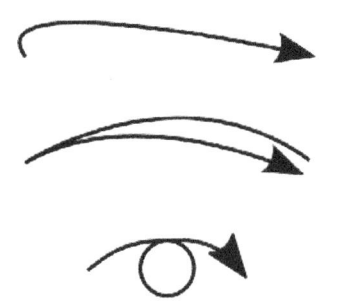

Direction arrow. Shows the direction to which paper will be folded.

Fold and unfold arrow. Shows that only creased line needs to be done.

Turn over arrow. Indicates that model should be turn over for futher steps.

Squash arrow. Shows that paper has to be pushed down.

Rotation arrow. Shows the direction to which model should be rotated.

Folds

Valley Fold

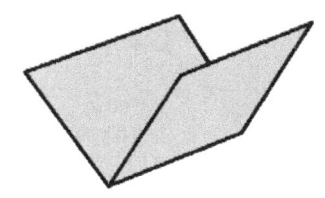

Folding the sides up while making the fold edge go down. Paper forms figure similar to the valley.

Mountain Fold

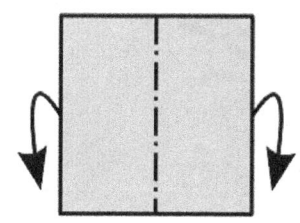

Folding the sides down while making the fold edge go up. Paper forms figure similar to the mountain.

Squash Fold

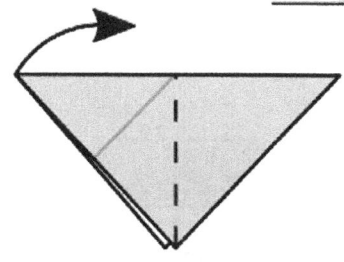

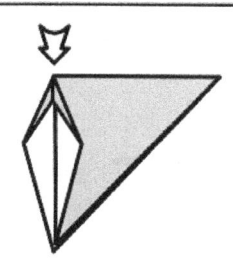

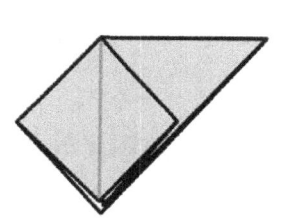

Fold containing two steps. First the corner is folded vertically up and then it is pushed down using already precreased lines.

Model List

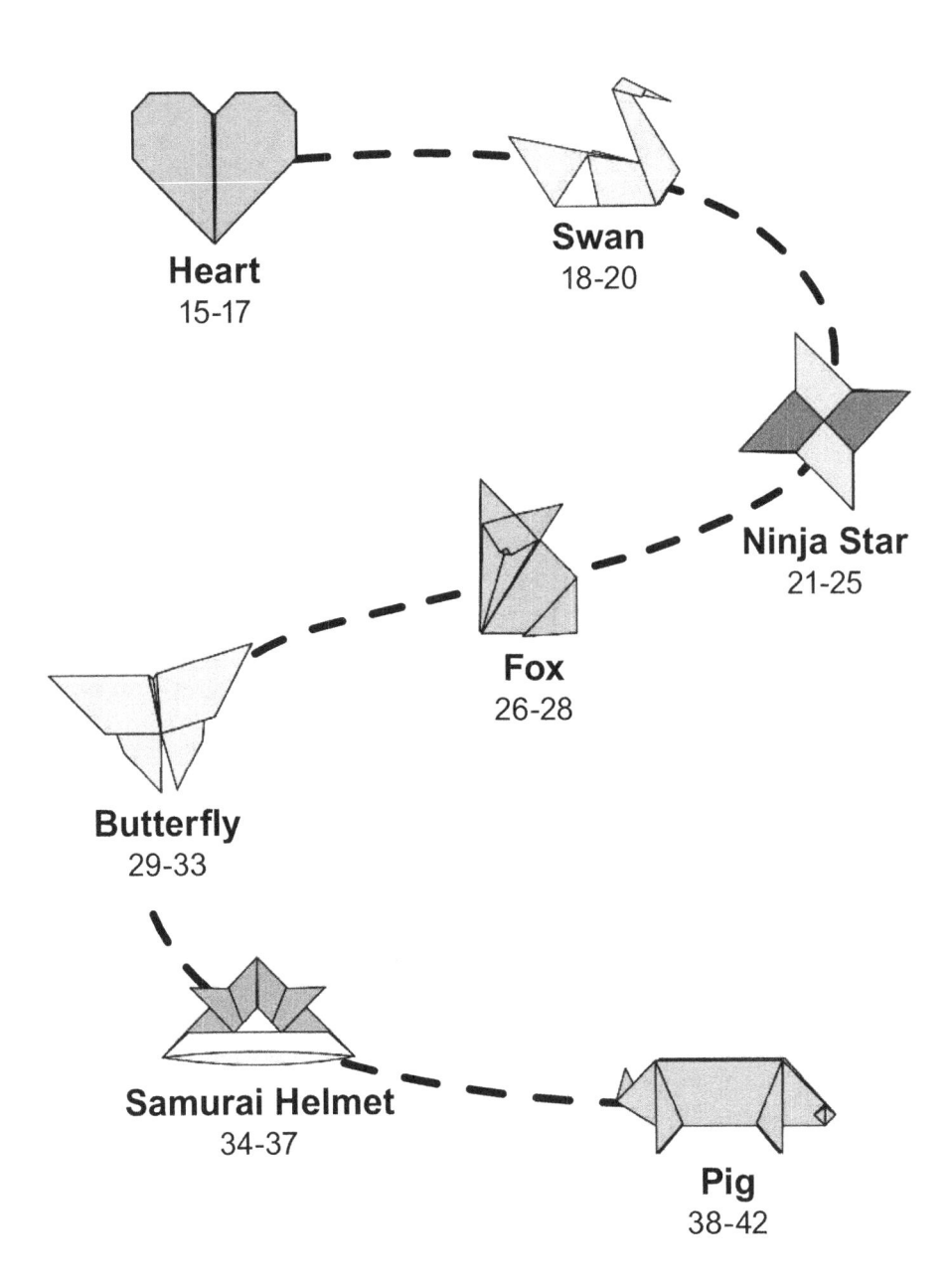

Heart
15-17

Swan
18-20

Ninja Star
21-25

Fox
26-28

Butterfly
29-33

Samurai Helmet
34-37

Pig
38-42

Cicade
43-46

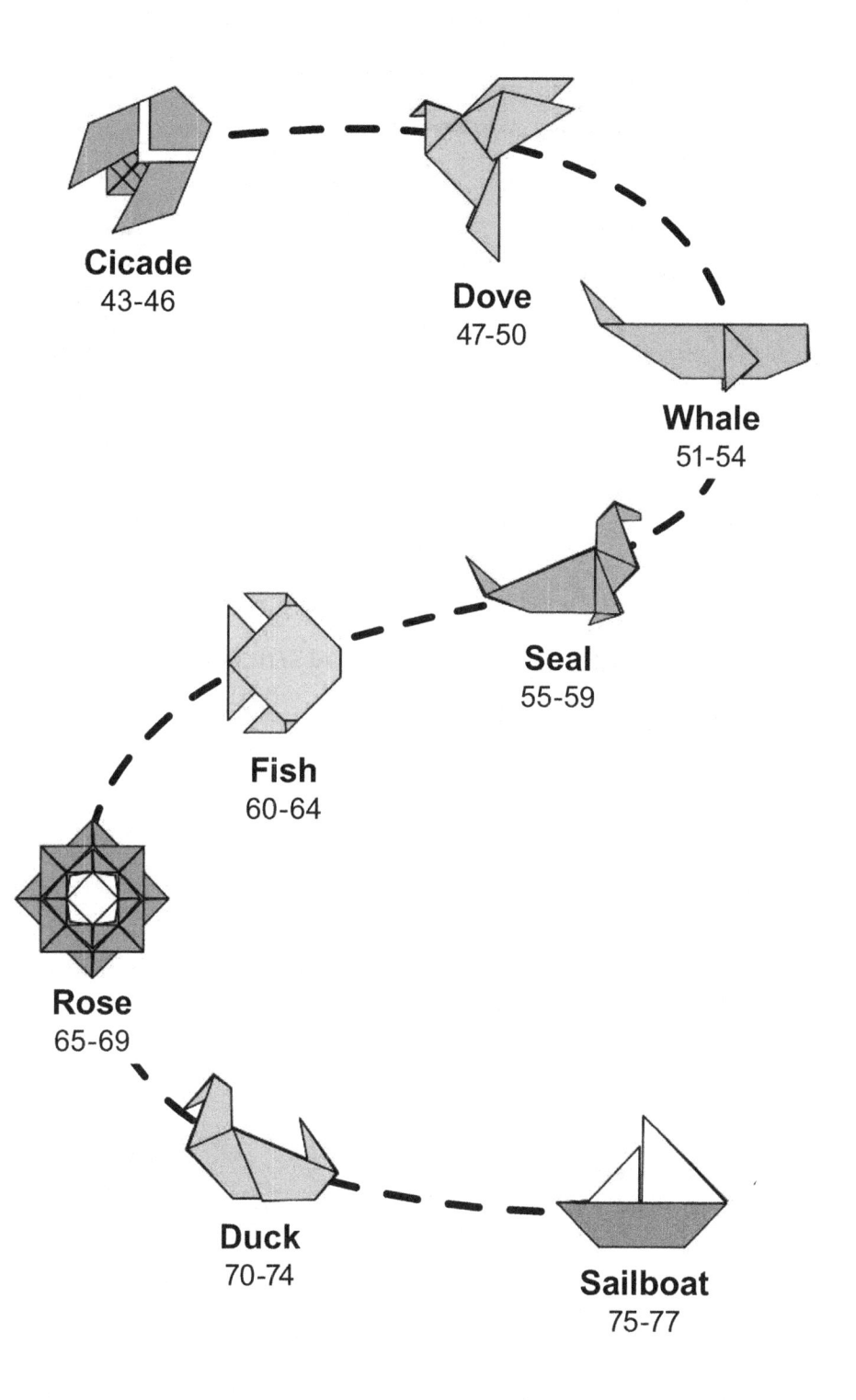

Dove
47-50

Whale
51-54

Seal
55-59

Fish
60-64

Rose
65-69

Duck
70-74

Sailboat
75-77

Parrot
78-81

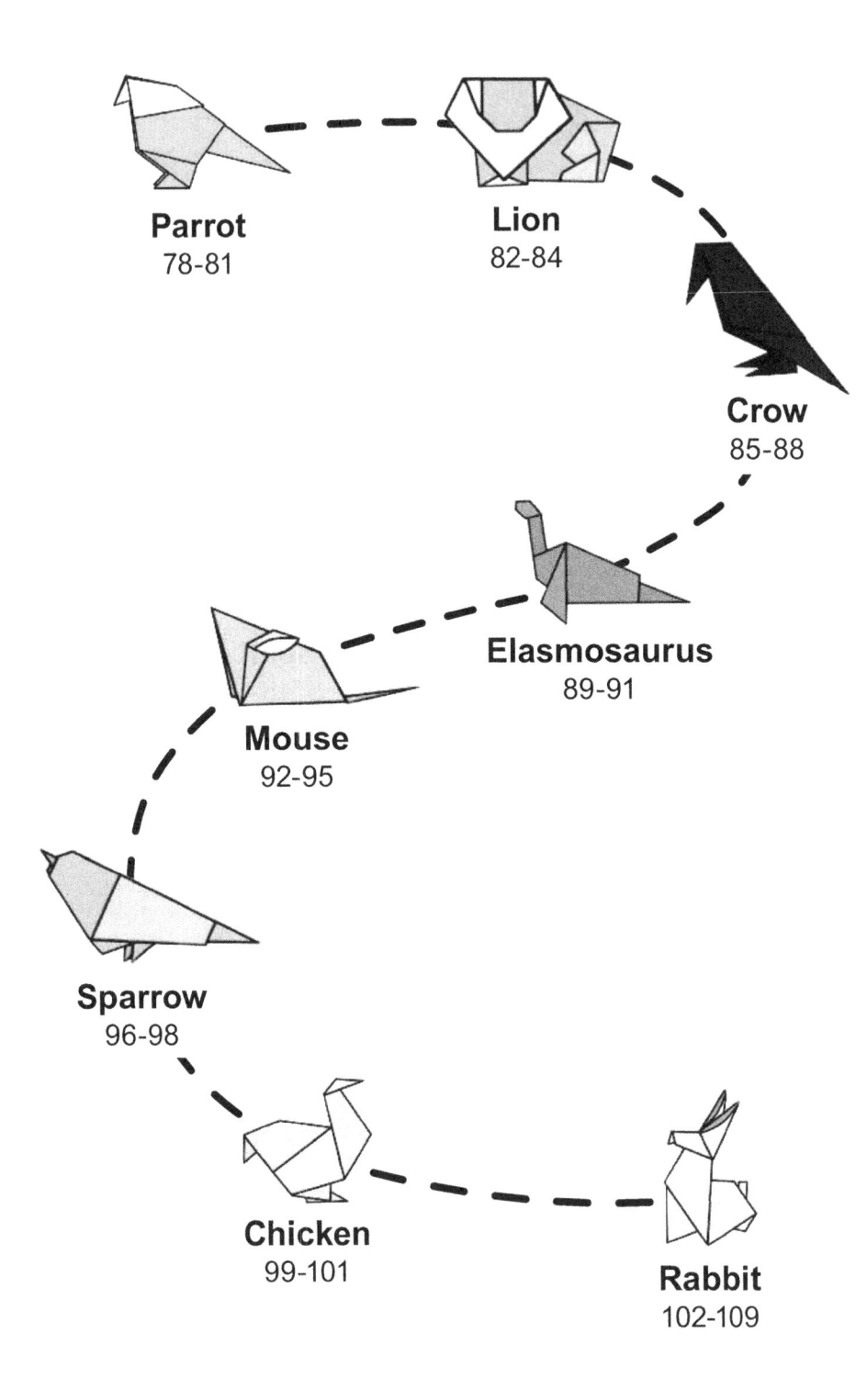

Lion
82-84

Crow
85-88

Elasmosaurus
89-91

Mouse
92-95

Sparrow
96-98

Chicken
99-101

Rabbit
102-109

Sea Horse
110-113

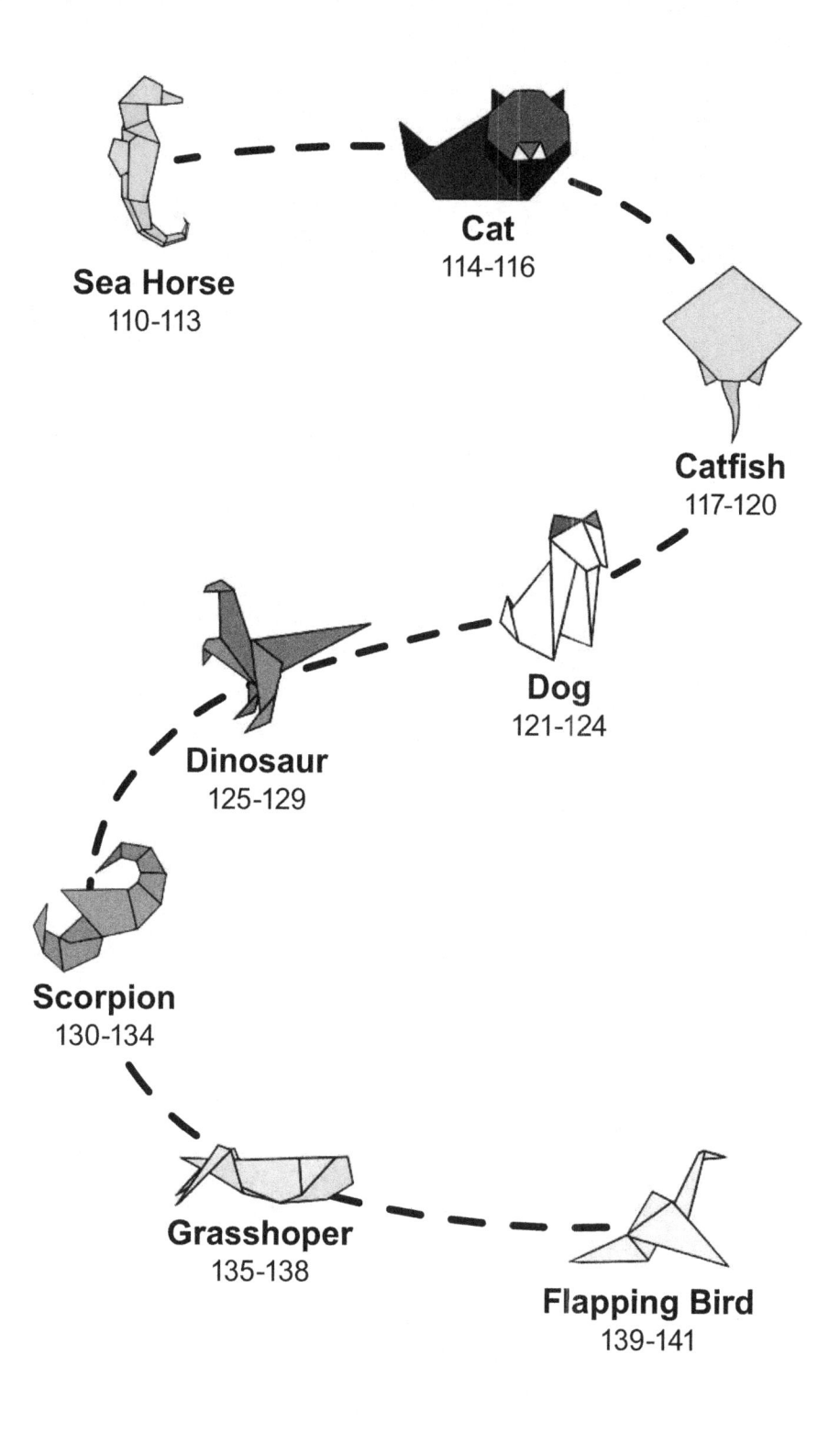

Cat
114-116

Catfish
117-120

Dog
121-124

Dinosaur
125-129

Scorpion
130-134

Grasshoper
135-138

Flapping Bird
139-141

Elephant
142-144

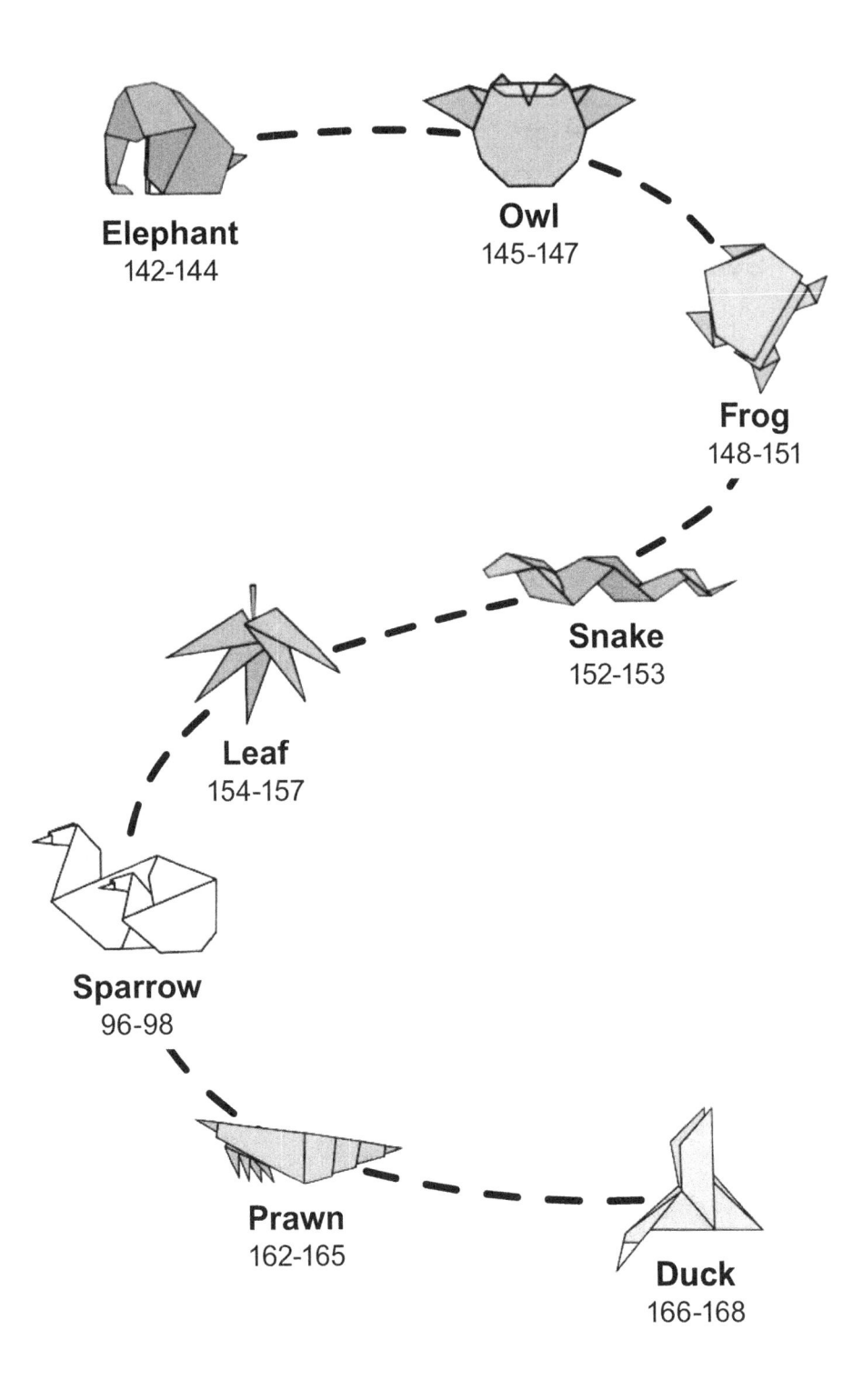

Owl
145-147

Frog
148-151

Snake
152-153

Leaf
154-157

Sparrow
96-98

Prawn
162-165

Duck
166-168

Penguin
169-172

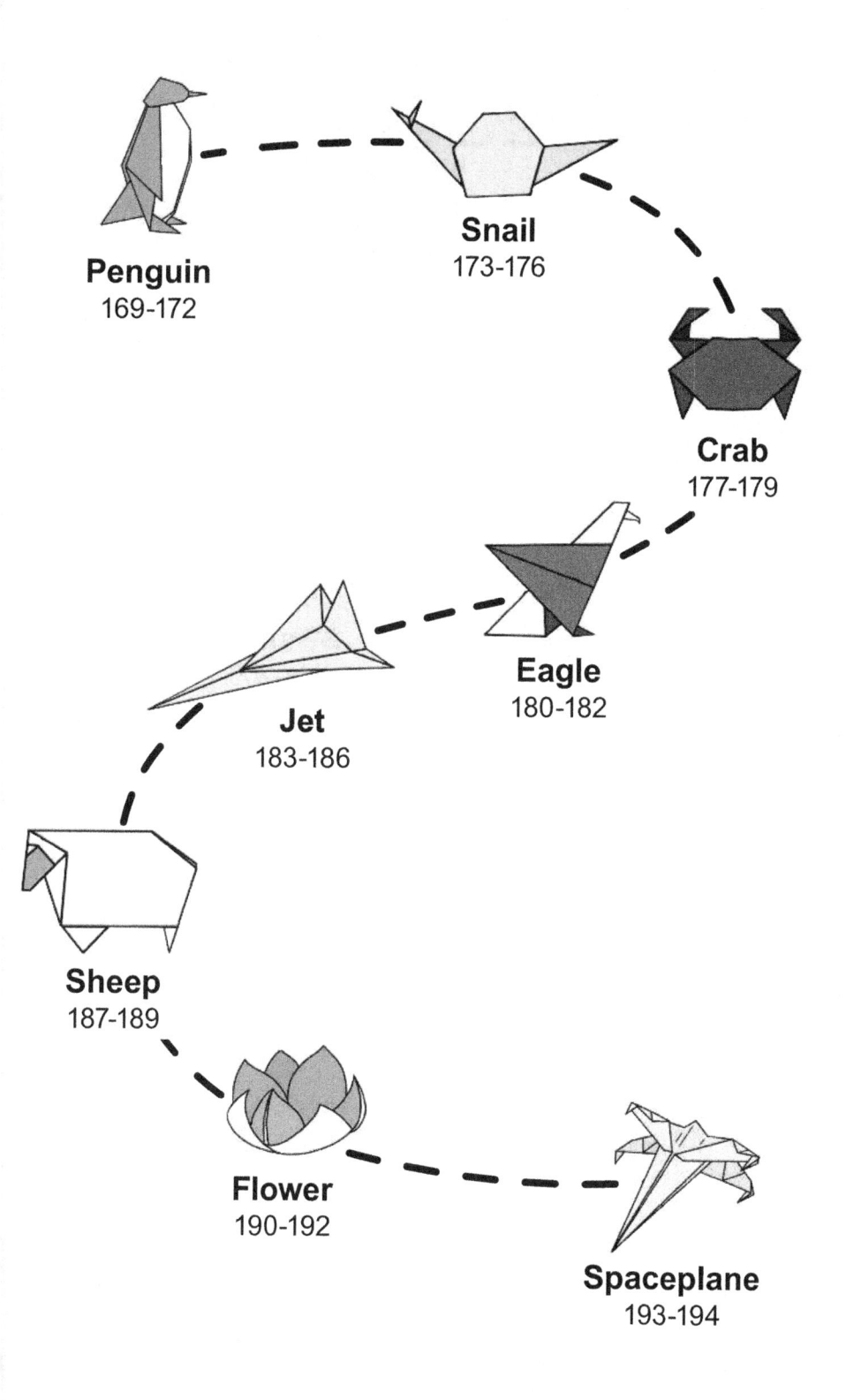

Snail
173-176

Crab
177-179

Eagle
180-182

Jet
183-186

Sheep
187-189

Flower
190-192

Spaceplane
193-194

Dress
195-197

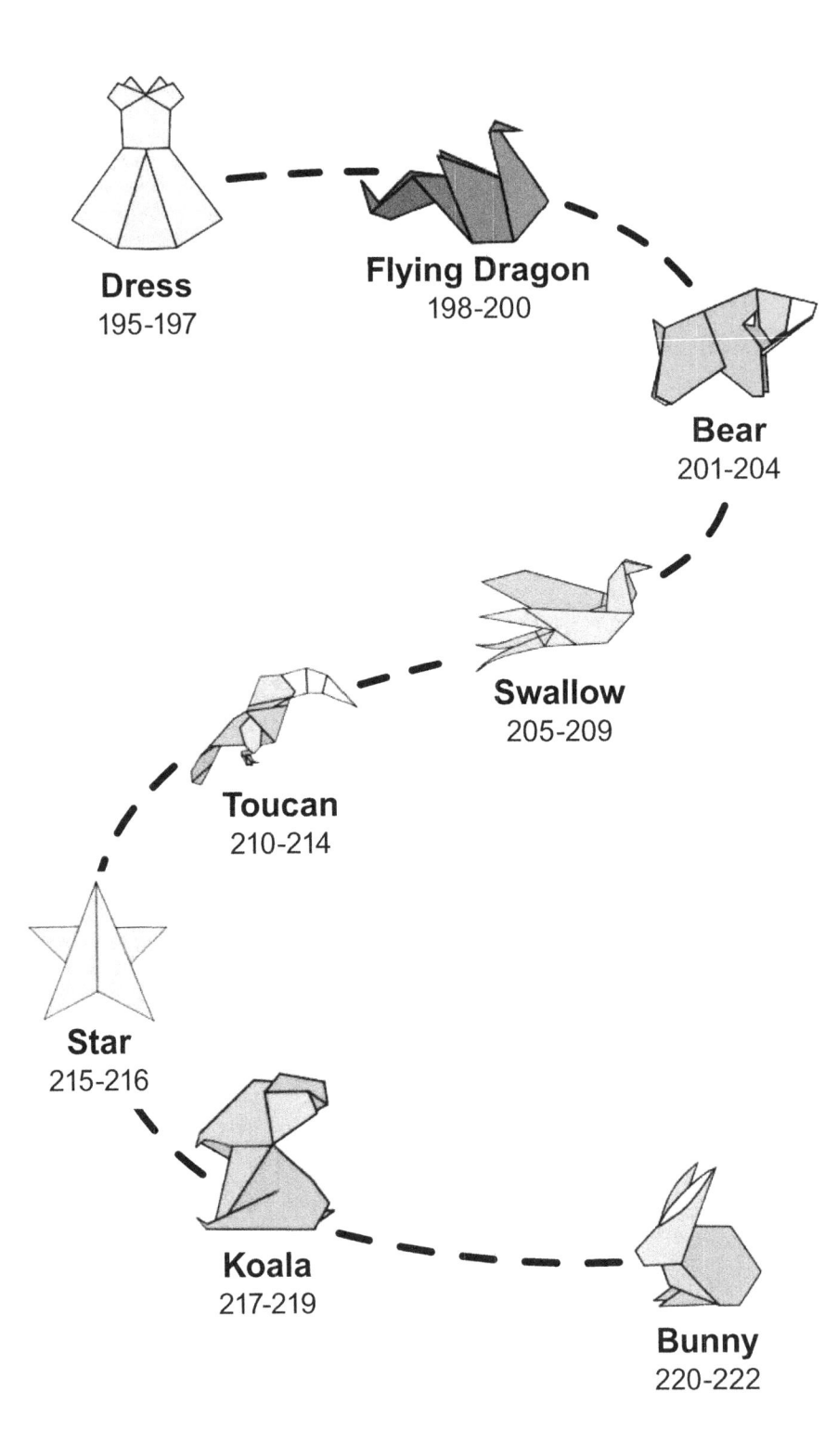

Flying Dragon
198-200

Bear
201-204

Swallow
205-209

Toucan
210-214

Star
215-216

Koala
217-219

Bunny
220-222

Boat
223-225

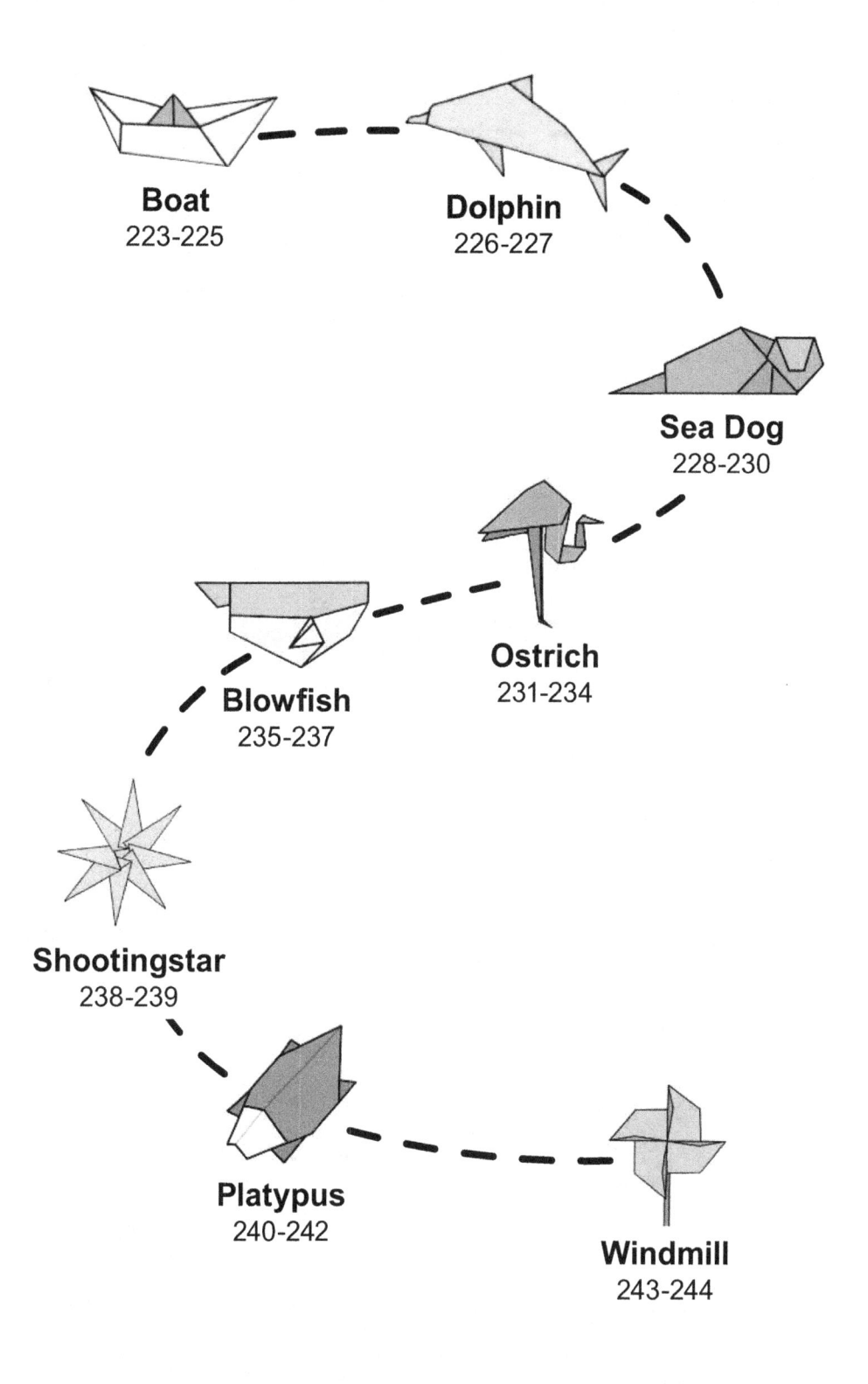

Dolphin
226-227

Sea Dog
228-230

Ostrich
231-234

Blowfish
235-237

Shootingstar
238-239

Platypus
240-242

Windmill
243-244

Pumpkin
245-247

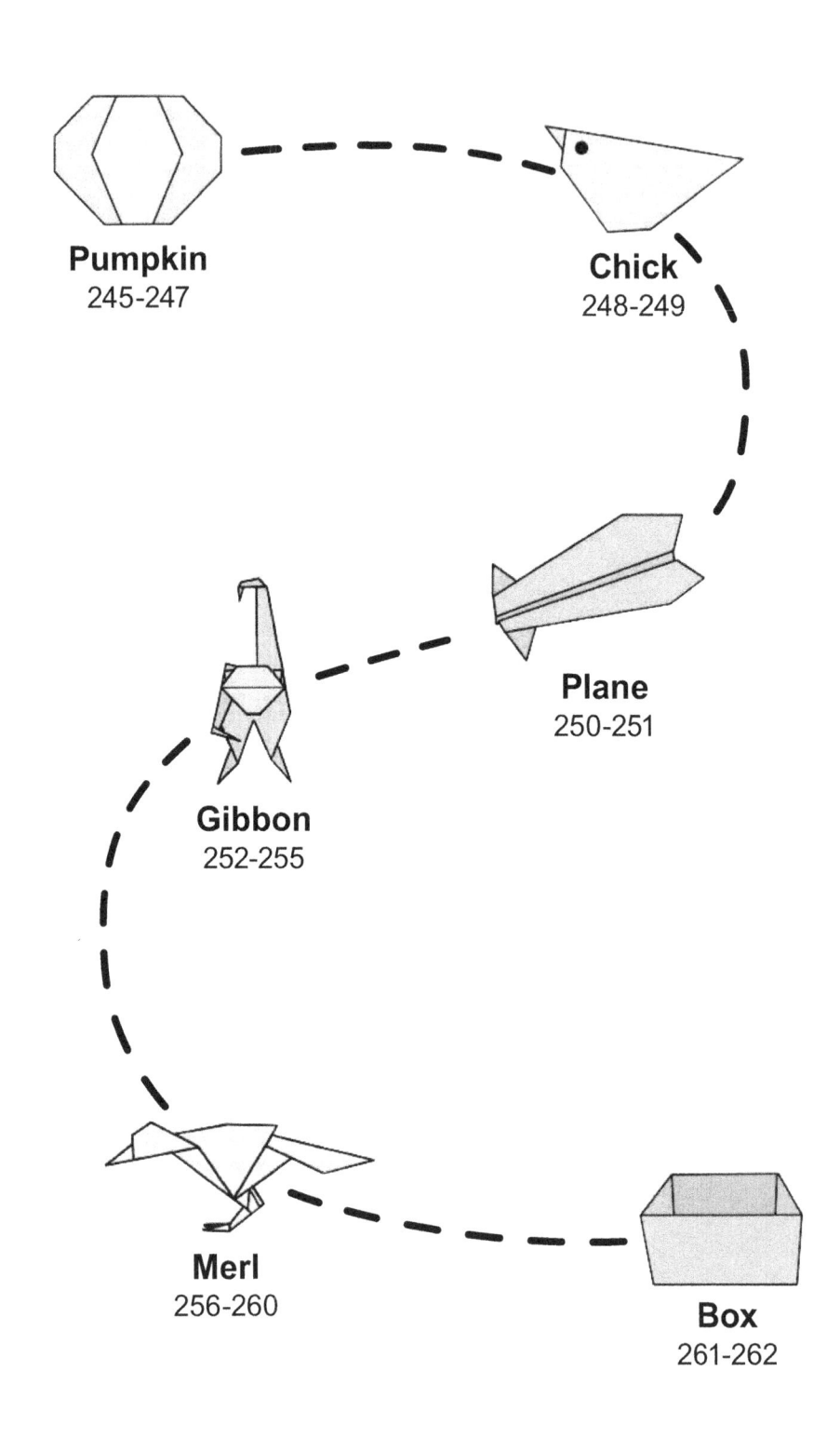

Chick
248-249

Plane
250-251

Gibbon
252-255

Merl
256-260

Box
261-262

Heart

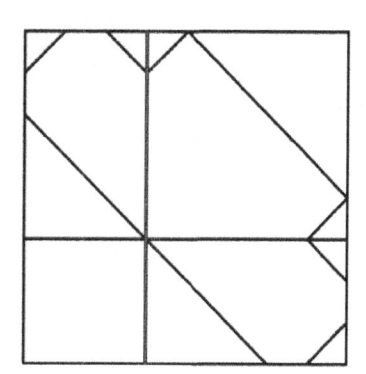

1. Start with the white side up.
2. Fold and unfold in the half diagonally. 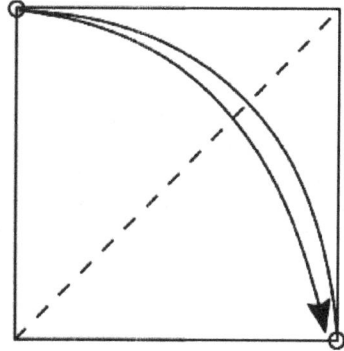
3. Fold and unfold in the half to the other direction. 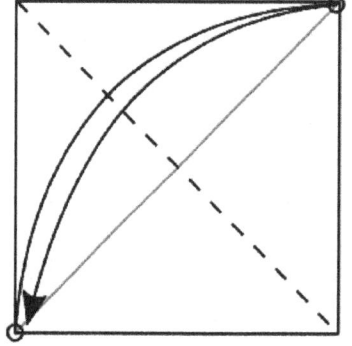
4. Fold the corner to the center point. 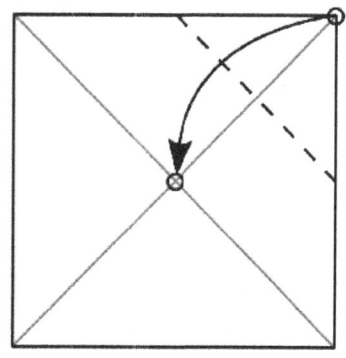

15

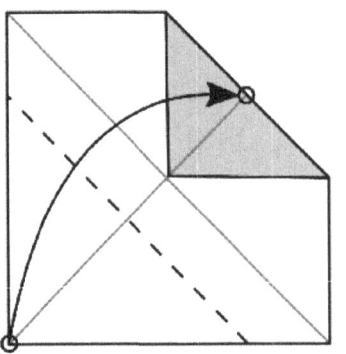

5 Fold the corner to the top middle point.

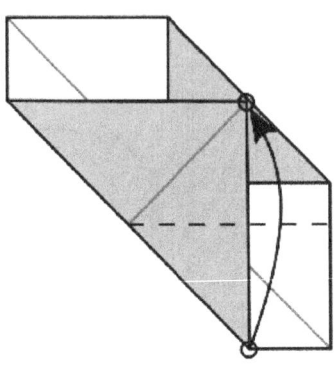

6 Fold the corner to the top middle point.

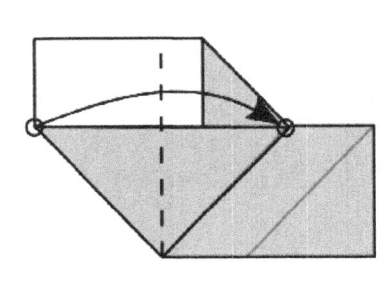

7 Fold the other corner accordingly.

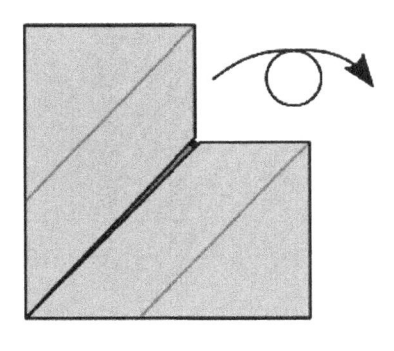

8 Turn the model over.

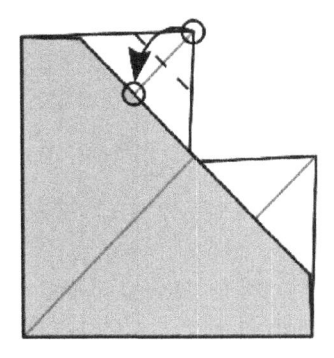

9 Fold the corner to the marked point.

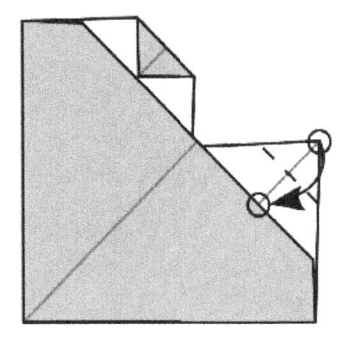

10 Fold the other corner accordingly.

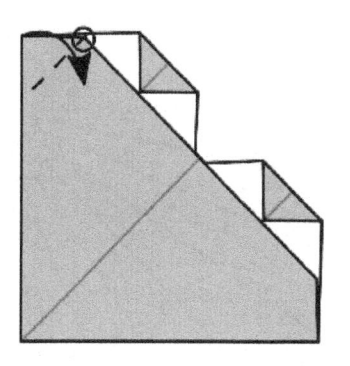

11 Fold corner according to the marked point.

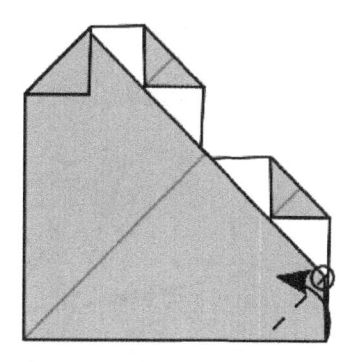

12 Fold the other corner accordingly.

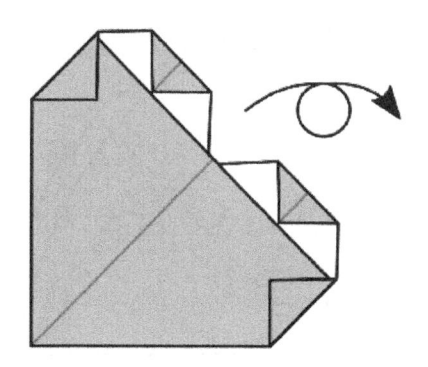

13 Turn the model over.

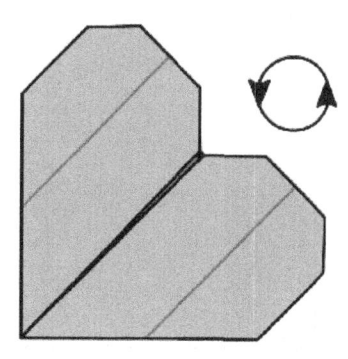

14 Rotate the model to the left.

15 Finished heart!

Swan

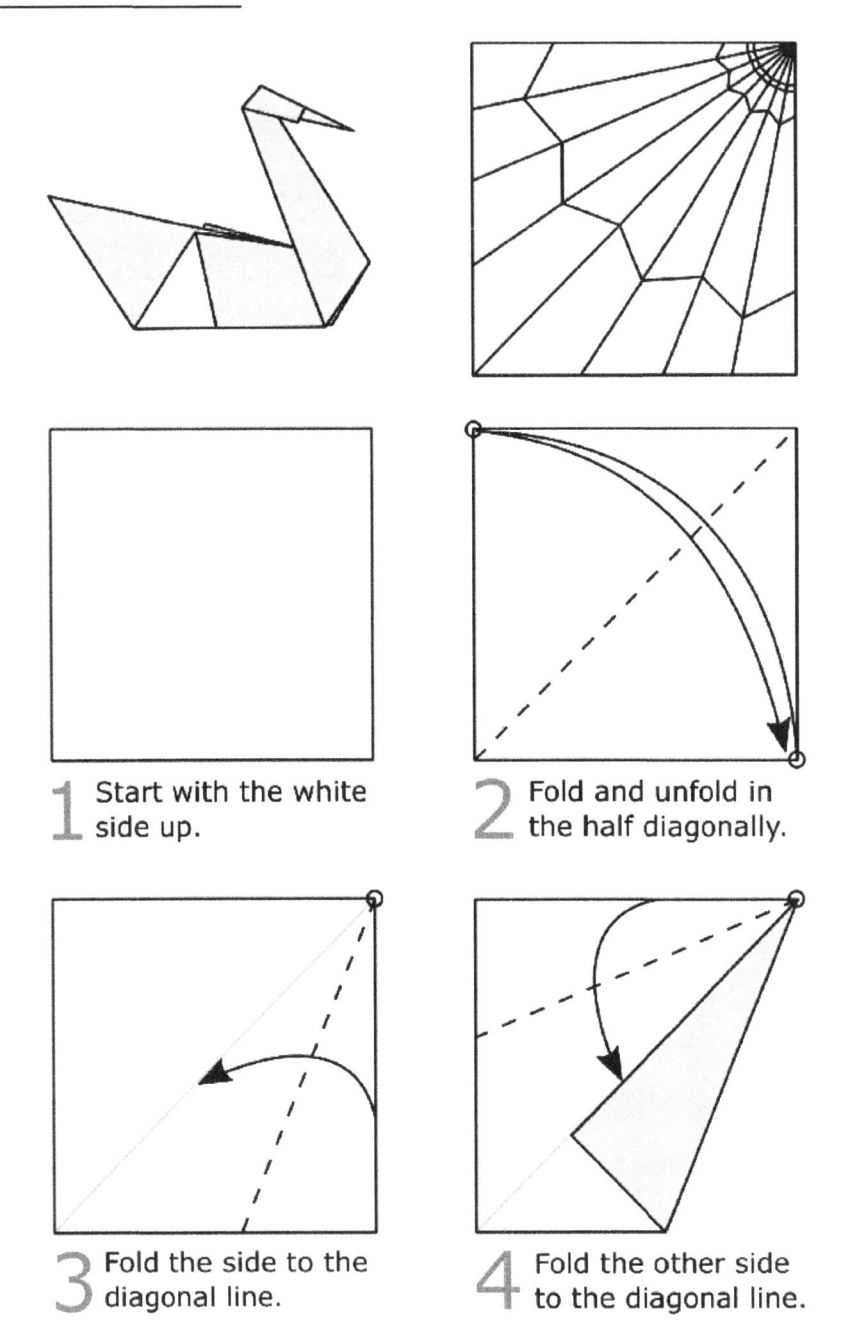

1. Start with the white side up.

2. Fold and unfold in the half diagonally.

3. Fold the side to the diagonal line.

4. Fold the other side to the diagonal line.

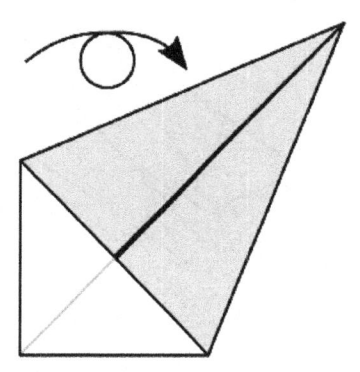

5 Turn the model over.

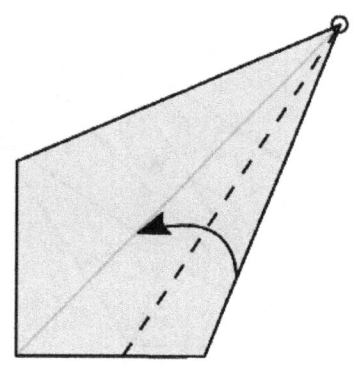

6 Fold the side to the digonal line.

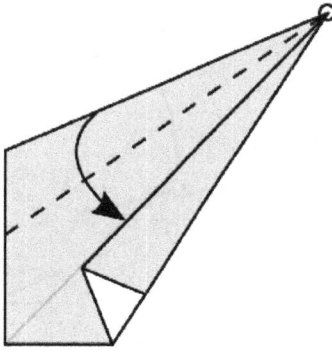

7 Fold the other side to the diagonal line.

8 Fold the top corner to the bottom one.

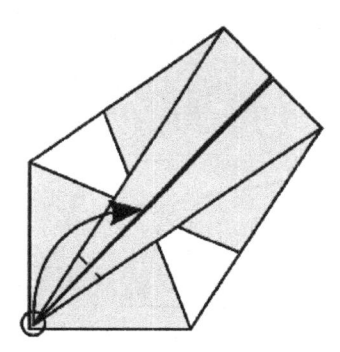

9 Fold the corner up.

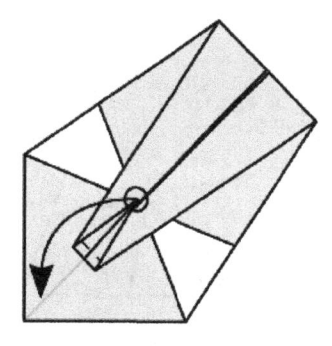

10 Fold the corner down.

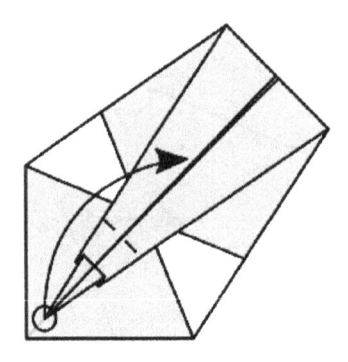

11 Fold the corner up to form the head.

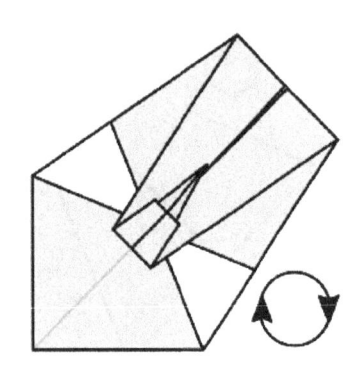

12 Rotate the model.

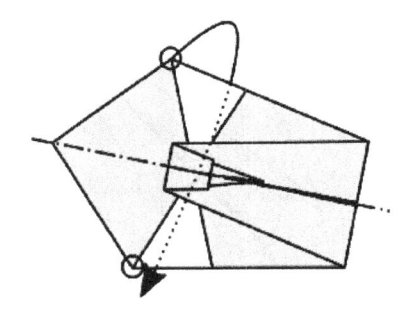

13 Fold the model in half behind.

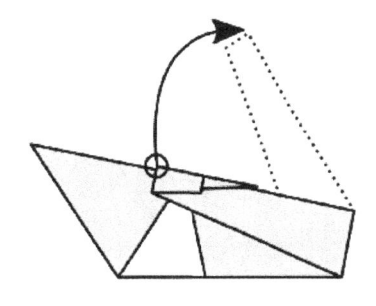

14 Lift the neck and head up.

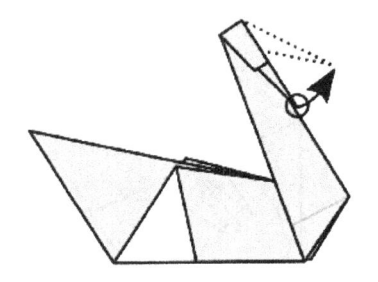

15 Lift the head up.

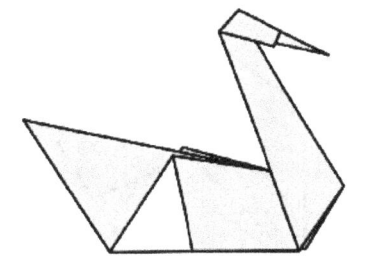

16 Finished swan!

Ninja Star

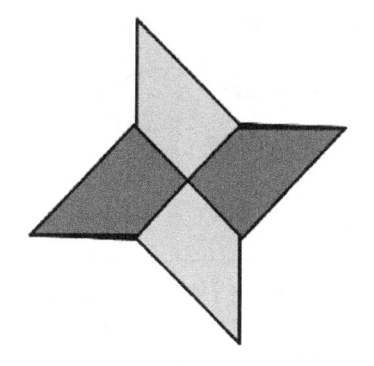

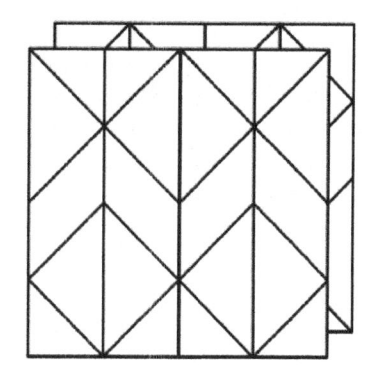

1 You will need two same size piece of papers.

2 Start with the white side up.

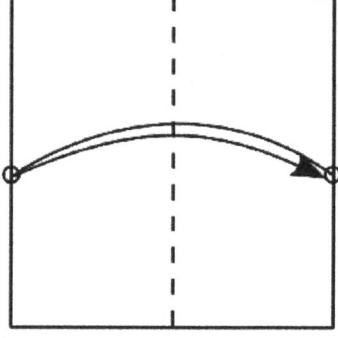

3 Fold and unfold vertically in the half.

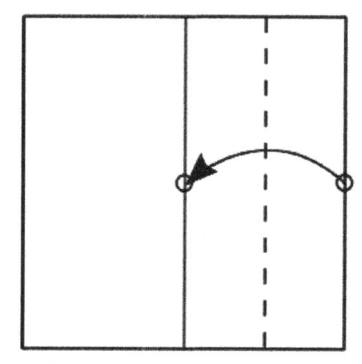

4 Fold the side to the center line.

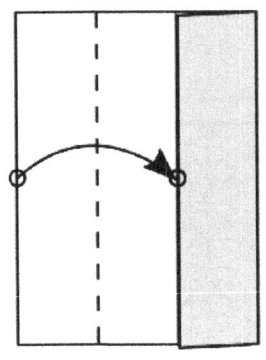

5 Fold the other side to the center line.

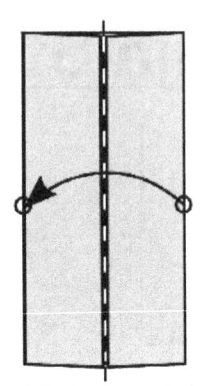

6 Fold the model in the half to the left.

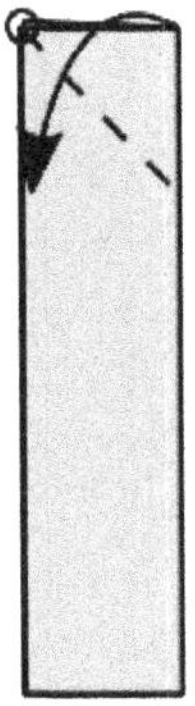

7 Fold the corner diagonally down.

8 Fold the corner diagonally up.

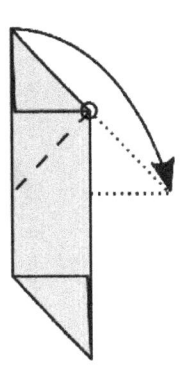

9 Fold the corner down as marked.

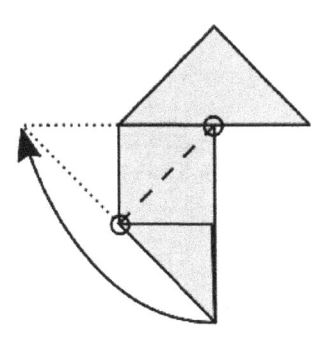

10 Fold the corner up as marked.

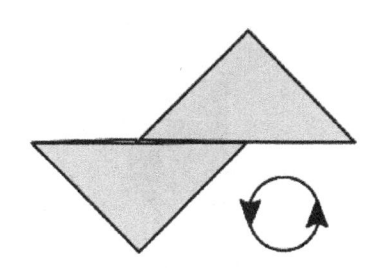

11 Rotate the model.

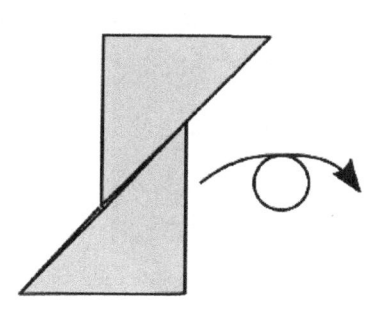

12 Turn the model over.

13 Finished first piece!

14 Start from step 7 with the other piece of paper.

15 Fold the corner diagonally down.

16 Fold the corner diagonally up.

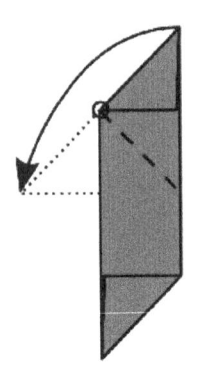

17 Fold the corner down as marked.

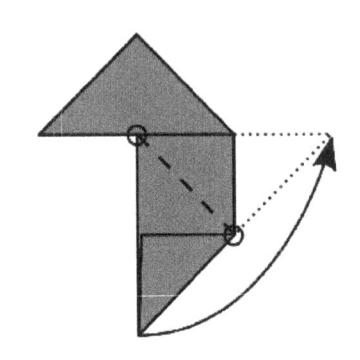

18 Fold the corner up as marked.

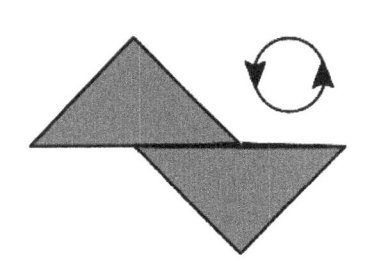

19 Rotate the model.

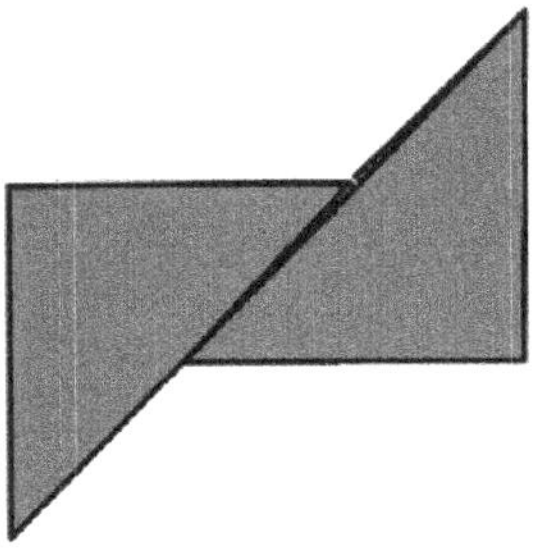

20 Finished second piece!

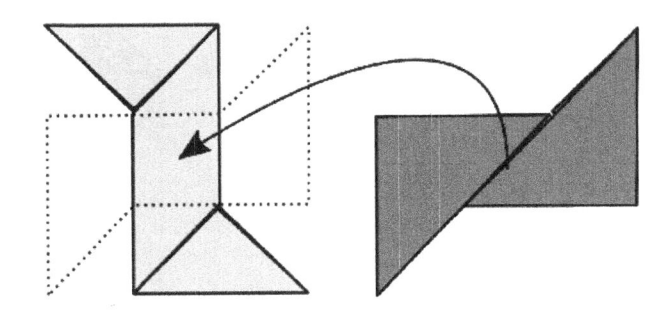

21 Put the second pieces on the top of the first one as indicated

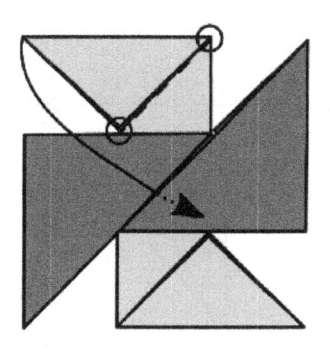

22 Tuck the corner inside the pocket.

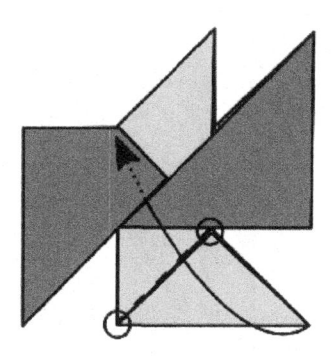

23 Tuck the other corner inside the pocket.

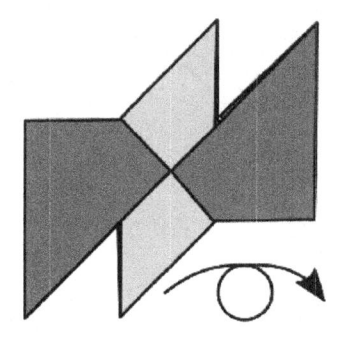

24 Turn the model over.

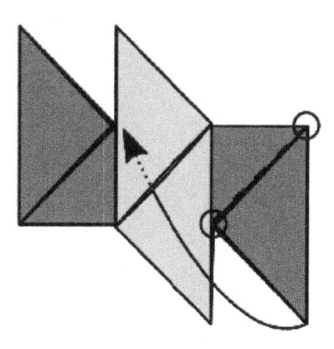

25 Tuck the corner inside the pocket.

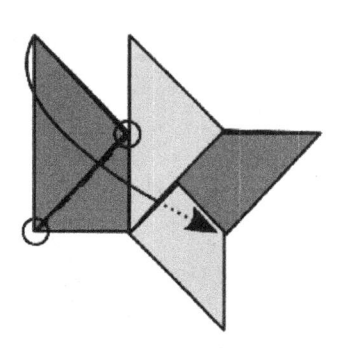

26 Tuck the last corner inside the pocket.

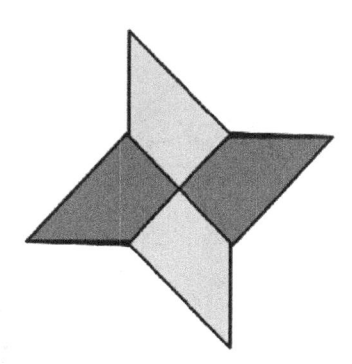

27 Finished ninja star!

Fox

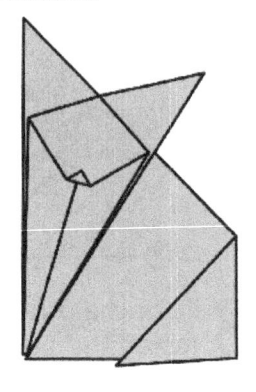

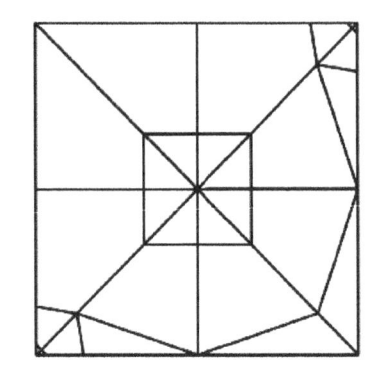

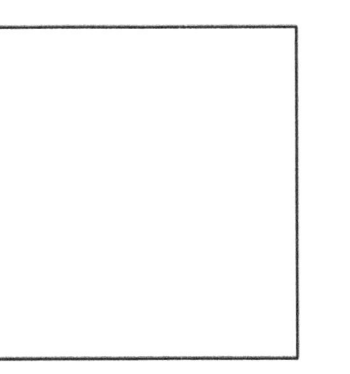

1. Start with the white side up.

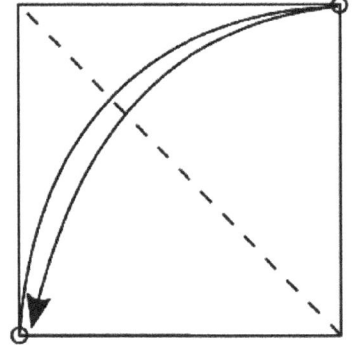

2. Fold and unfold in the half diagonally.

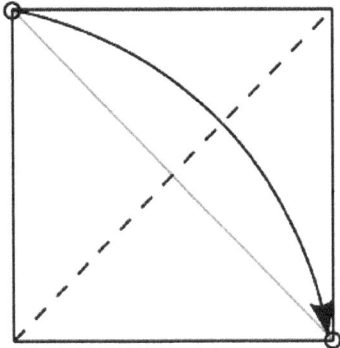

3. Fold diagonally in half to the other direction.

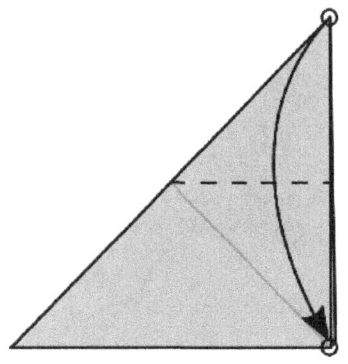

4. Fold the corner down to the bottom point.

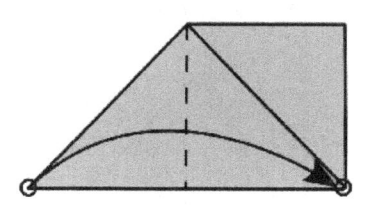

5 Fold the other corner to the same point.

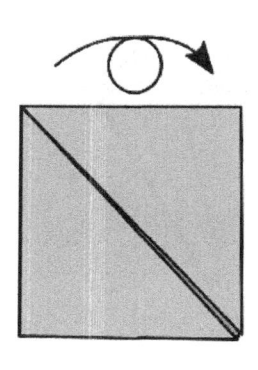

6 Turn the model over.

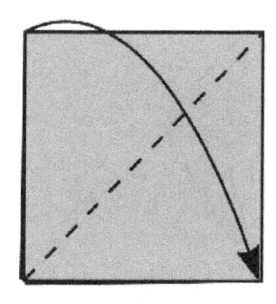

7 Fold the model diagonally in half.

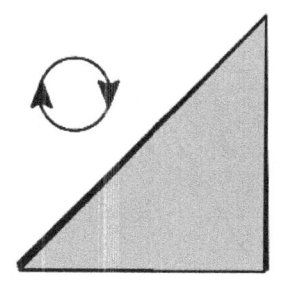

8 Rotate the model.

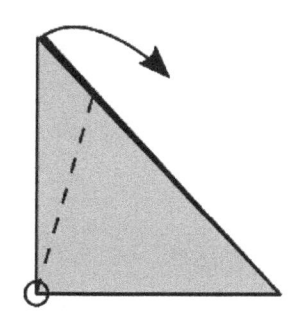

9 Fold through all the layers to the right.

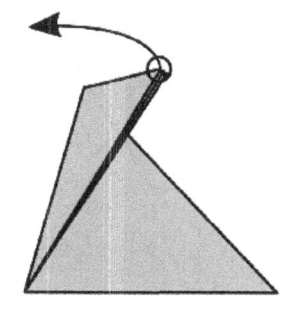

10 Unfold the top layer back to the previous position.

27

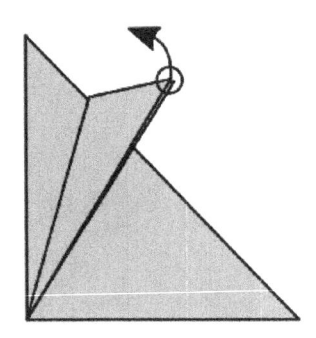

11 Fold the top layer perpendicularly up.

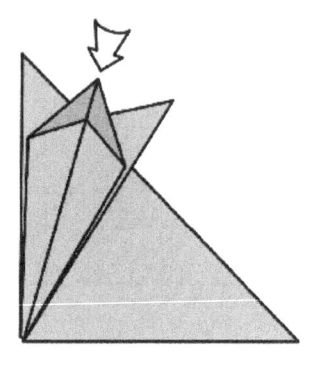

12 Squash fold down by separating layers to sides and pushing down the top part.

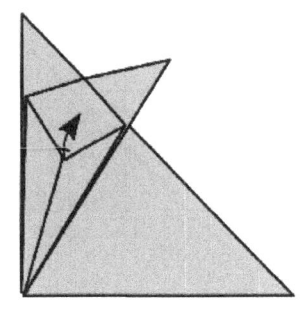

13 Fold the tip through the both layers up.

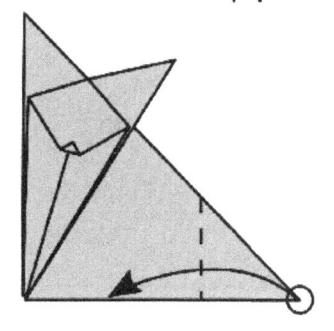

14 Fold the corner to the left.

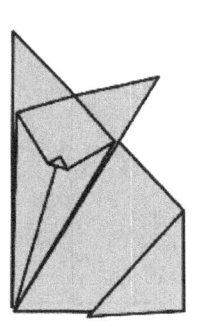

15 Finished fox!

Butterfly

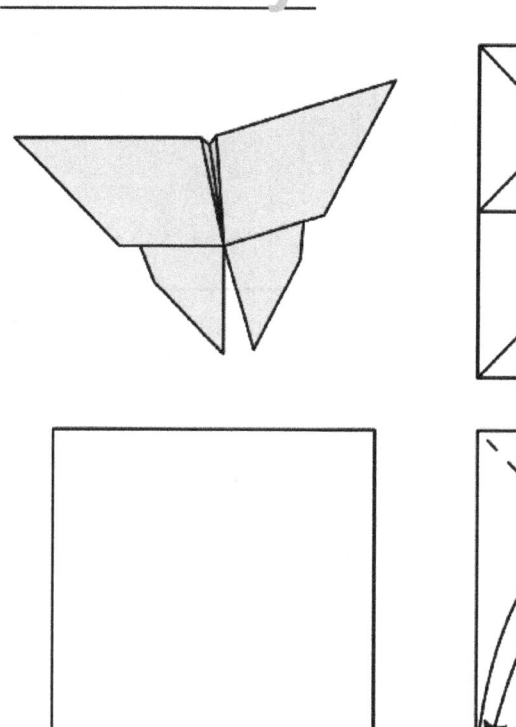

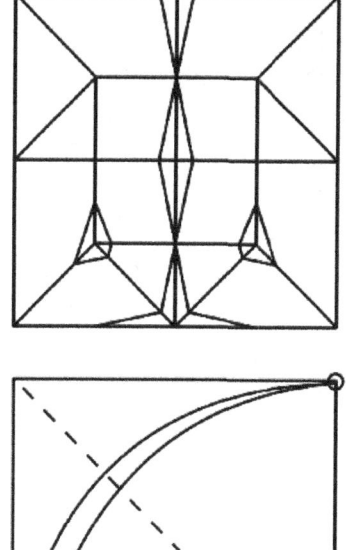

1. Start with the white side up.
2. Fold and unfold diagonally in the half.
3. Fold and unfold diagonally in the half to the other direction. 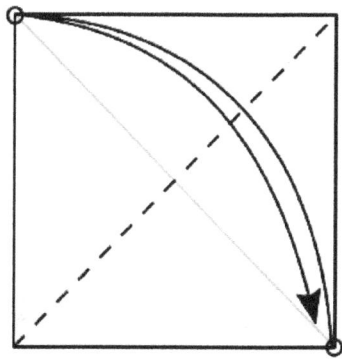
4. Fold and unfold vertically in the half.

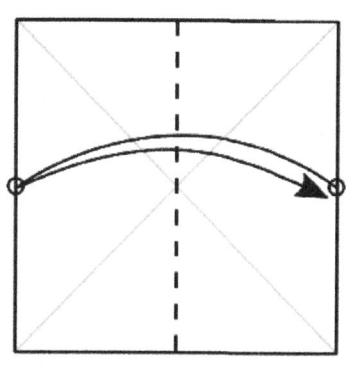

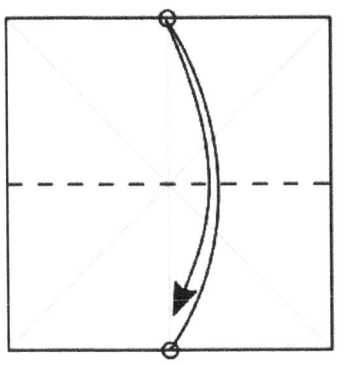

5. Fold and unfold horizontally in the half.

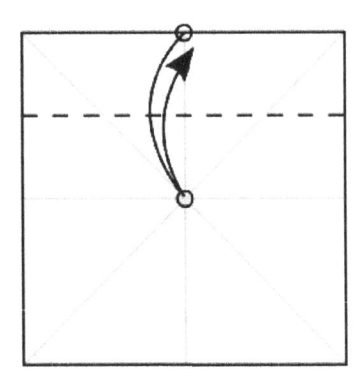

6. Fold and unfold the top edge to the center line.

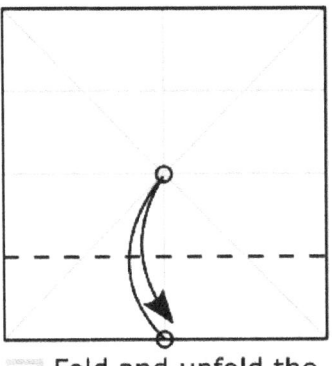

7. Fold and unfold the bottom edge to the center line.

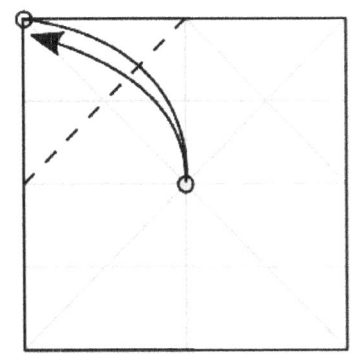

8. Fold and unfold the first corner to the center point.

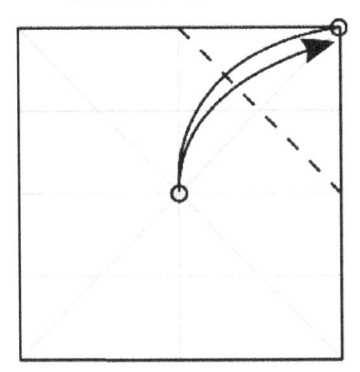

9. Fold and unfold the second corner to the center point.

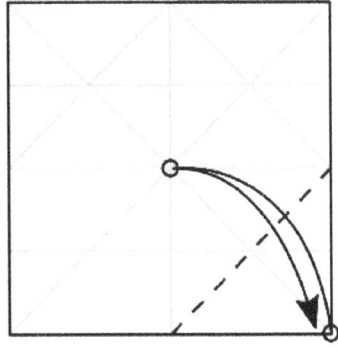

10. Fold and unfold the third corner to the center point.

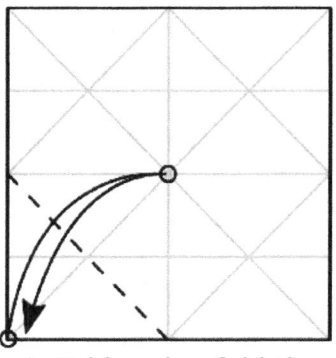

11 Fold and unfold the forth corner to the center point.

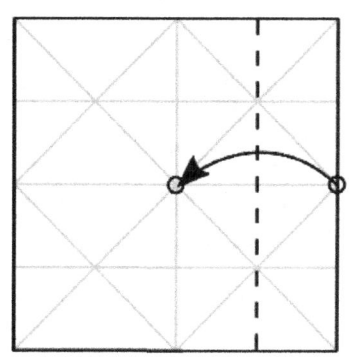

12 Fold the right edge to the center line.

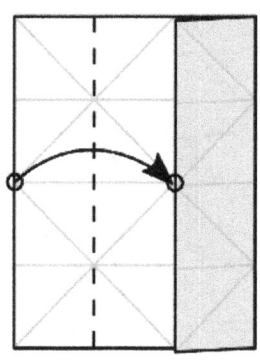

13 Fold the left edge to the center line.

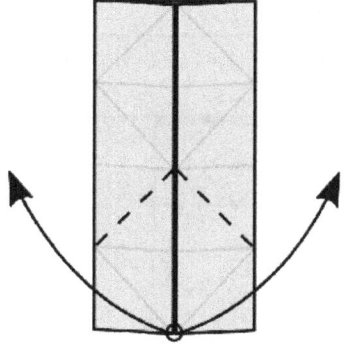

14 Fold the corners to the sides according to the marked lines.

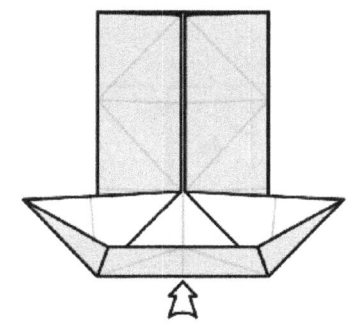

15 Squash the paper down to make it flat.

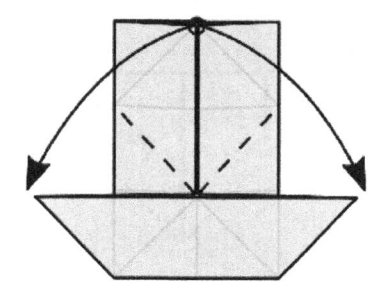

16 Fold the top corners to the sides.

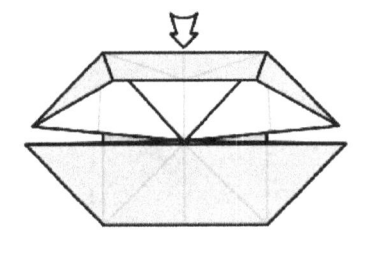

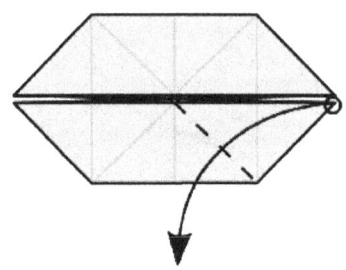

17 Squash the paper down to make it flat.

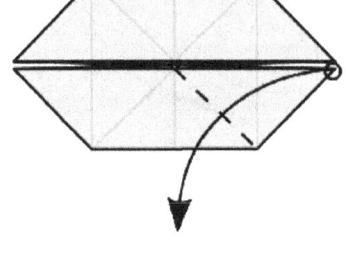

18 Fold the corner down.

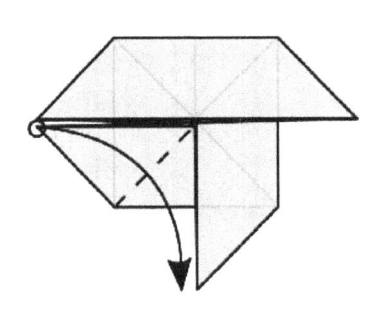

19 Fold the opposite corner down.

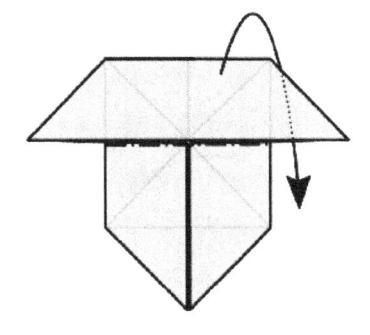

20 Fold the top part horizontally behind.

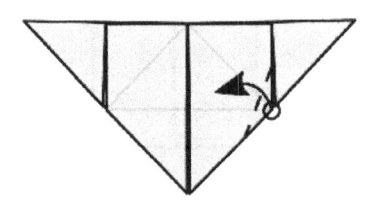

21 Fold the corner to the left.

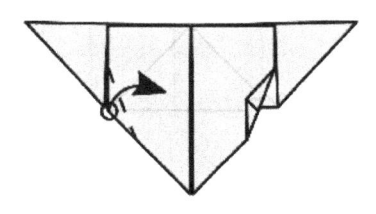

22 Fold the opposite corner to the right.

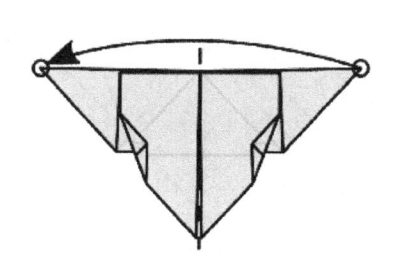

23 Fold the model in the half to the left.

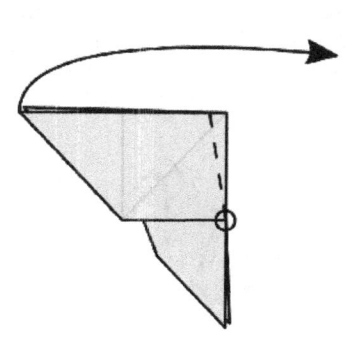

24 Fold the top layer to the right.

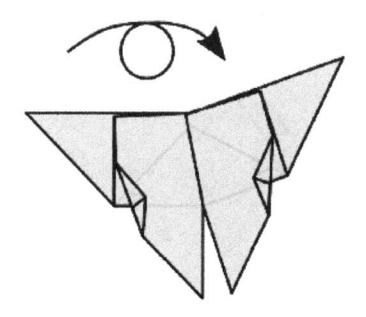

25 Turn the model over.

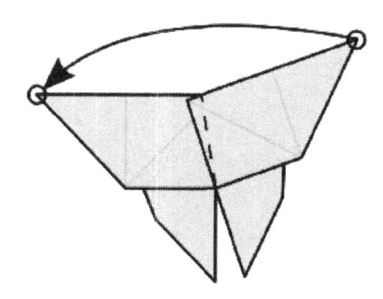

26 Fold the one corner to the other.

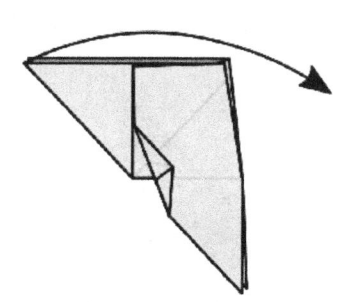

27 Open up the model by folding top layer to the right.

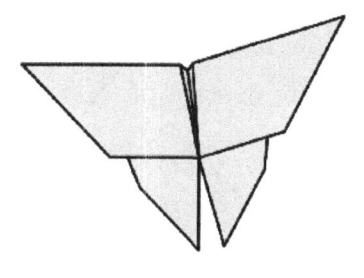

28 Finished butterfly!

Samurai Helmet

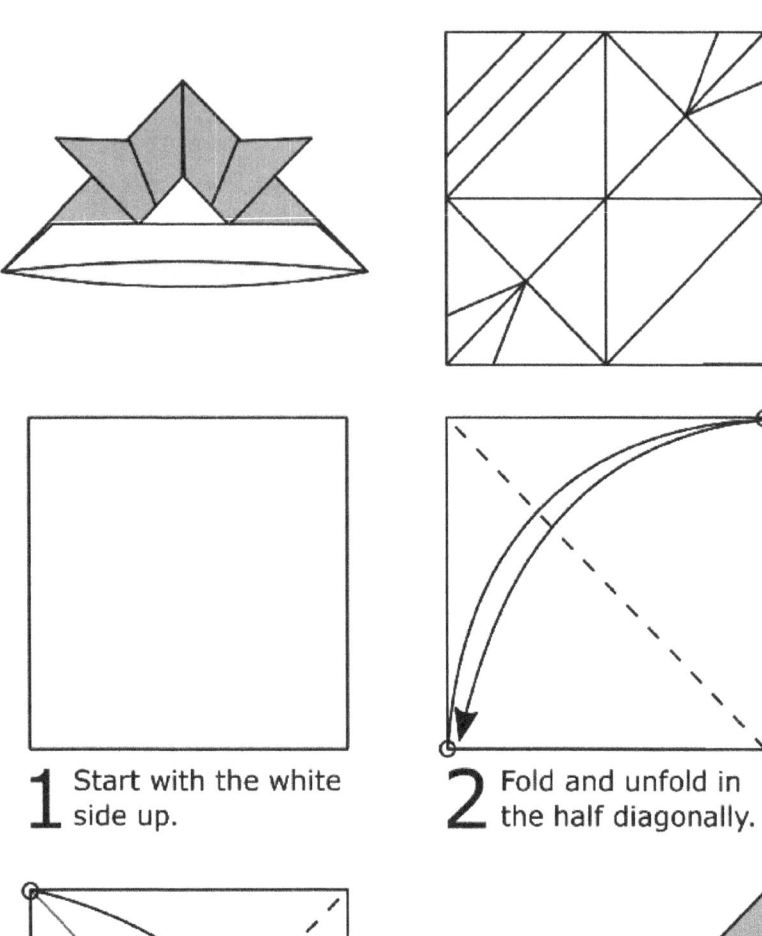

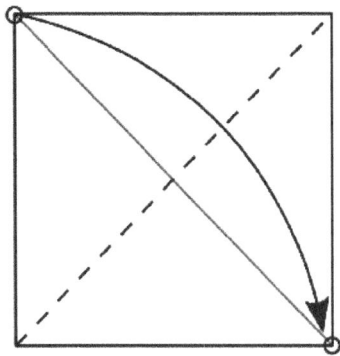

1. Start with the white side up.

2. Fold and unfold in the half diagonally.

3. Fold diagonally in half to the other direction.

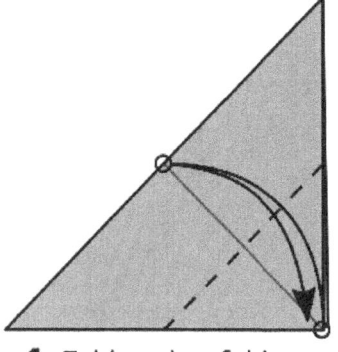

4. Fold and unfold corner to the top point.

34

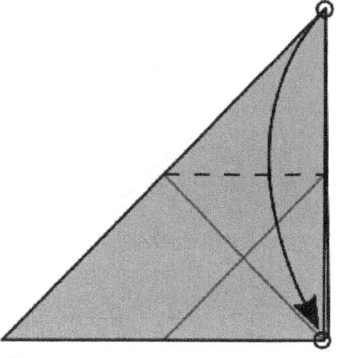

5 Fold the corner to the bottom point.

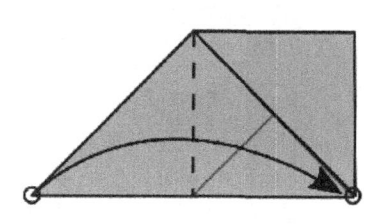

6 Fold the opposite corner to the bottom point.

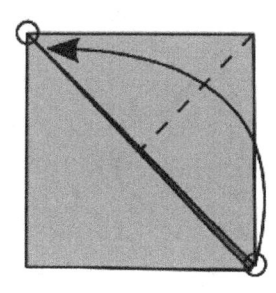

7 Fold the corner to the top point.

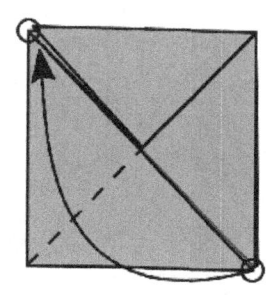

8 Fold the opposite corner to the top point.

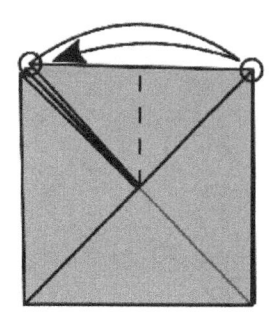

9 Fold and unfold the flap to the right corner.

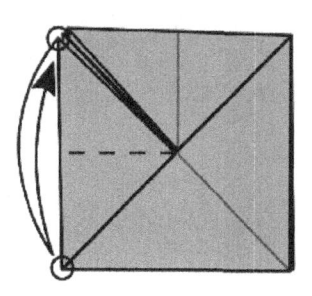

10 Fold and unfold the flap to the bottom corner.

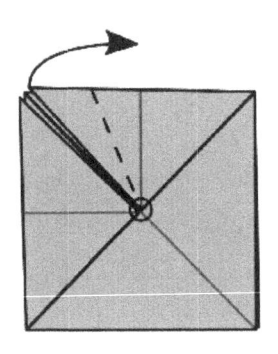

11 Fold the flap to the right on the line.

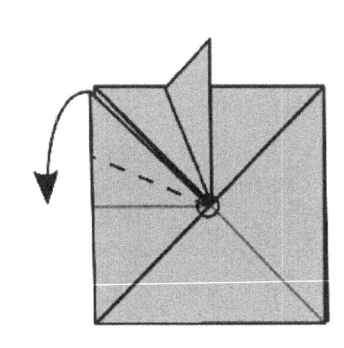

12 Fold the flap down on the line.

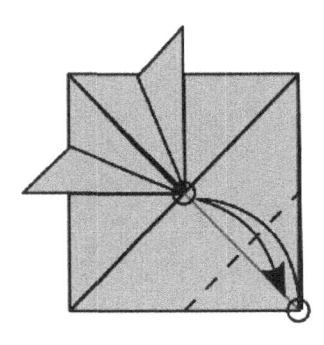

13 Fold and unfold the top layer to the top point.

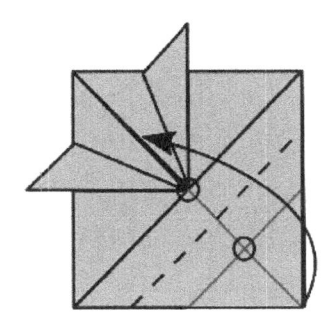

14 Fold the top layer up according to the marked points.

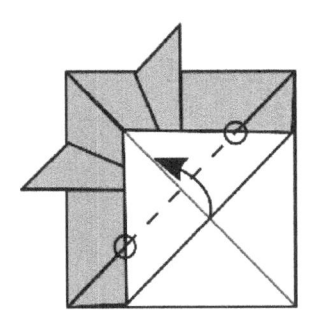

15 Fold the top layer up again according to the marked points.

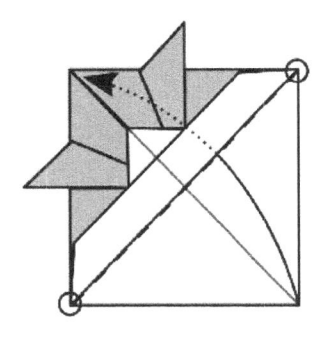

16 Fold the corner inside the model.

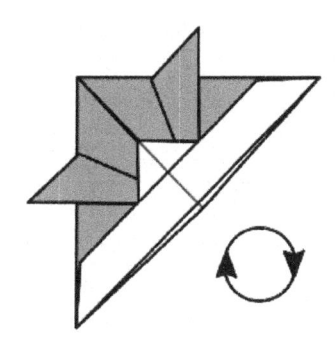

17 Rotate the model.

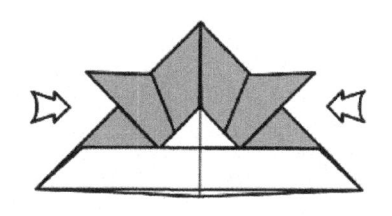

18 Push the sides to make the model 3D.

19 Finished samurai helmet!

Pig

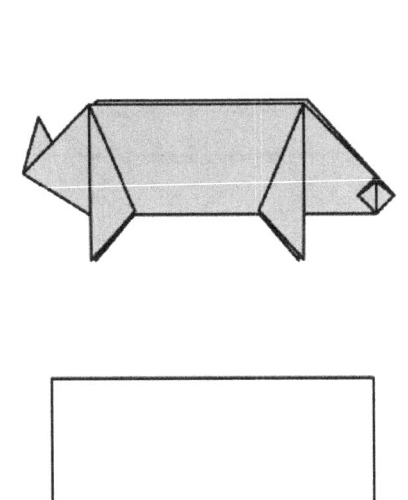

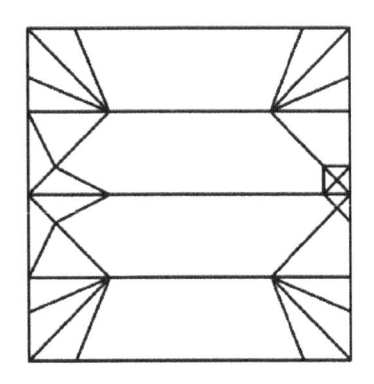

1. Start with the white side up.

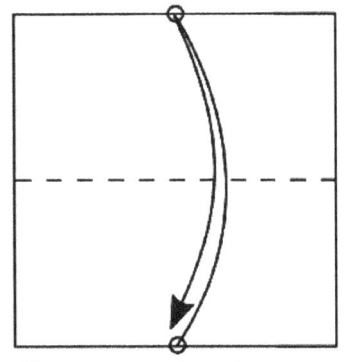

2. Fold and unfold horizontally in the half.

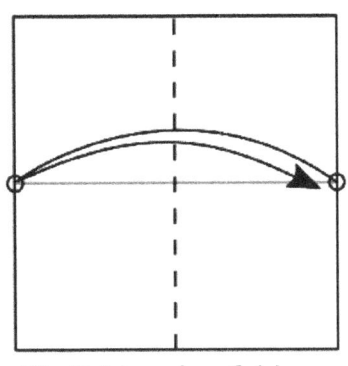

3. Fold and unfold vertically in the half.

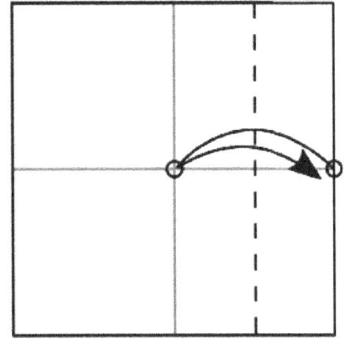

4. Fold and unfold the right side to the center line.

38

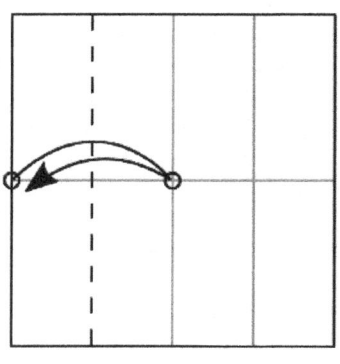

5. Fold and unfold the left side to the center line.

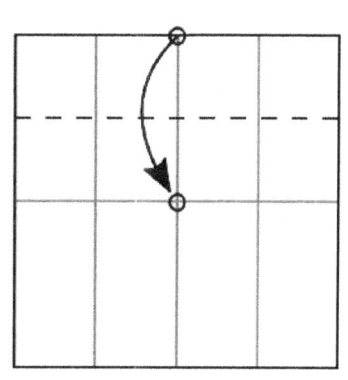

6. Fold the top edge to the center line.

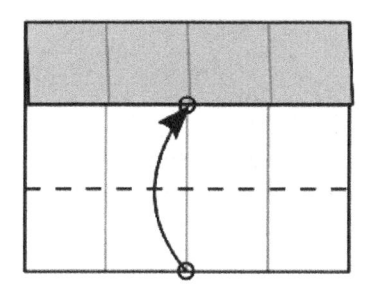

7. Fold the bottom edge to the center line.

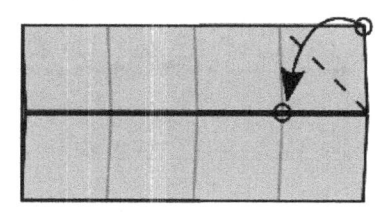

8. Fold the top right corner to the marked point.

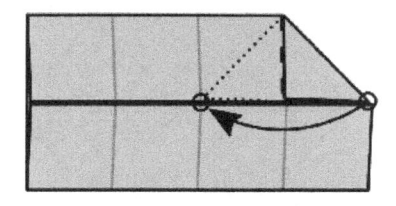

9. Take out the hidden corner to the left.

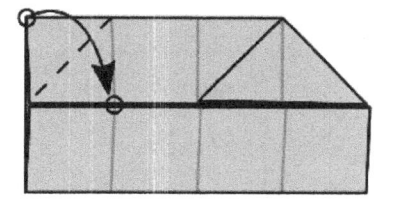

10. Fold the top left corner to the marked point.

39

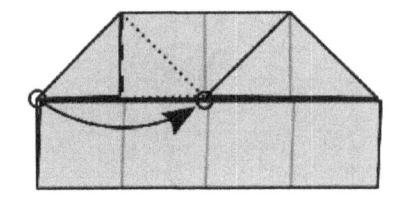

11 Take out the hidden corner to the right.

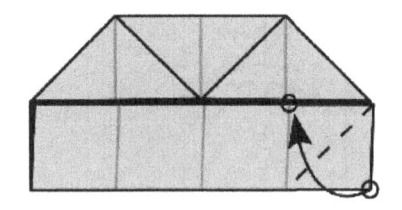

12 Fold the bottom right corner to the marked point.

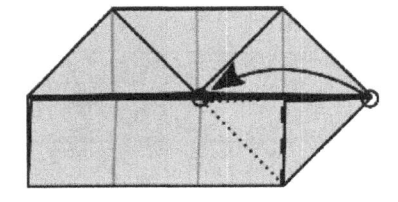

13 Take out the hidden corner ro the left.

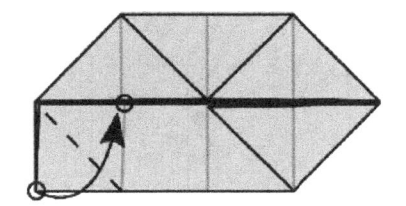

14 Fold the bottom left corner to the marked point.

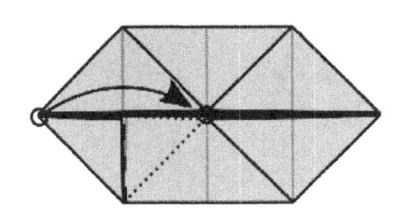

15 Take out the hidden corner to the right.

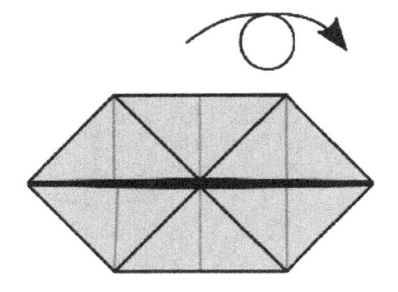

16 Turn the model over.

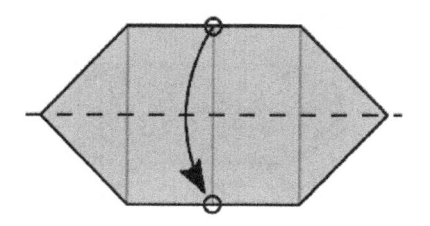

17 Fold the model horizontally in the half.

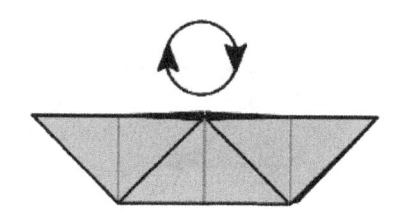

18 Rotate the model.

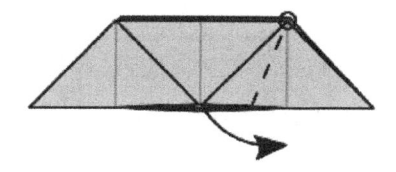

19 Fold the corner down to the right.

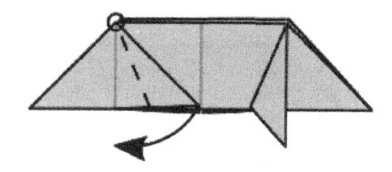

20 Fold the corner down to the left.

21 Fold the corner up.

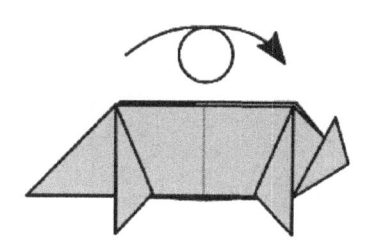

22 Turn the model over.

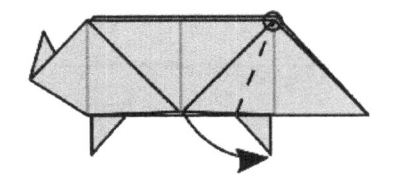

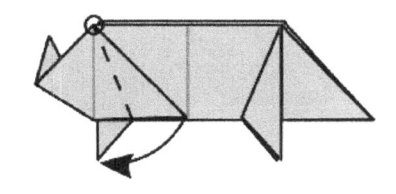

23 Fold the corner down to the right.

24 Fold the corner down to the left.

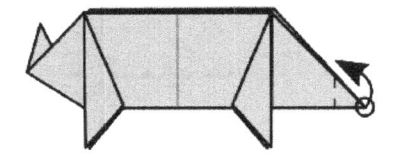

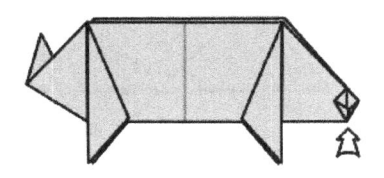

25 Fold the corner perpendicularly up.

26 Squash fold the corner down by separating layers to the sides.

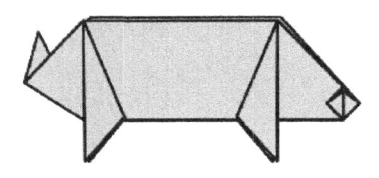

27 Finished pig!

Cicada

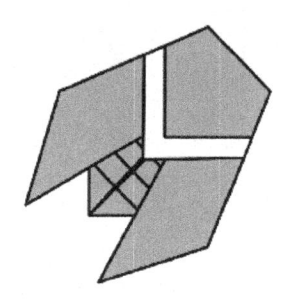

1. Start with the white side up.
2. Fold and unfold in the half diagonally. 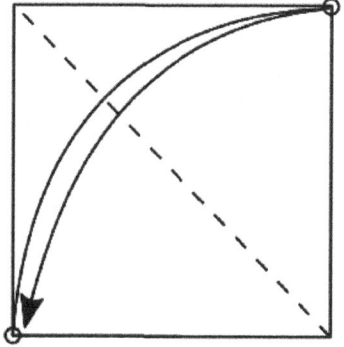
3. Fold diagonally in half to the other direction. 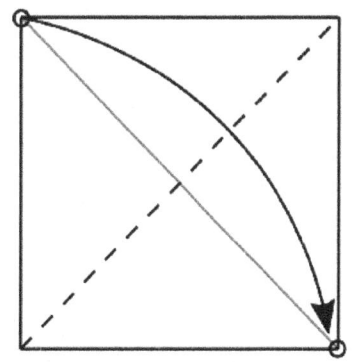
4. Fold the corner down to the bottom point. 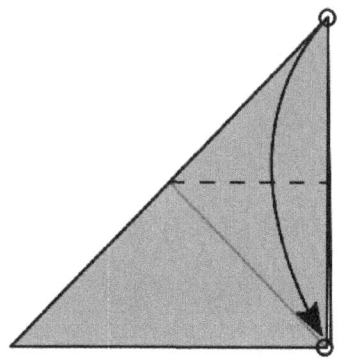

43

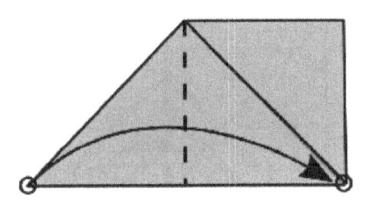

5 Fold the corner to the same point.

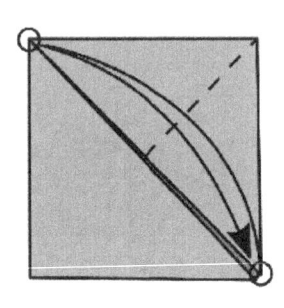

6 Fold and unfold the corner to the top point.

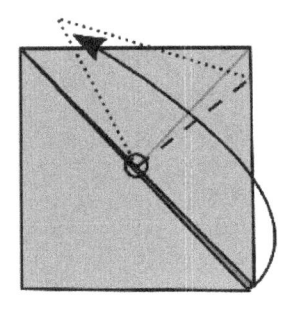

7 Fold the corner up according to the marked point.

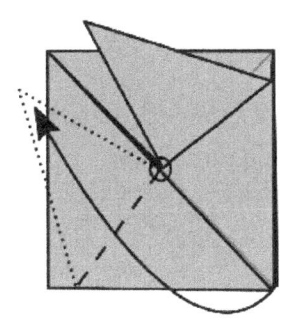

8 Fold the other corner up according to the marked point.

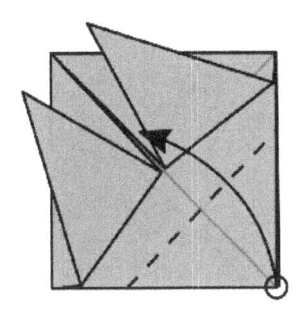

9 Fold the top layer up on the center line.

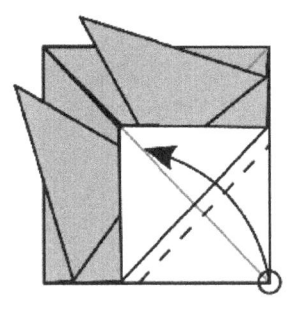

10 Fold the bottom layer up on the center line.

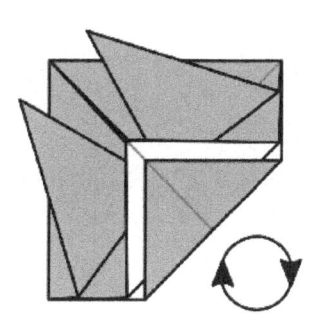

11 Rotate the model.

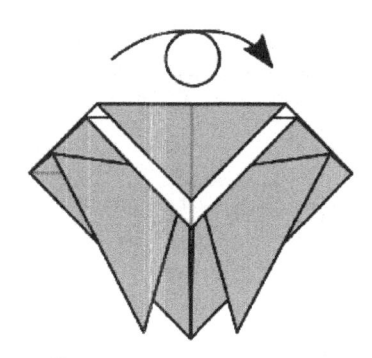

12 Turn the model over.

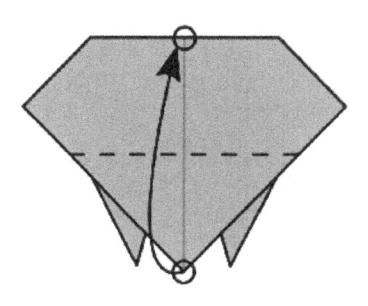

13 Fold the corner to the top middle point.

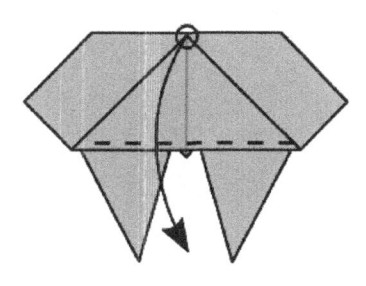

14 Fold the corner down leaving a little space between the folds.

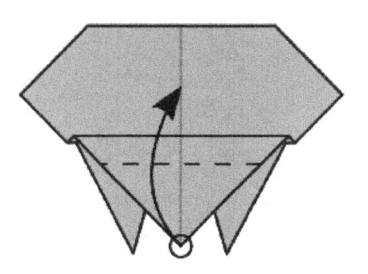

15 Fold the corner up on the middle line.

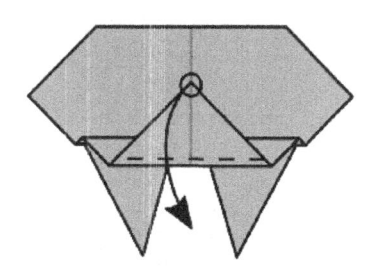

16 Fold the corner down leaving a little space between the folds.

45

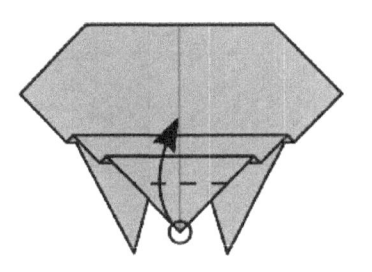

17 Fold the corner up on the middle line.

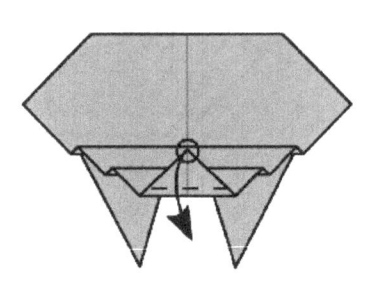

18 Fold the corner down leaving a little space between the folds.

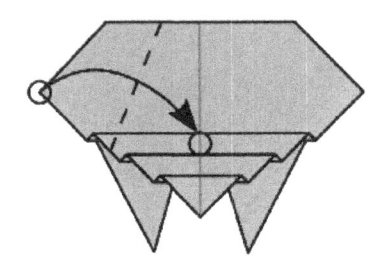

19 Fold the left edge on the center line.

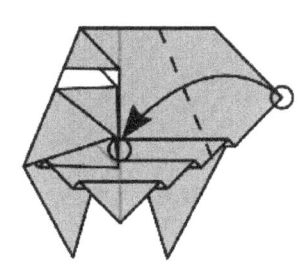

20 Fold the right edge on the center line.

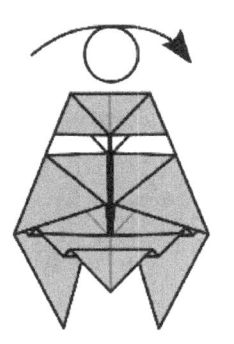

21 Turn the model over.

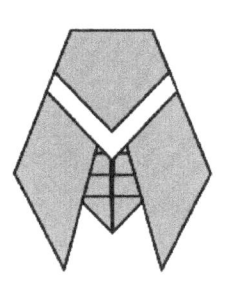

22 Finished cicada!

Dove

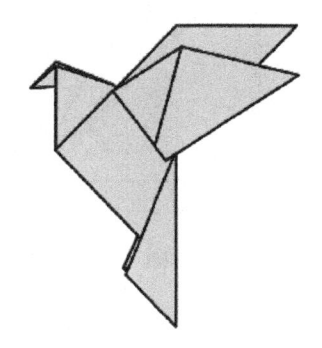

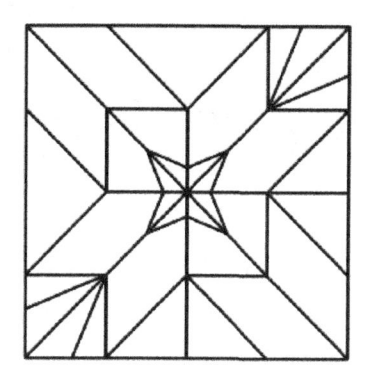

1. Start with the white side up.
2. Fold and unfold in the half diagonally. 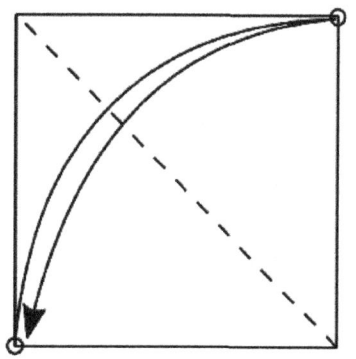
3. Fold diagonally in half to the other direction. 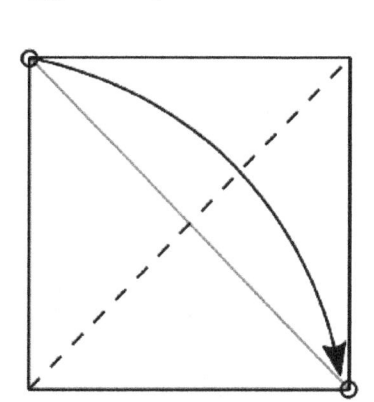
4. Fold the corner down to the bottom point.

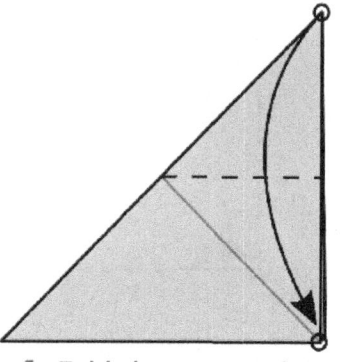

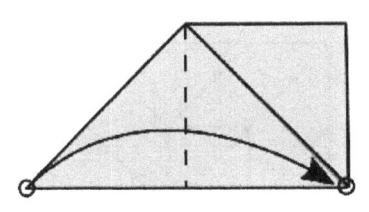

5 Fold the other corner to the same point.

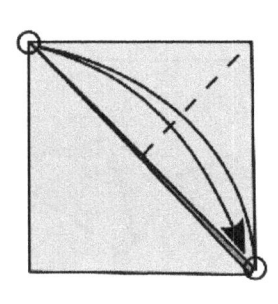

6 Fold and unfold the corner to the top point.

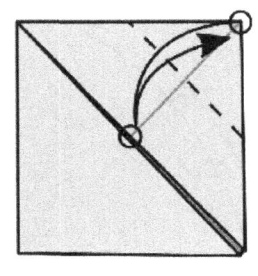

7 Fold and unfold the top right corner to the marked point.

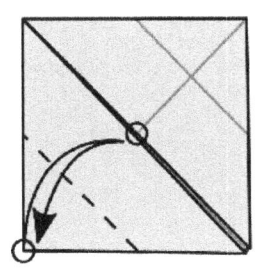

8 Fold and unfold the bottom left corner to the marked point.

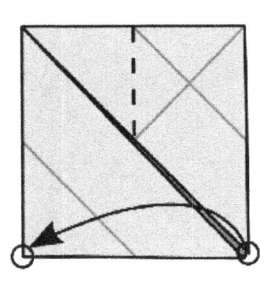

9 Fold the bottom right corner to the bottom left corner.

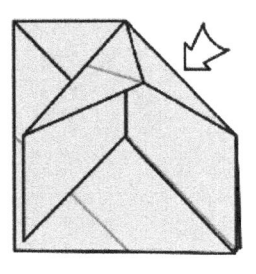

10 Squash the paper down to make the model lie flat.

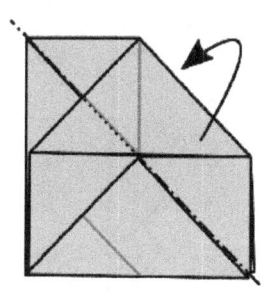

11 Fold the model in the half by folding right part behind.

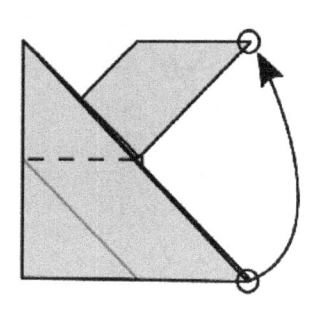

12 Fold the bottom right corner to the top right corner.

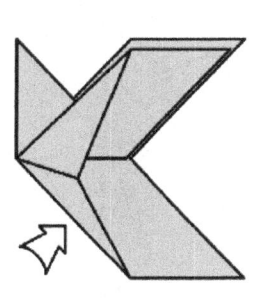

13 Squash the paper down to make the model lie flat.

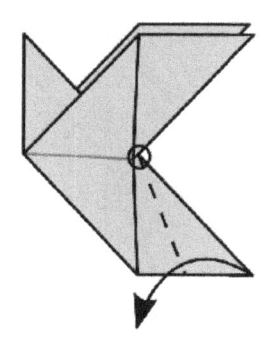

14 Fold the corner down according to the marked point.

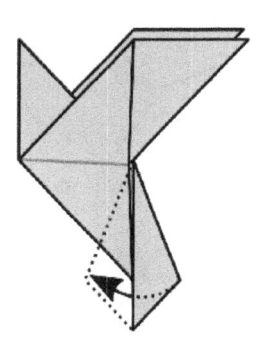

15 Take out the hidden paper layer to the left.

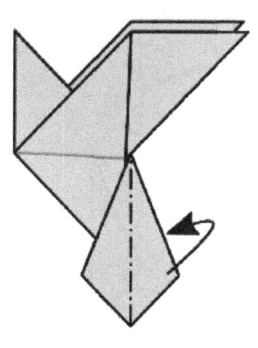

16 Fold the right edge behind.

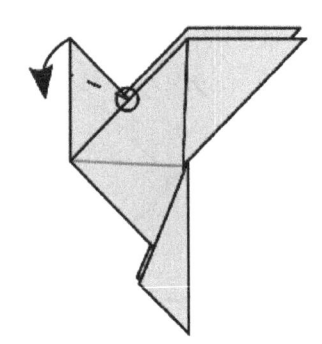

17 Fold the corner down according to the marked point.

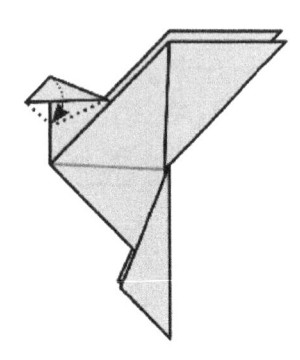

18 Take out the hidden paper layer down.

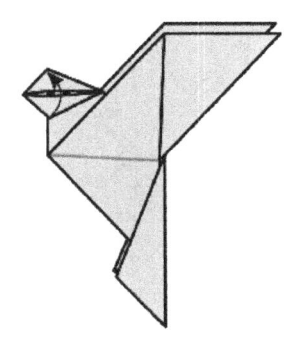

19 Fold the bottom edge to the top.

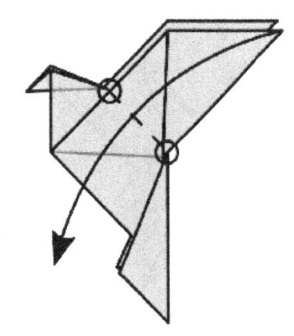

20 Fold the corner down according to the marked points.

21 Fold the corner back up according to the marked point.

22 Finished dove!

Whale

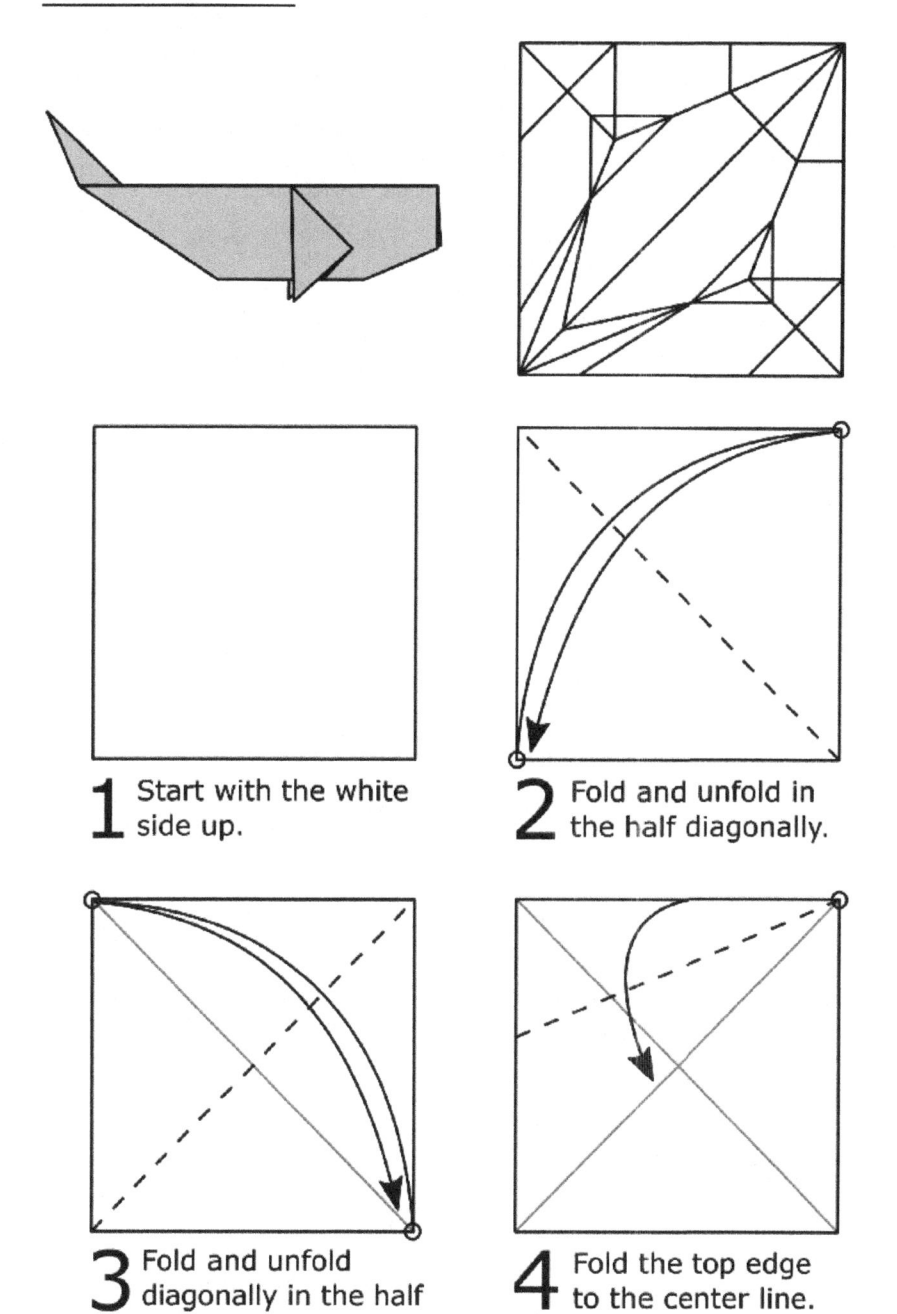

1. Start with the white side up.
2. Fold and unfold in the half diagonally.
3. Fold and unfold diagonally in the half to the other direction.
4. Fold the top edge to the center line.

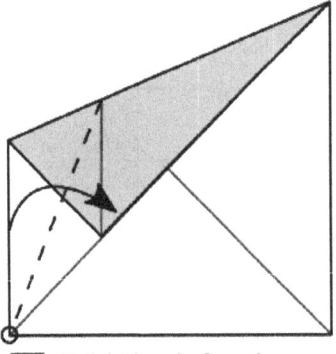

5 Fold the left edge to the center line.

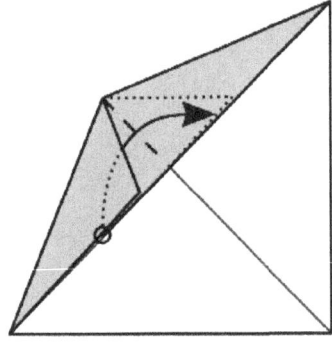

6 Take out the hidden corner to the top.

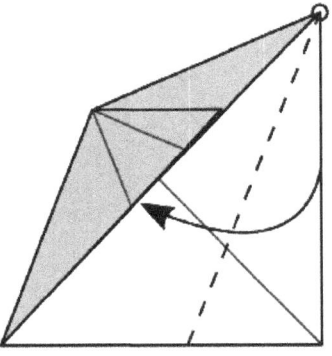

7 Fold the right edge to the center line.

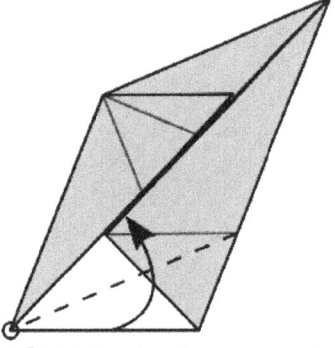

8 Fold the bottom edge to the center line.

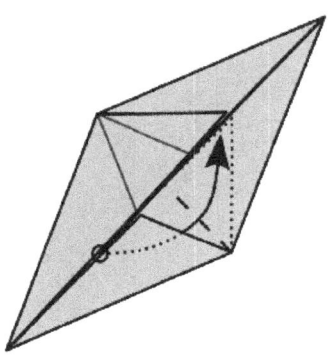

9 Take out the hidden corner to the top.

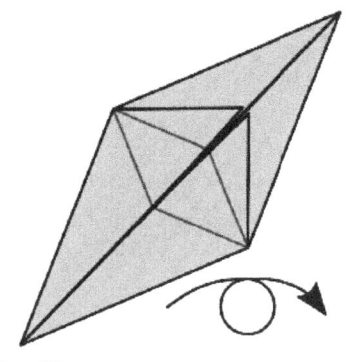

10 Turn the model over.

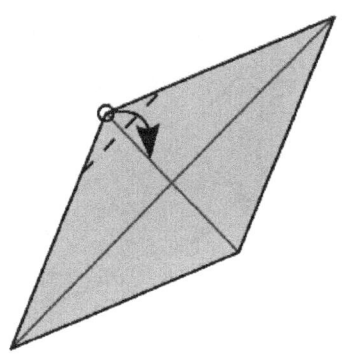

11 Fold the corner on the center line.

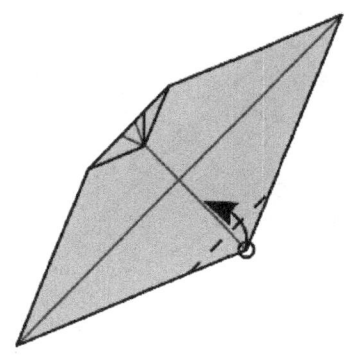

12 Fold the opposite corner on the center line.

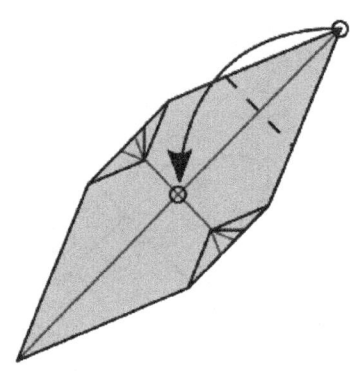

13 Fold the top corner to the center point.

14 Fold the model in the half.

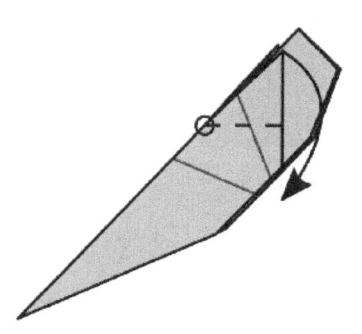

15 Fold the corner down accroding to the marked point.

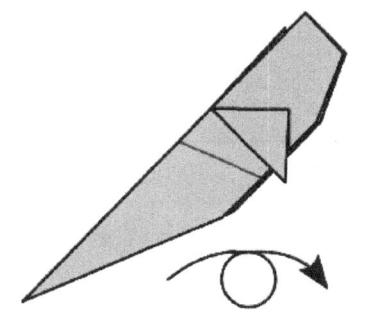

16 Turn the model over.

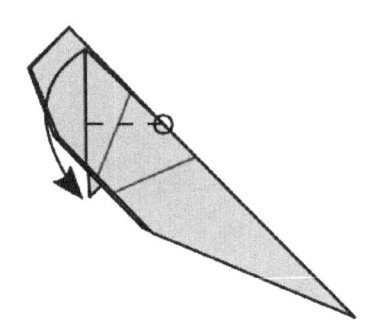

17 Fold the corner down according to the marked point.

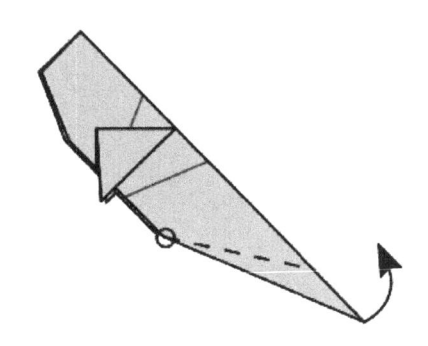

18 Fold the corner up according to the marked point.

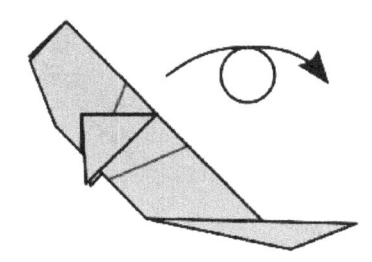

19 Turn the model over.

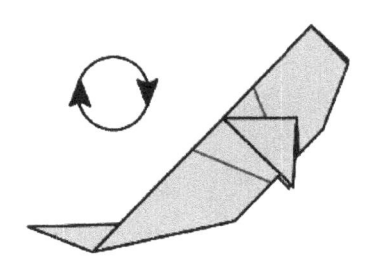

20 Rotate the model.

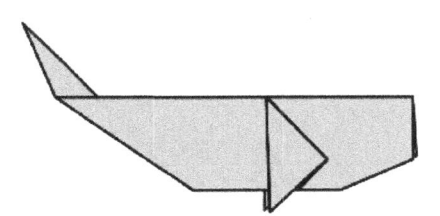

21 Finished whale!

Seal

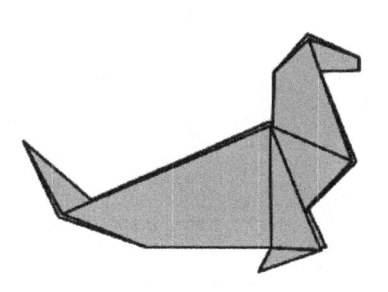

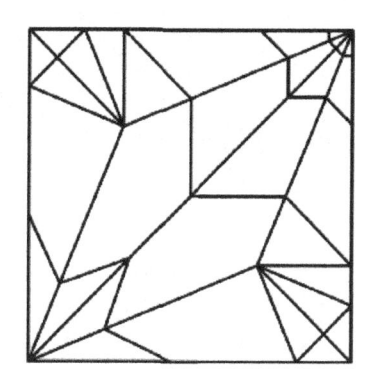

1. Start with the white side up.
2. Fold and unfold in the half diagonally. 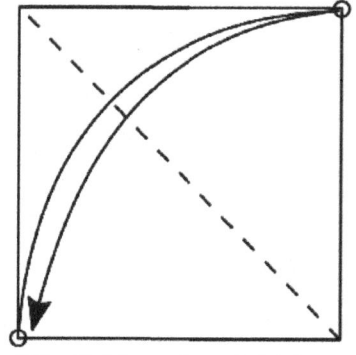
3. Fold and unfold diagonally in the half to the other direction. 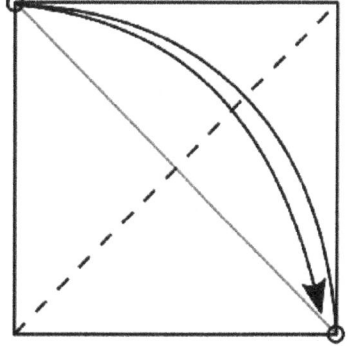
4. Fold the top edge to the center line.

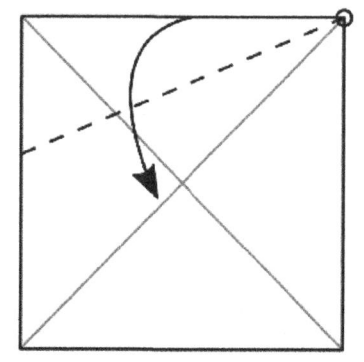

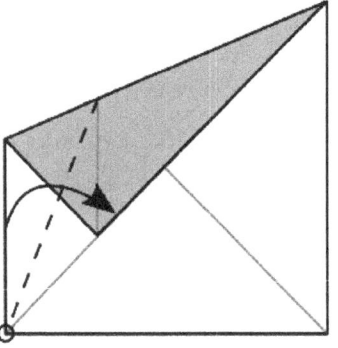

5 Fold the left edge to the center line.

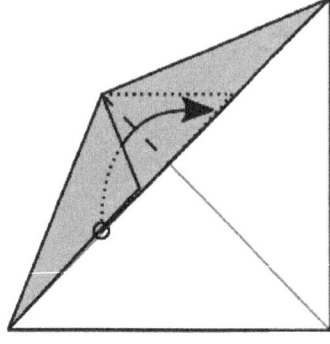

6 Take out the hidden corner to the top.

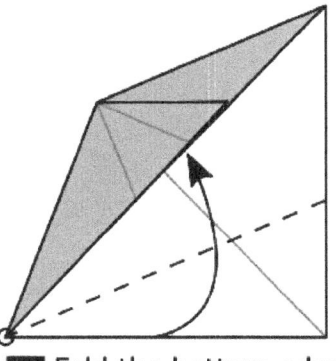

7 Fold the bottom edge to the center line.

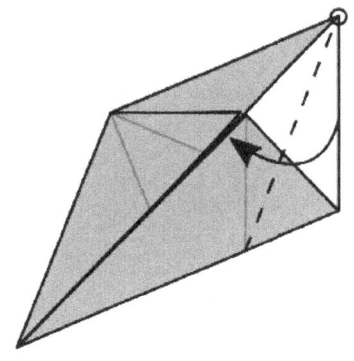

8 Fold the right edge to the center line.

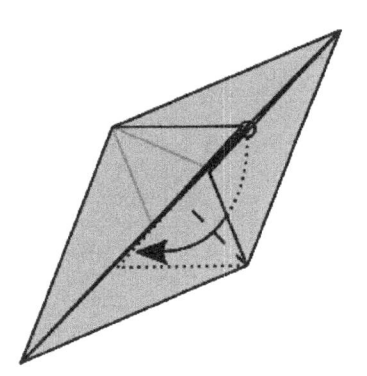

9 Take out the hidden corner to the bottom.

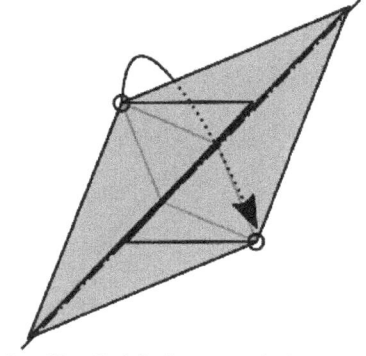

10 Fold the model behind in the half.

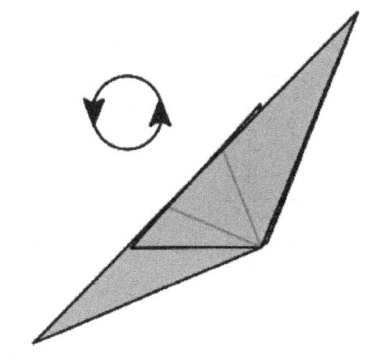

11 Rotate the model.

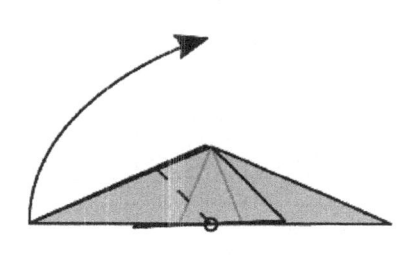

12 Fold the corner up according to the market point.

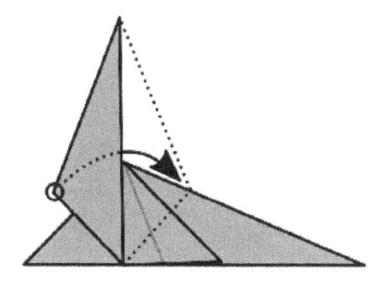

13 Take out the hidden corner to the right.

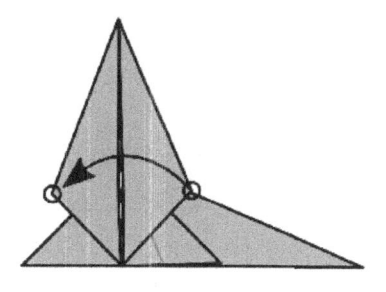

14 Fold the corner to the left.

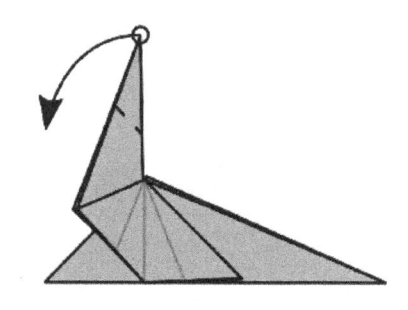

15 Fold the corner vertically down.

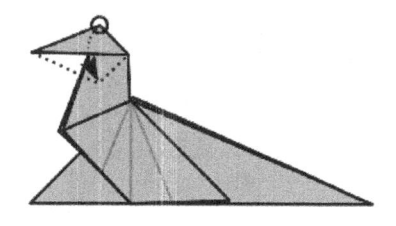

16 Take out the hidden corner down.

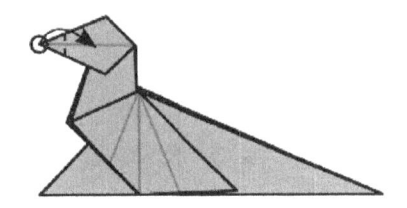

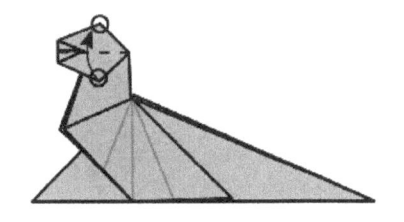

17 Fold the corner on the middle line.

18 Fold the corner to the top point.

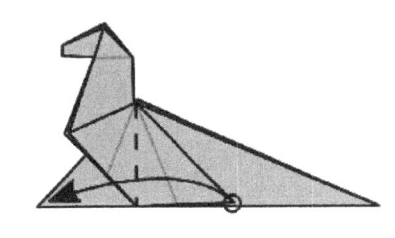

19 Fold the corner to the left.

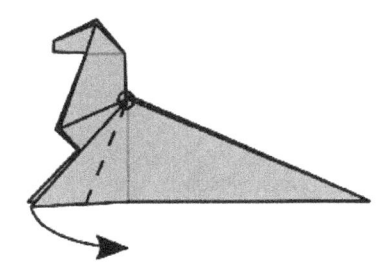

20 Fold the corner down according to the marked point.

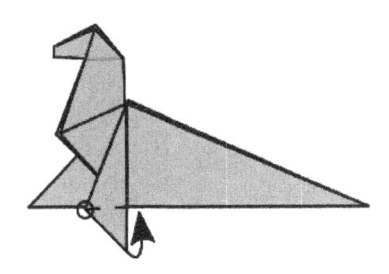

21 Fold the corner vertically up.

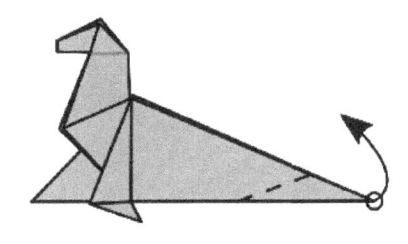

22 Fold the corner up.

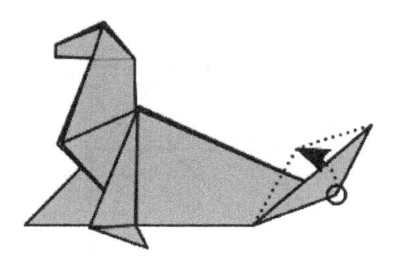

23 Take out the hidden corner to the left.

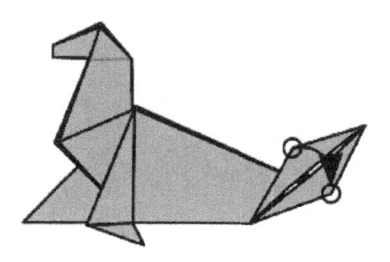

24 Fold the corner to the left.

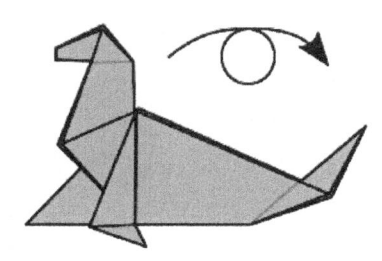

25 Turn over the model.

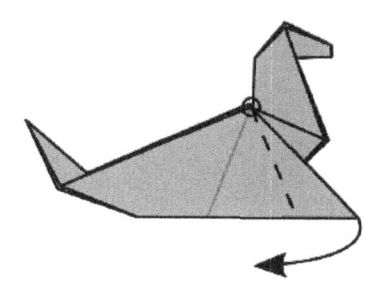

26 Fold the corner down according to the marked point.

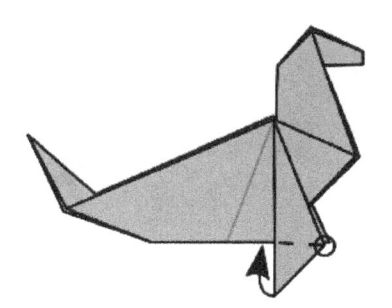

27 Fold the coroner vertically up.

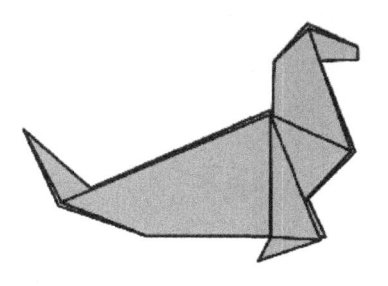

28 Finished seal!

Fish

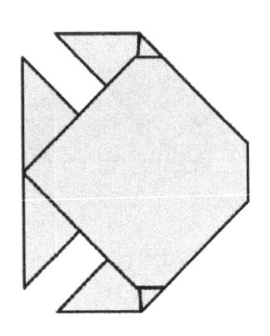

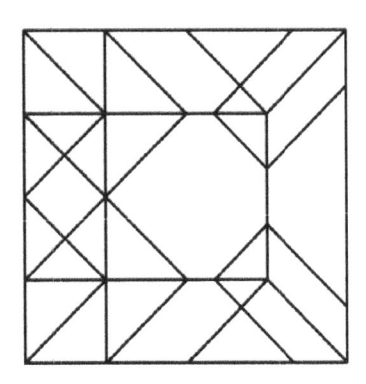

1 Start with the white side up.

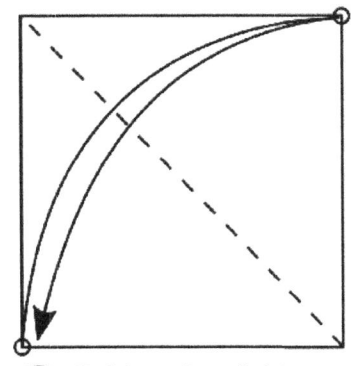

2 Fold and unfold diagonally in the half.

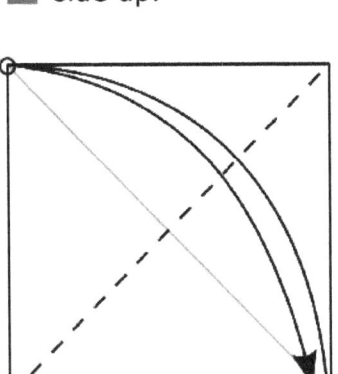

3 Fold and unfold diagonally in the half to the other direction.

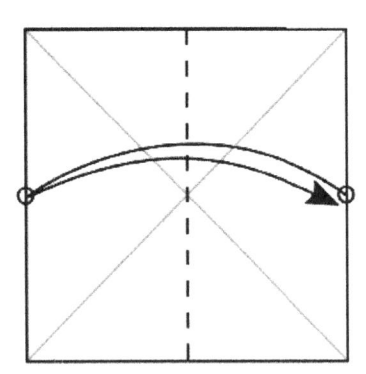

4 Fold and unfold vertically in the half.

60

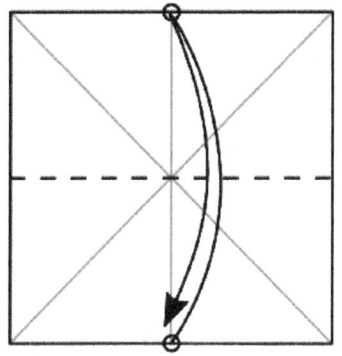

5 Fold and unfold horizontally in the half.

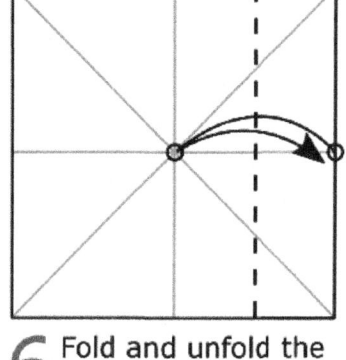

6 Fold and unfold the right edge to the center line.

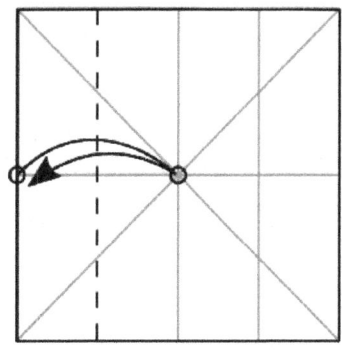

7 Fold and unfold the left edge to the center line.

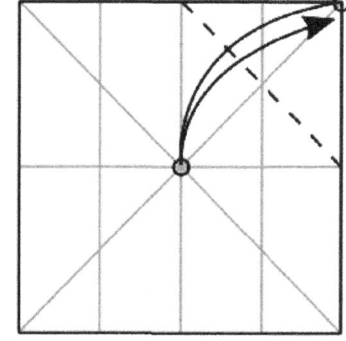

8 Fold and unfold the top right corner to the center point.

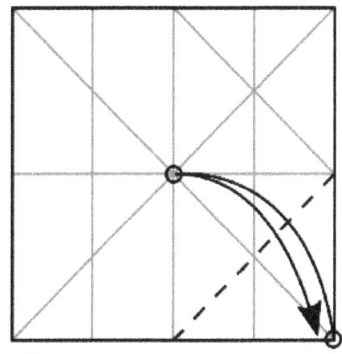

9 Fold and unfold the bottom right corner to the center point.

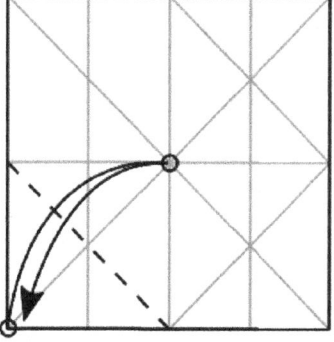

10 Fold and unfold the bottom left corner to the center point.

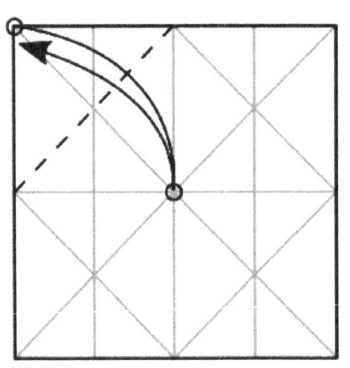

11 Fold and unfold the top left corner to the center point.

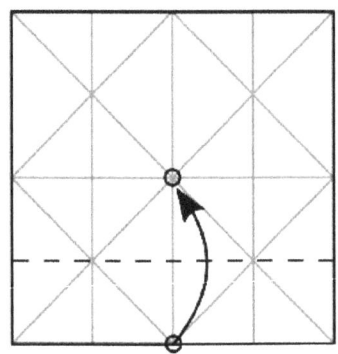

12 Fold the bottom edge to the center line.

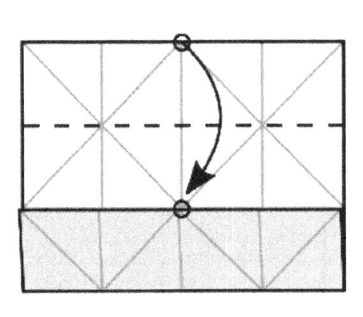

13 Fold the top edge to the center line.

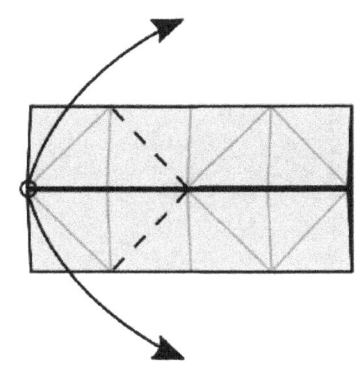

14 Fold the corners to the sides according to the marked lines.

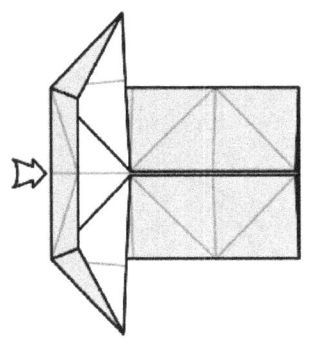

15 Squash the paper down to make it flat.

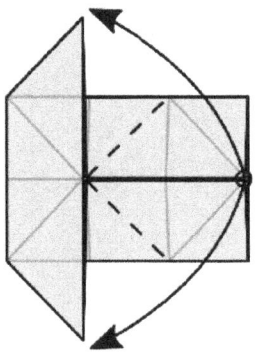

16 Fold the corner to the sides according to the marked lines.

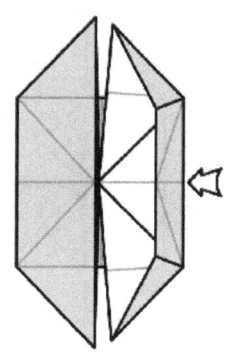

17 Squash the paper down to make it flat.

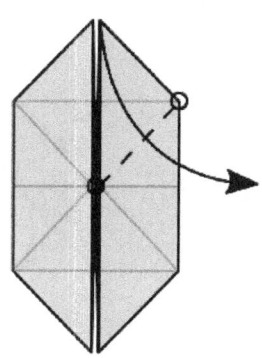

18 Fold the corner down according to the marked point.

19 Fold the corner up according to the marked points.

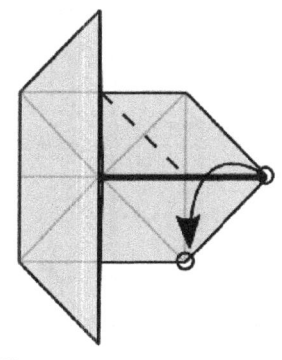

20 Fold the corner to the bottom point.

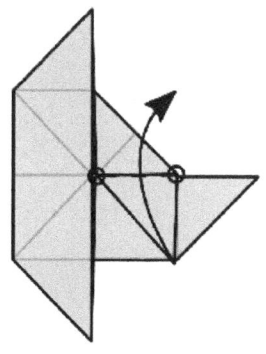

21 Fold the corner up according to the marked points.

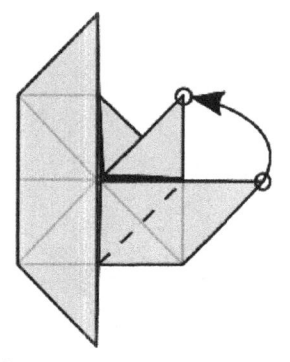

22 Fold the corner to the top point.

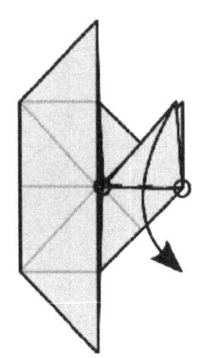

23 Fold the corner down according to the marked points.

24 Fold the corner diagonally down.

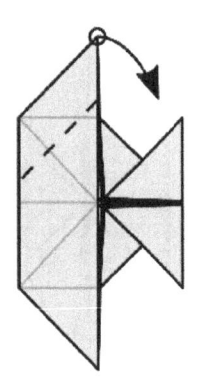

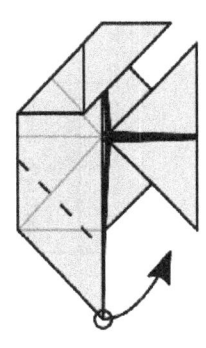

25 Fold the corner diagonally up.

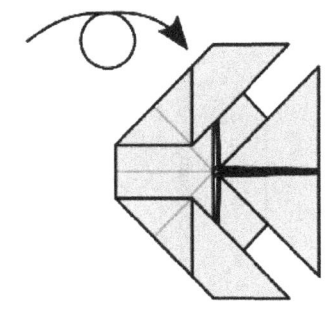

26 Turn the model over.

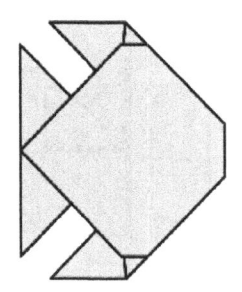

27 Finished fish!

Rose

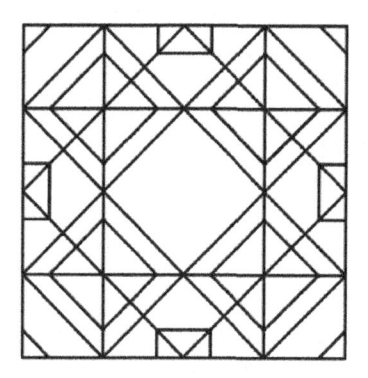

1. Start with the white side up.
2. Fold and unfold in the half diagonally. 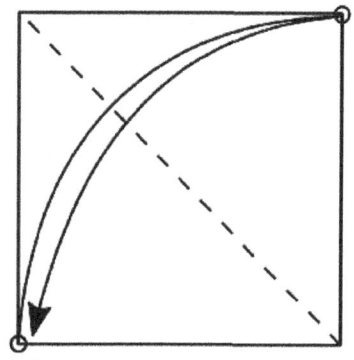
3. Fold and unfold diagonally in the half to the other direction. 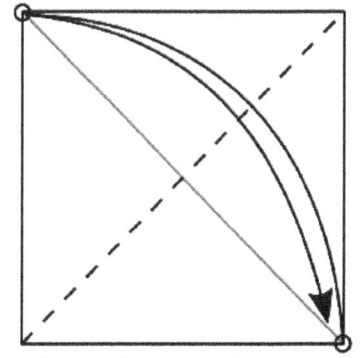
4. Fold the top right corner to the center point.

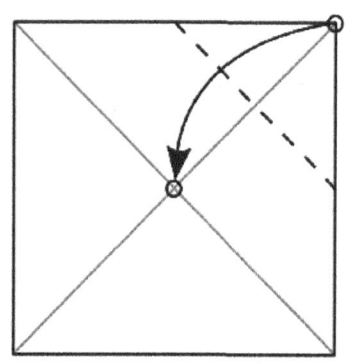

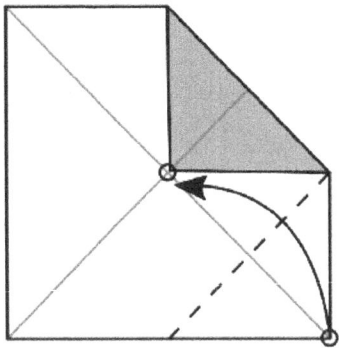

5 Fold the bottom right corner to the center point.

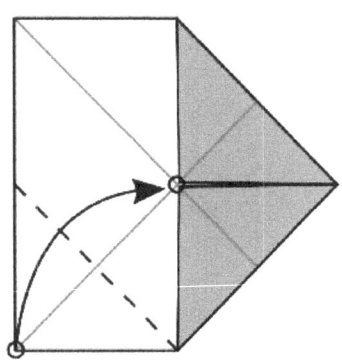

6 Fold the bottom left corner to the center point.

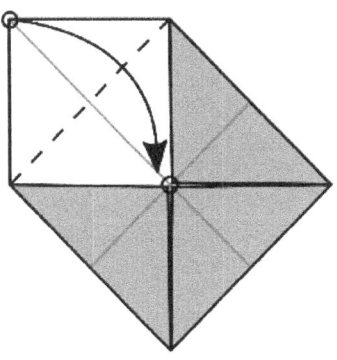

7 Fold the top left corner to the center point.

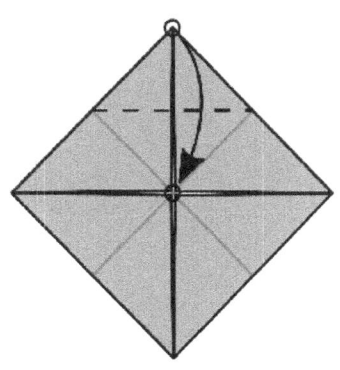

8 Fold the top corner to the center point.

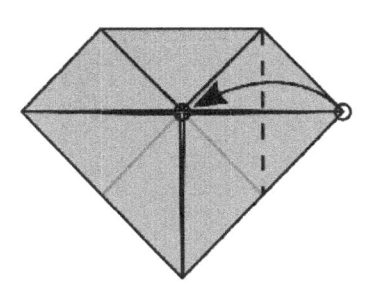

9 Fold the right corner to the center point.

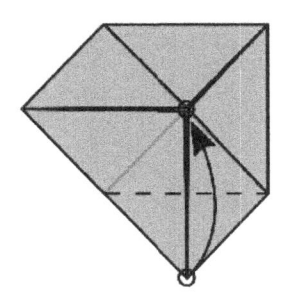

10 Fold the bottom corner to the center point.

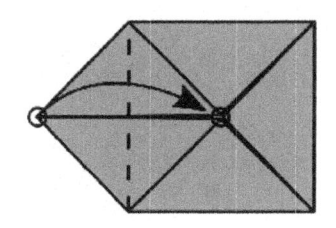

11 Fold the left corner to the center point.

12 Fold the top right corner to the center point.

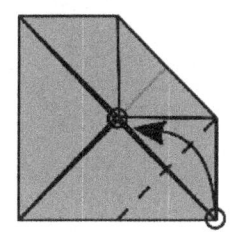

13 Fold the bottom right corner to the center point.

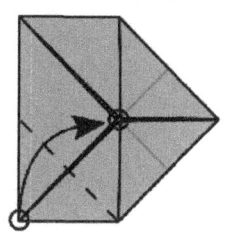

14 Fold the bottom left corner to the center point.

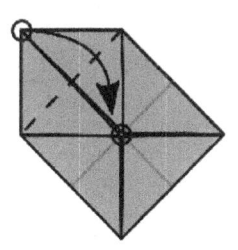

15 Fold the top left corner to the center point.

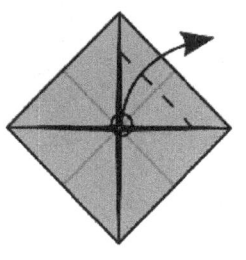

16 Fold the corner outside to the top right.

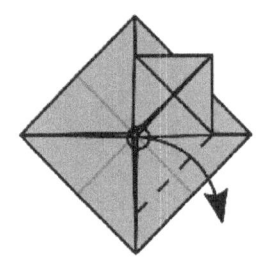

17 Fold the corner outside to the bottom right.

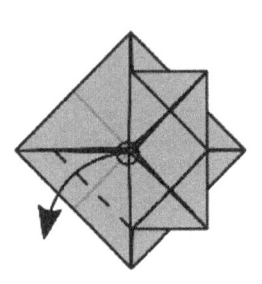

18 Fold the corner outside to the bottom left.

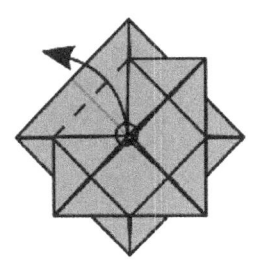

19 Fold the corner outside to the top left.

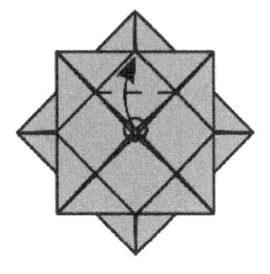

20 Fold the corner from the center to the top.

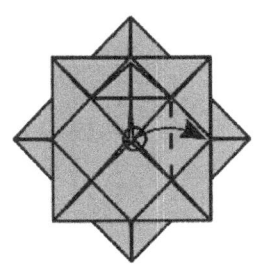

21 Fold the corner from the center to the right.

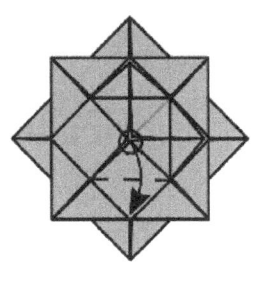

22 Fold the corner from the center to the bottom.

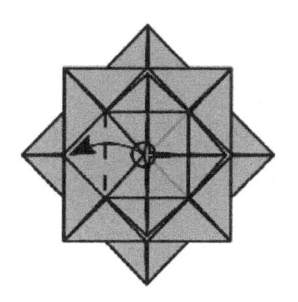

23 Fold the corner from the center to the left.

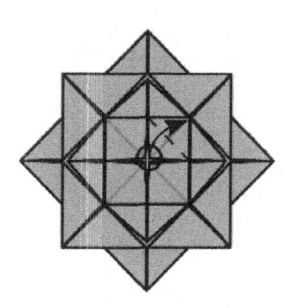

24 Fold the corner to the top right.

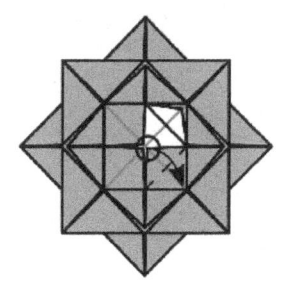

25 Fold the corner to the bottom right.

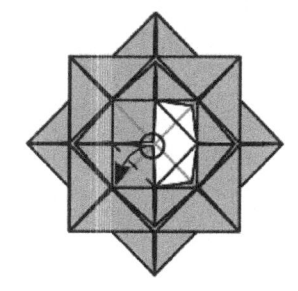

26 Fold the corner to the bottom left.

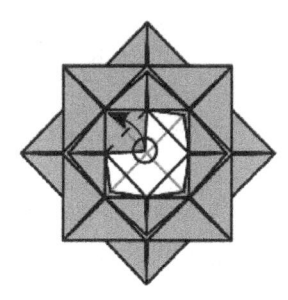

27 Fold the corner to the top left.

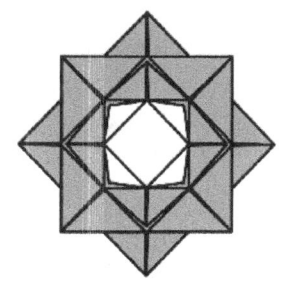

28 Finished rose!

Duck

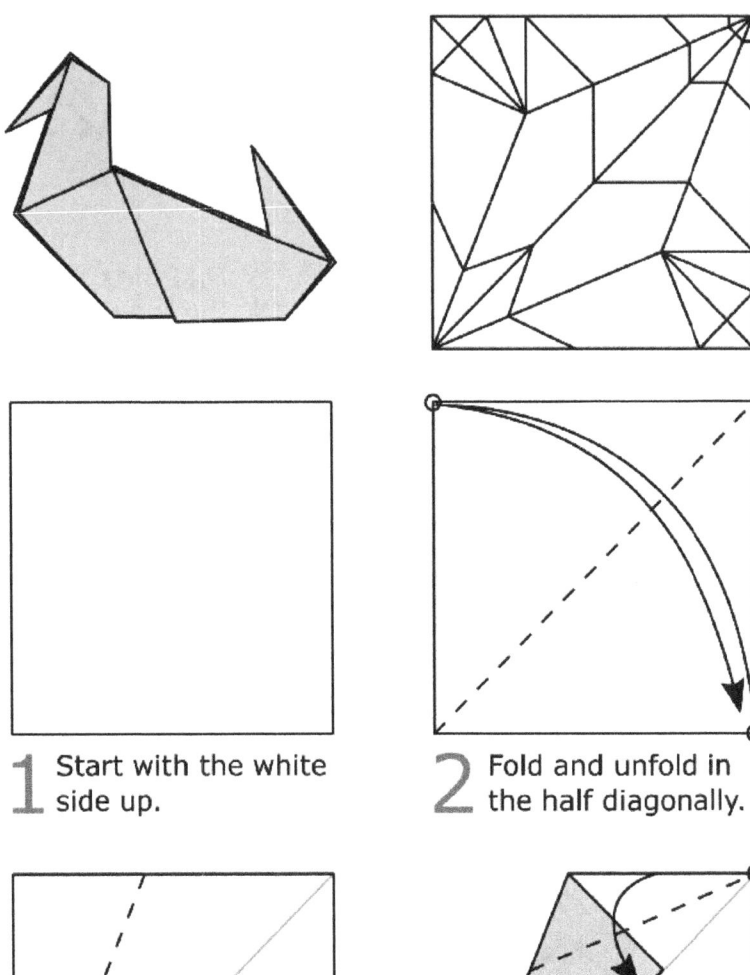

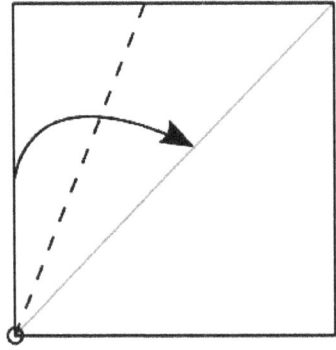

1. Start with the white side up.

2. Fold and unfold in the half diagonally.

3. Fold the left edge to the center line.

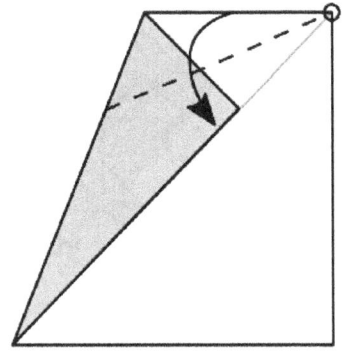

4. Fold the top edge to the center line.

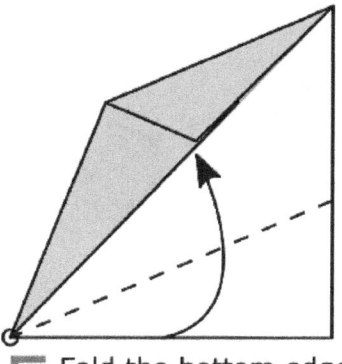

5 Fold the bottom edge to the center line.

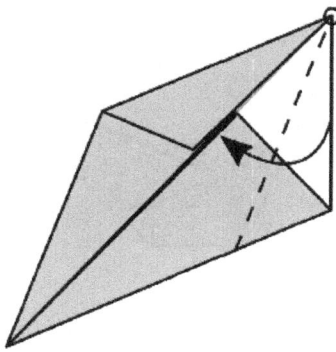

6 Fold the right edge to the center line.

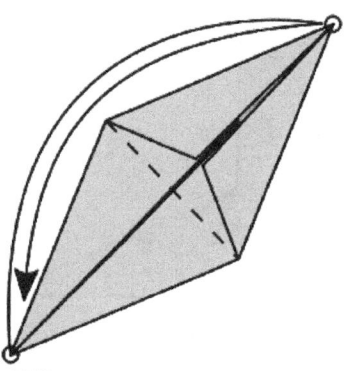

7 Fold and unfold diagonally in the half.

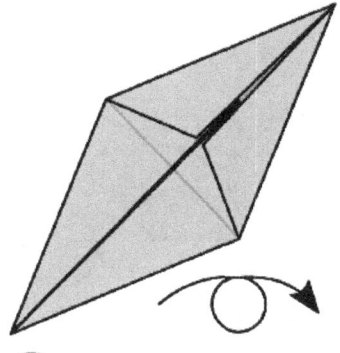

8 Turn the model over.

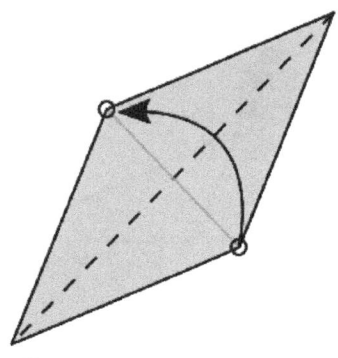

9 Fold the model in half to the top point.

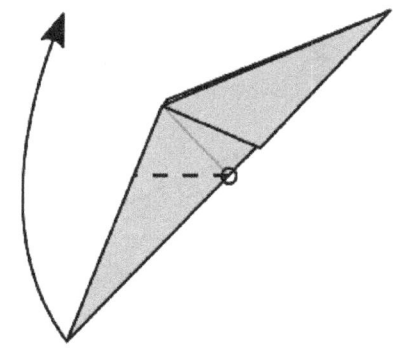

10 Fold the corner up according to the marked point.

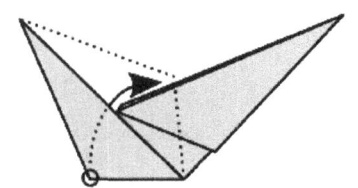

11 Take out the hidden corner to the right.

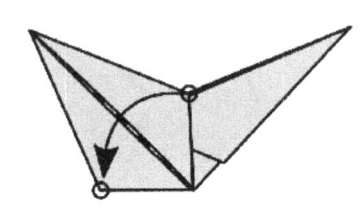

12 Fold the corner to the left.

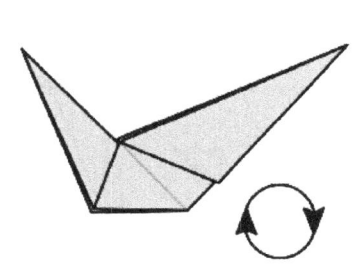

13 Rotate the model.

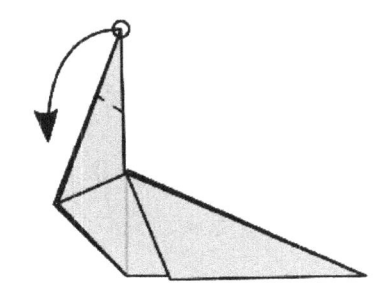

14 Fold the corner down.

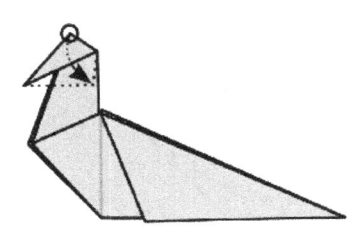

15 Take out the hidden corner down.

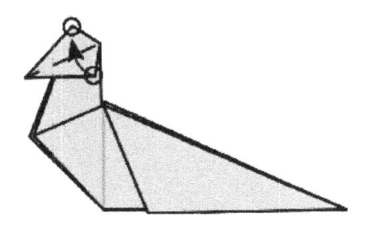

16 Fold the corner up.

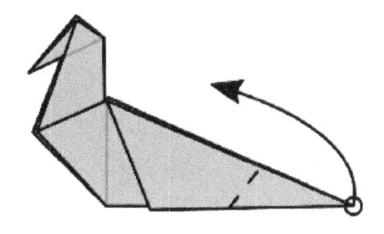

17 Fold the corner up.

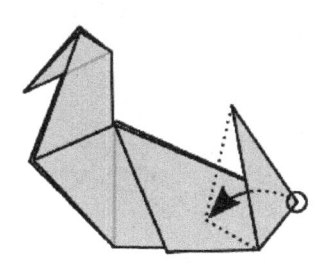

18 Take out the hidden corner to the left.

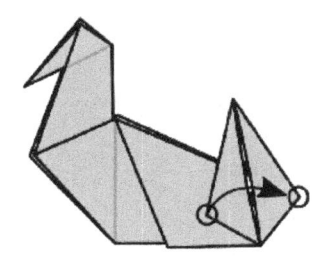

19 Fold the corner to the right.

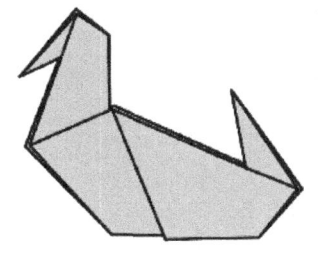

20 Finished duck!

Sailboat

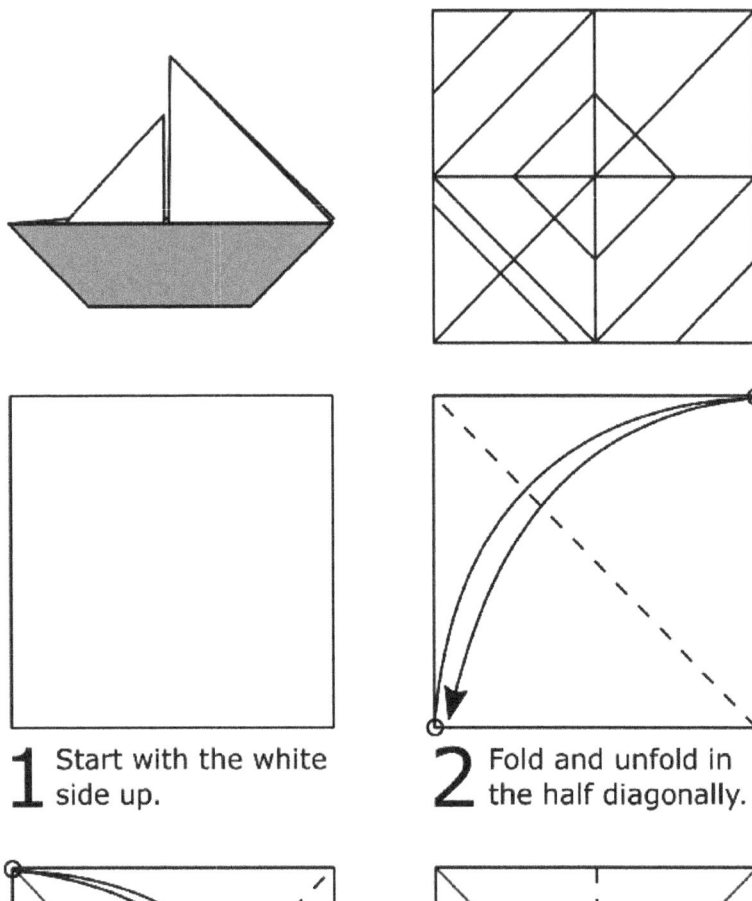

1. Start with the white side up.
2. Fold and unfold in the half diagonally.
3. Fold and unfold diagonally in the half to the other direction. 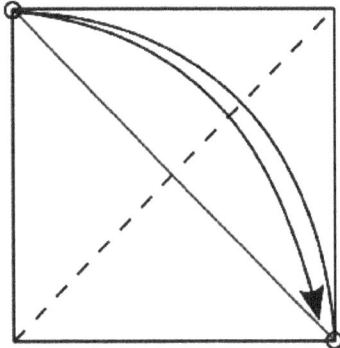
4. Fold and unfold vertically in the half.

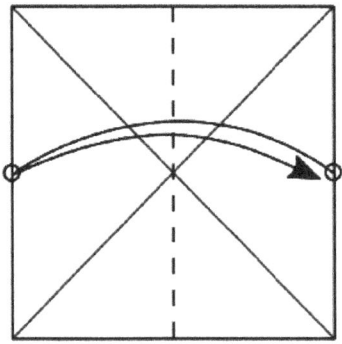

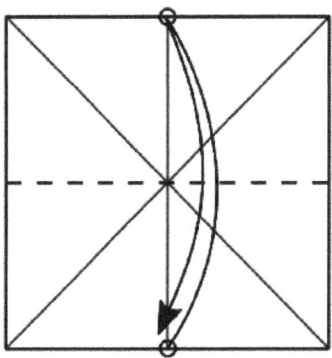

5 Fold and unfold horizontally in the half.

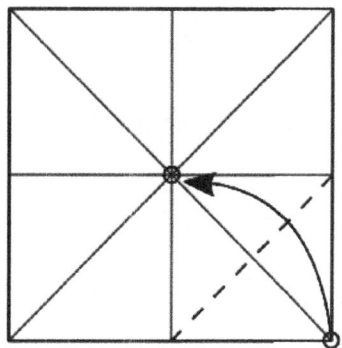

6 Fold the bottom right corner to the center point.

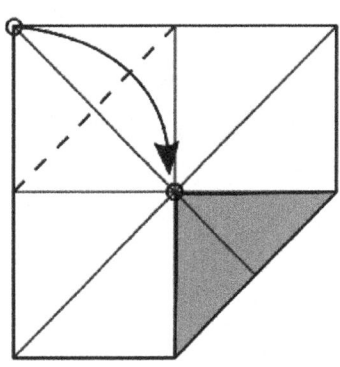

7 Fold the top left corner to the center point.

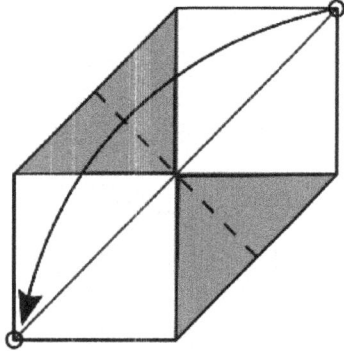

8 Fold the top right corner to the bottom left corner.

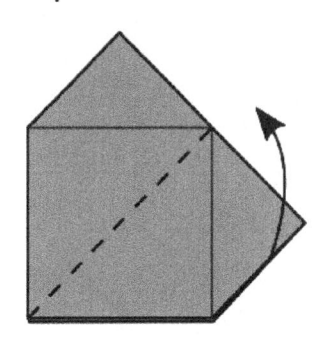

9 Fold the left edge vertically up.

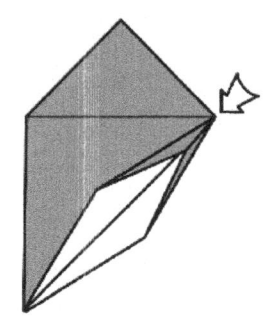

10 Squash fold the edge down to make the model flat.

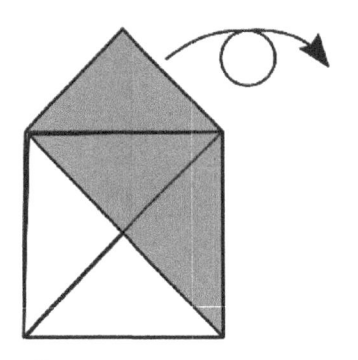

11 Turn the model over.

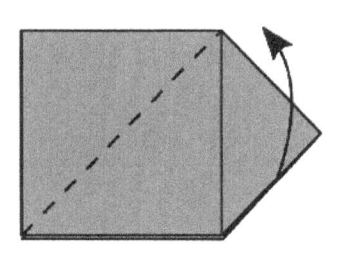

12 Fold the left edge vertically up.

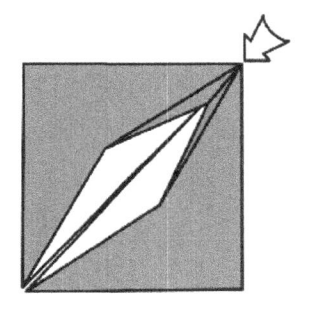

13 Squash fold the edge down to make the model flat.

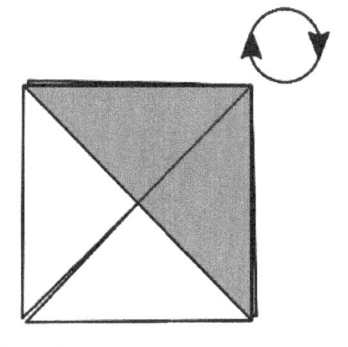

14 Rotate the model.

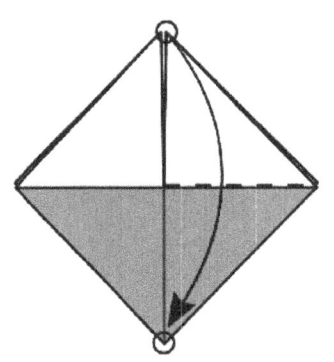

15 Fold the top left corner to the bottom point.

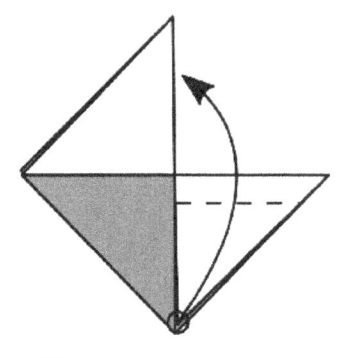

16 Fold the corner up.

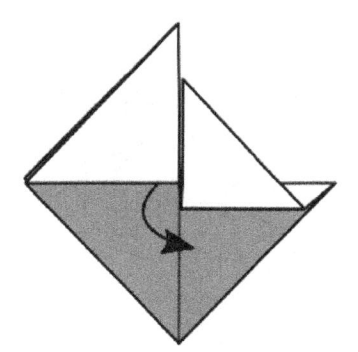

17 Bring the paper layer from behind to the front.

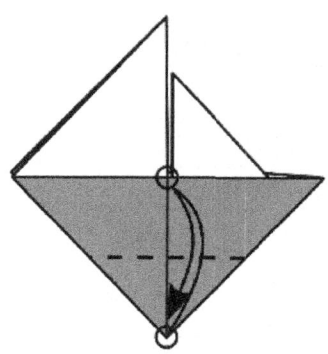

18 Fold and unfold the bottom corner to the center point.

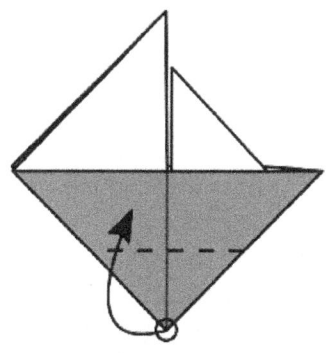

19 Fold the bottom corner vertically up.

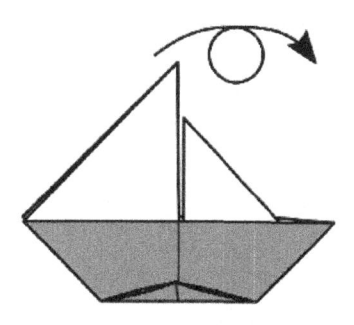

20 Turn the model over.

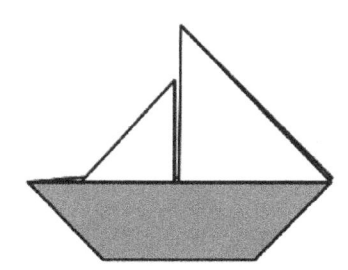

21 Finished sailboat!

Parrot

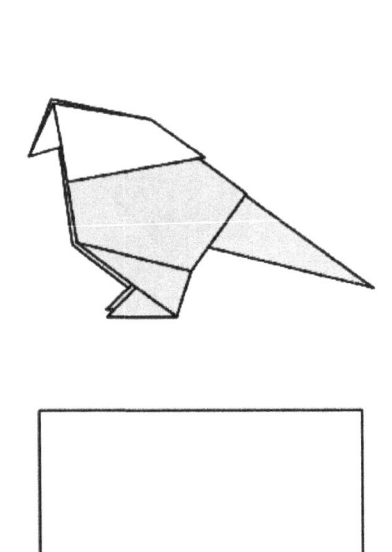

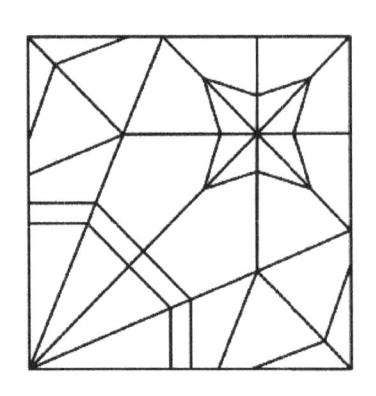

1. Start with the white side up.
2. Fold and unfold in the half diagonally. 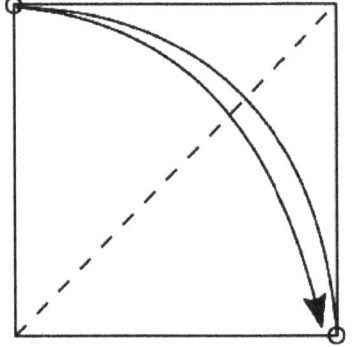
3. Fold the left edge to the center line. 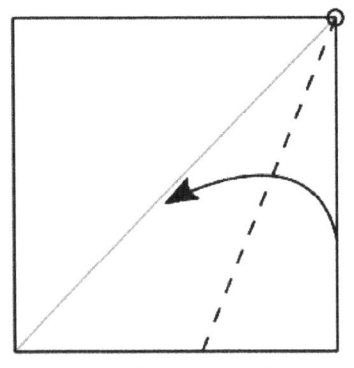
4. Fold the top edge to the center line.

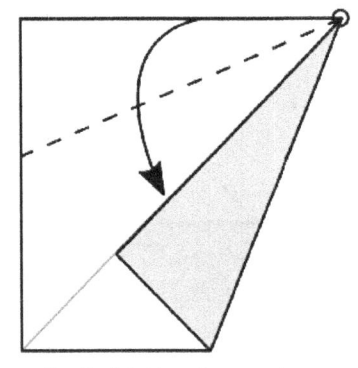

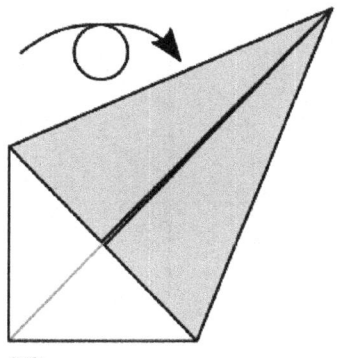

5 Turn the model over.

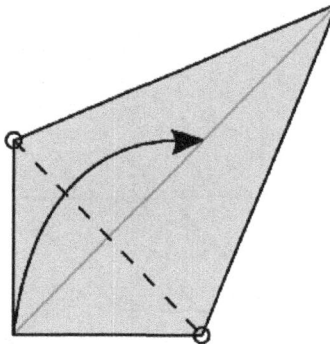

6 Fold the corner up according to the marked points.

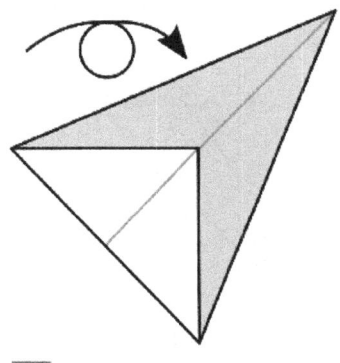

7 Turn the model over.

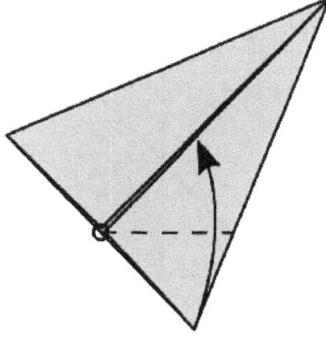

8 Fold the corner to the center line according to the marked point.

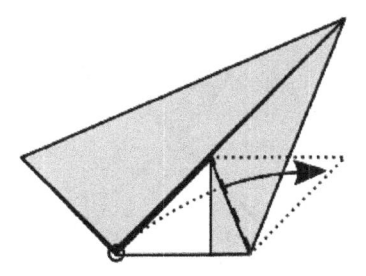

9 Take out the hidden corner to the right.

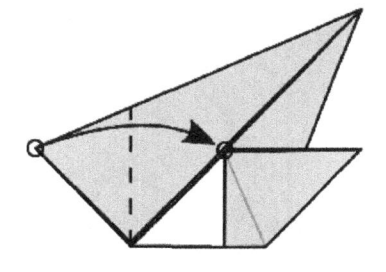

10 Fold the corner to the marked point.

79

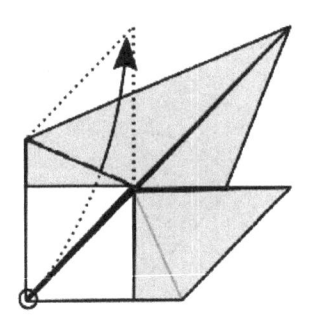

11 Take out the hidden corner to the top.

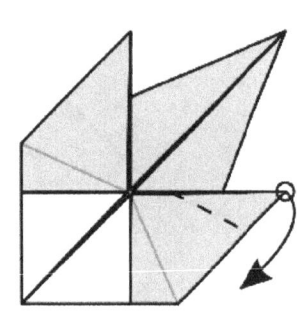

12 Fold the corner down.

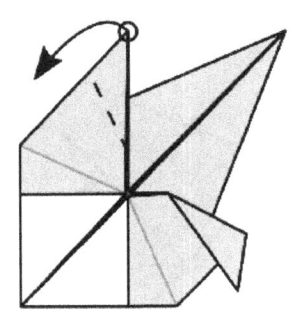

13 Fold the opposite corner symmetrically down.

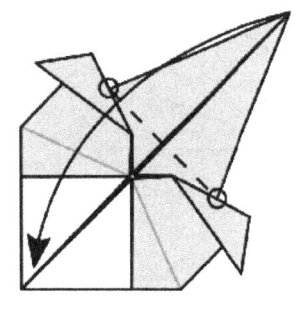

14 Fold the corner down according to the marked points.

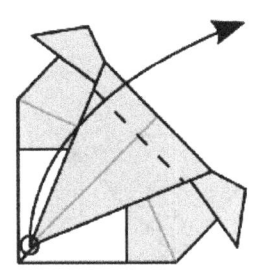

15 Fold the corner up.

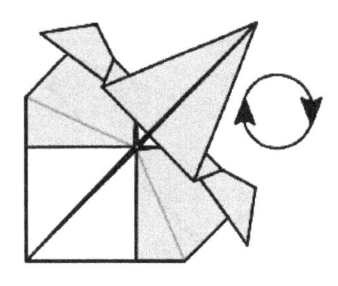

16 Rotate the model.

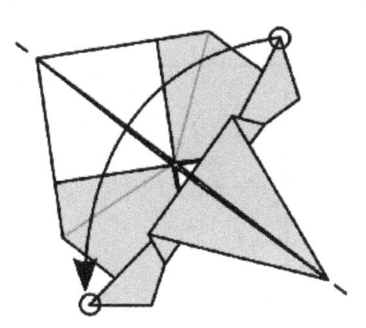

17 Fold the model in down in half.

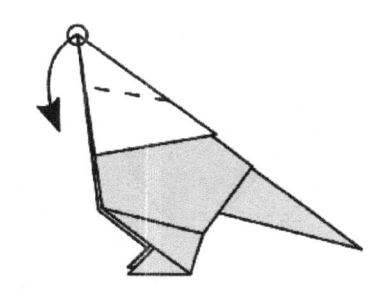

18 Fold the corner down.

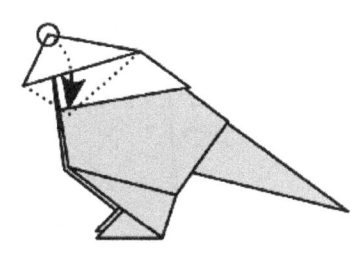

19 Take out the hidden corner to the bottom.

20 Fold the corner to the top point.

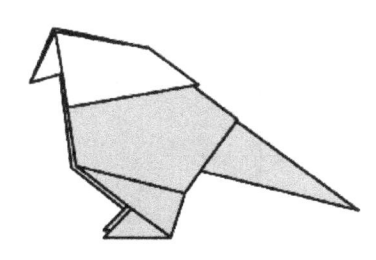

21 Finished parrot!

Lion

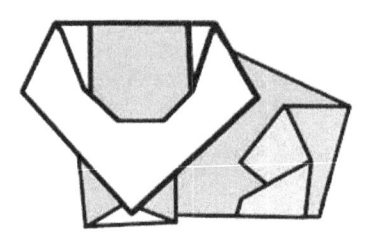

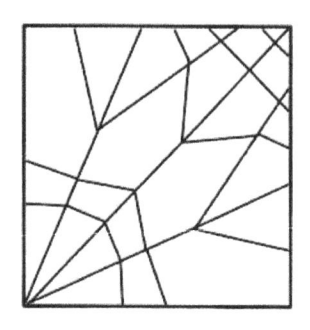

1. Start with the white side up.

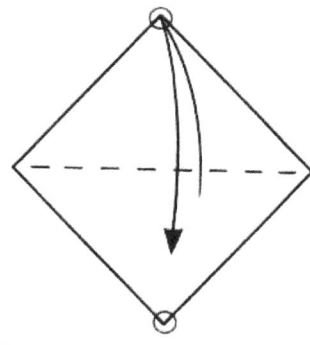

2. Fold and unfold in the half diagonally.

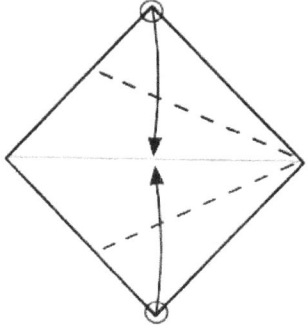

3. Fold the corners to the center.

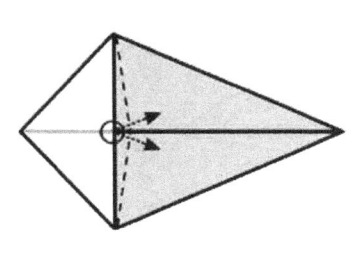

4. Fold the layers inside in the dotted lines.

82

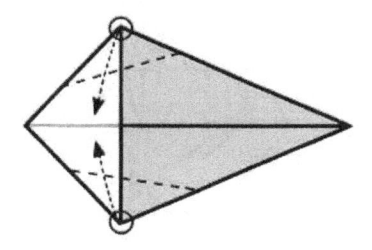

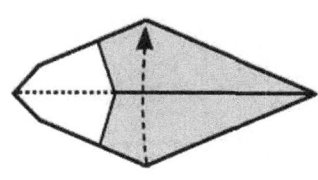

5 Fold back in the dotted lines.

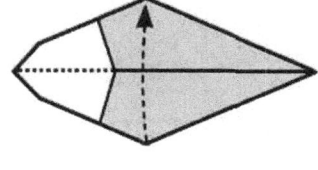

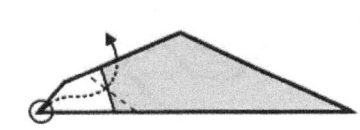

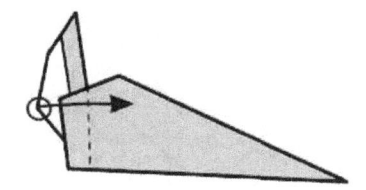

6 Fold in half.

7 Pocket fold in the dotted lines.

8 Open the front layer to the right in the dotted lines.

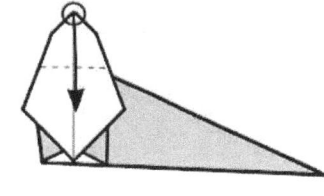

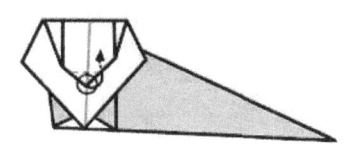

9 Fold to the marked point to form the head.

10 Fold back in the dotted line.

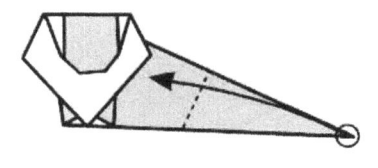

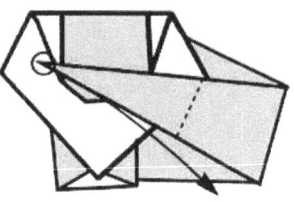

11 Fold to the left in the dotted line.

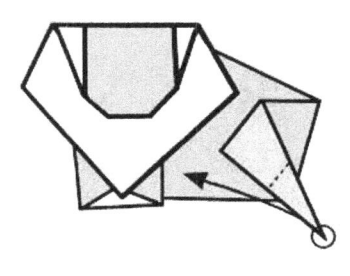

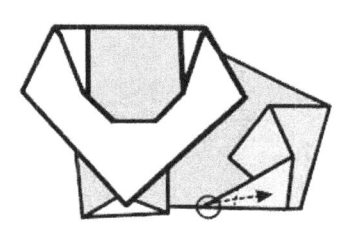

12 Fold diagonally down.

13 Fold to the marked point.

14 Pocket fold inside in the dotted line.

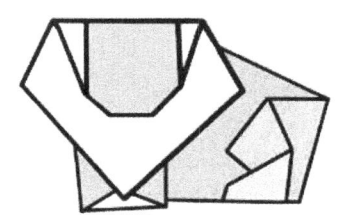

15 Finished Lion!

84

Crow

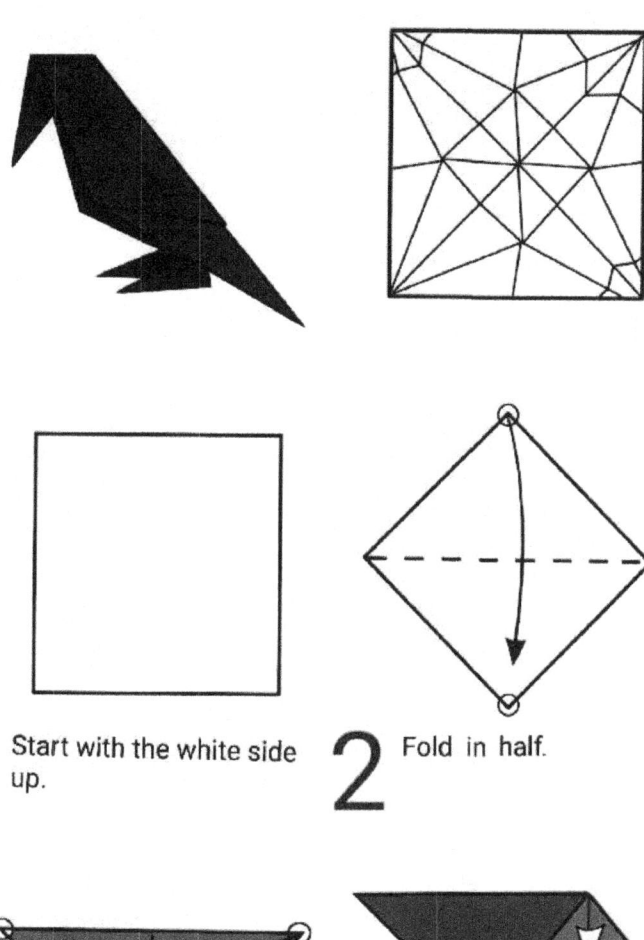

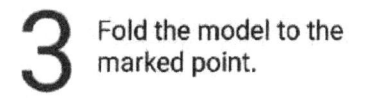

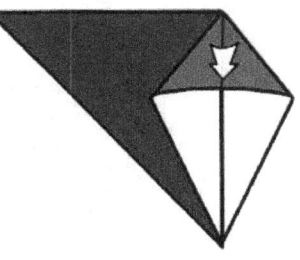

1. Start with the white side up.
2. Fold in half.
3. Fold the model to the marked point.
4. Squash fold the front layer.

85

5 Turn the model over.

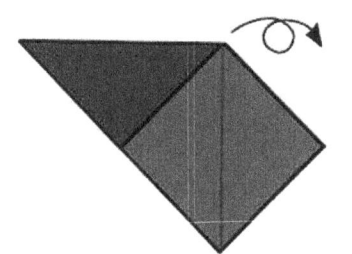

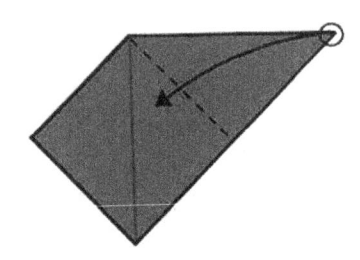

6 Squash fold the other side.

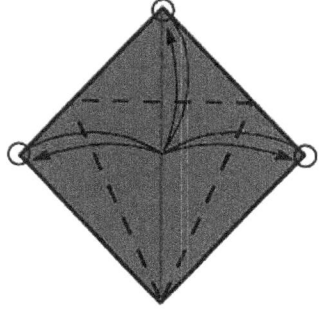

7 Fold and unfold the left, right and the top corners to the center.

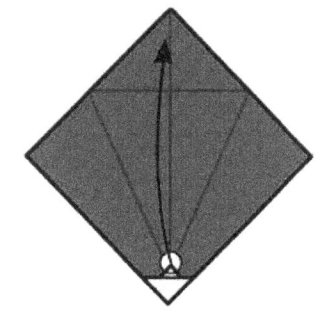

8 Lift the bottom corner up.

9 Squash fold the left and right side.

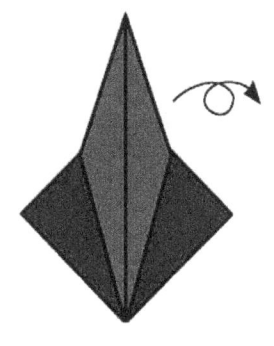

10 Turn the model over.

11 Lift the bottom corner up.

12 Pocket fold the bottom right and left corners in the dotted lines.

13 Fold the front layer down.

14 Fold the marked point down in the dotted line.

15 Fold in half.

16 Pocket fold to form the head.

17 Finished crow!

Elasmosaurus

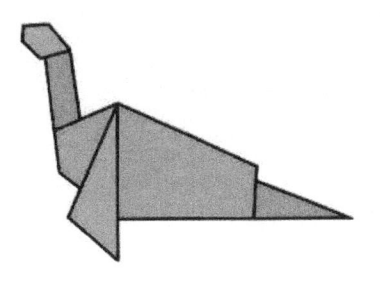

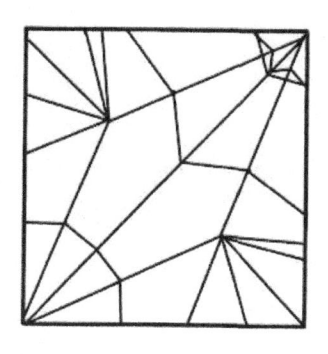

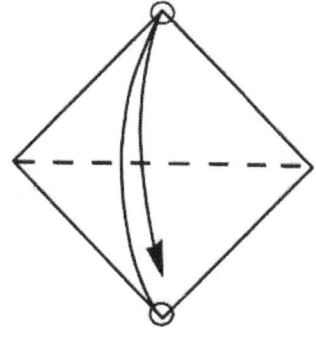

1 Start with the white side up.

2 Fold and unfold in the half diagonally.

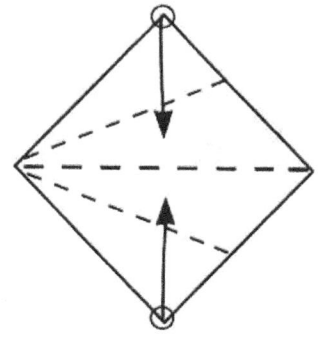

3 Fold the corners to the center.

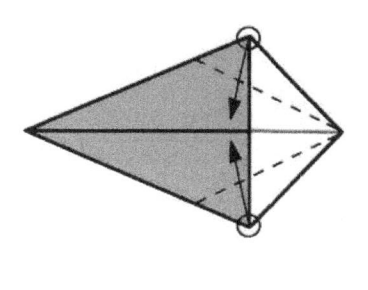

4 Fold in the dotted lines.

89

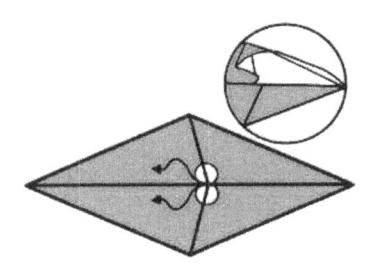

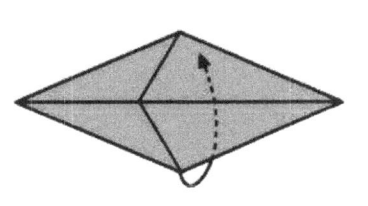

5 Open the pockets and fold as shown in the image.

6 Fold in half.

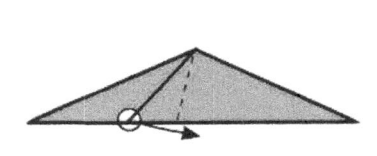

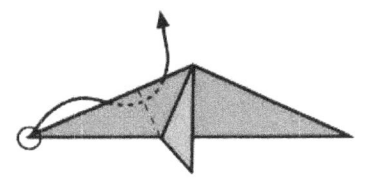

7 Fold to the right in the dotted lines.

8 Pocket fold to the marked point to form the neck.

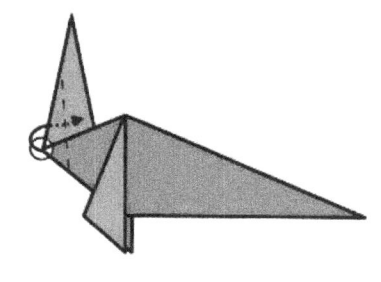

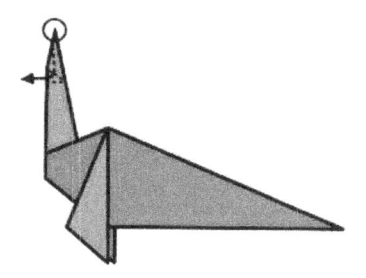

9 Fold inside in the dotted lines.

10 Fold the head down in the dotted lines doing a pocket fold.

11 Fold inside.

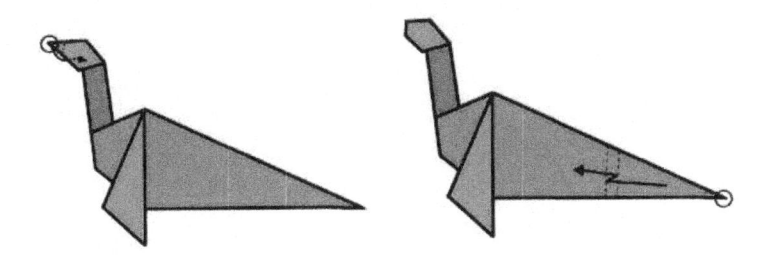

12 Do a step fold to form the tail.

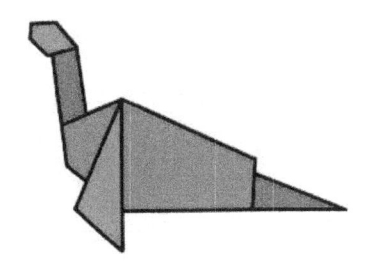

13 Finished elasmosaurus!

Mouse

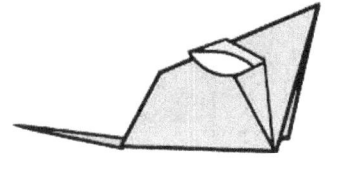

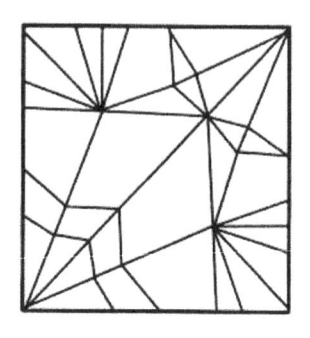

1. Start with the white side up.
2. Fold and unfold in the half diagonally. 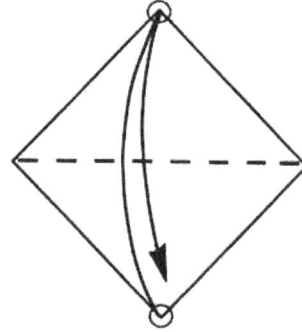
3. Fold the corners to the center. 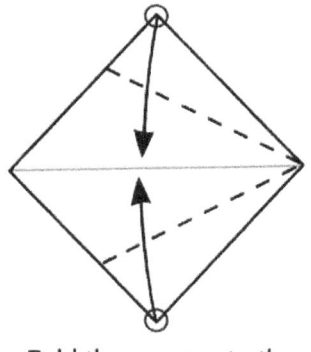
4. Fold in the dotted lines.

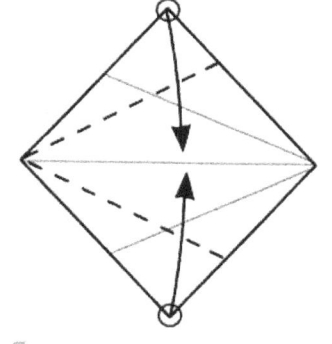

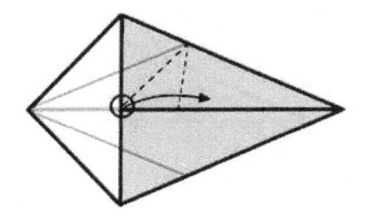

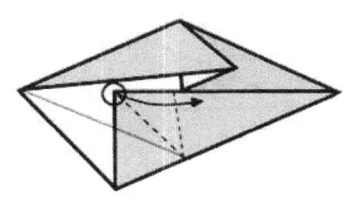

5 Fold down in the dotted lines creating a pocket.

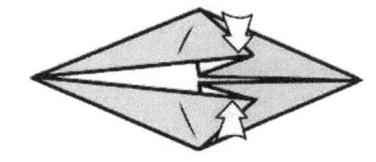

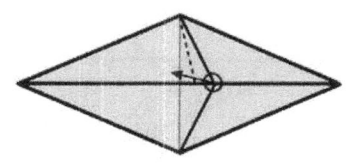

6 Fold the other side.

7 Flatten the pockets.

8 Mountain fold the flap behind.

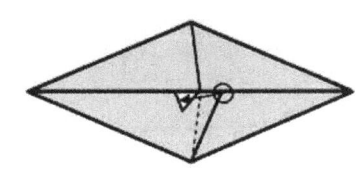

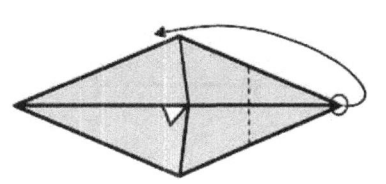

9 Fold the other flap accordingly.

10 Fold the tip behind.

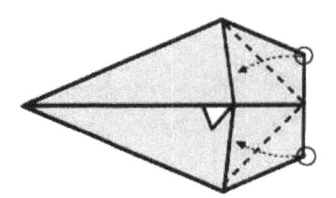

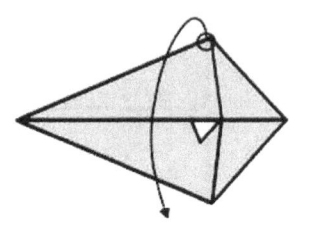

11 Fold back in the dotted lines.

12 Fold in half.

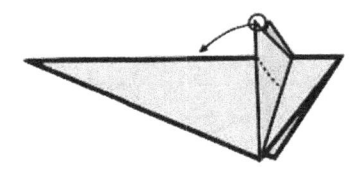

13 Fold the ears back opening the pockets.

14 Open the pockets to form the ears.

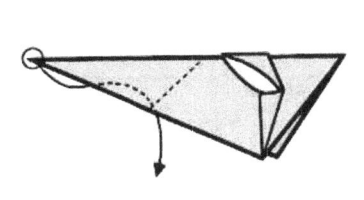

15 Pocket fold inside in the dotted lines.

16 Pocket fold to form a tail.

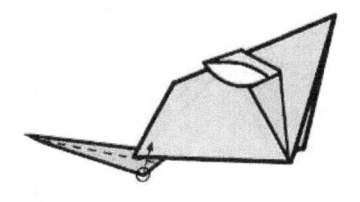

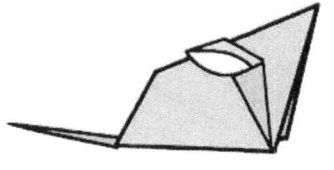

17 Fold the flaps inside. **18** Finished mouse!

Sparrow

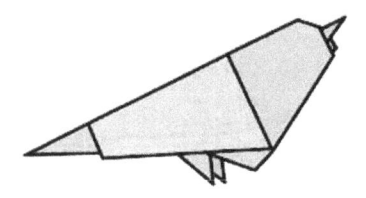

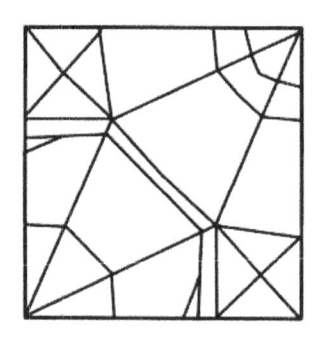

1. Start with the white side up.
2. Fold and unfold in the half diagonally. 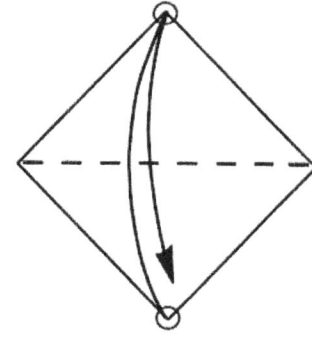
3. Fold the corners to the center. 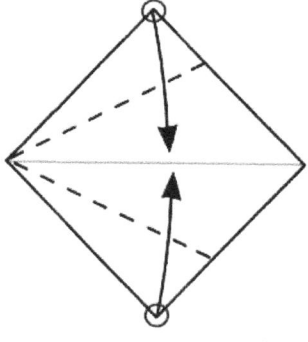
4. Fold in the dotted lines.

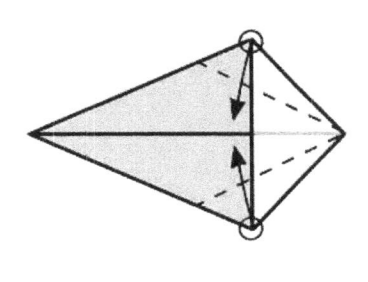

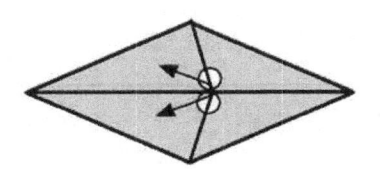

5 Open the pockets moving the corners to the marked points.

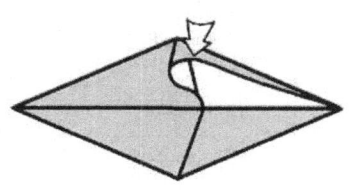

6 Flatten the pockets.

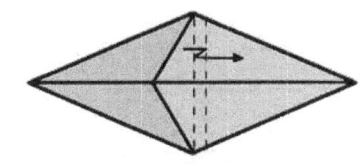

7 Step fold in the dotted lines.

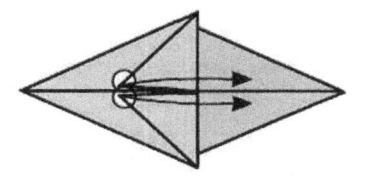

8 Fold forward.

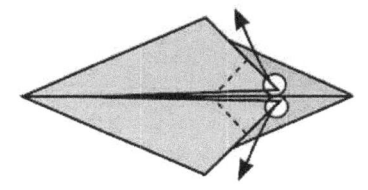

9 Fold the both sides in the dotted lines.

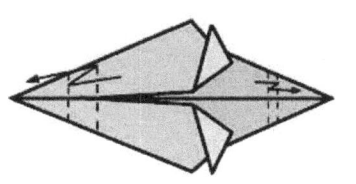

10 Step fold the both sides.

11 Fold in half.

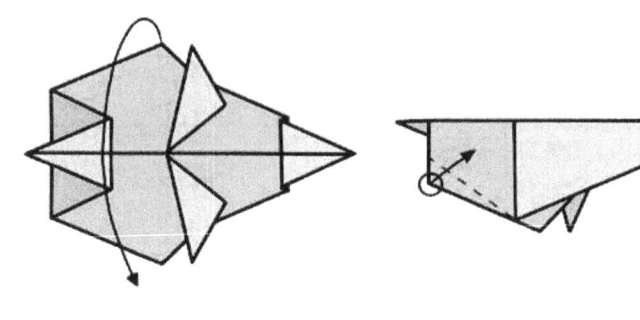

12 Fold both sides inside.

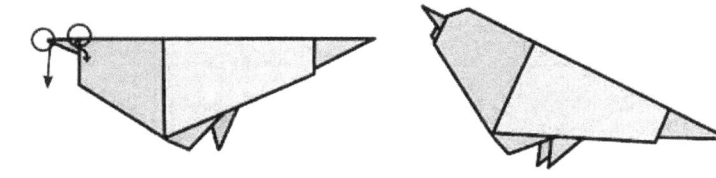

13 Pull down the beak and pocket fold inside the upper point on the head.

14 Finished sparrow!

Chicken

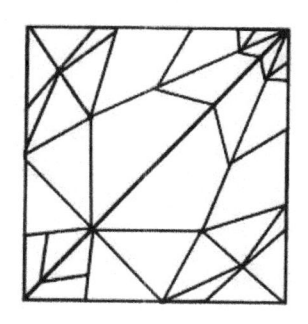

1. Start with the white side up.
2. Fold and unfold in the half diagonally. 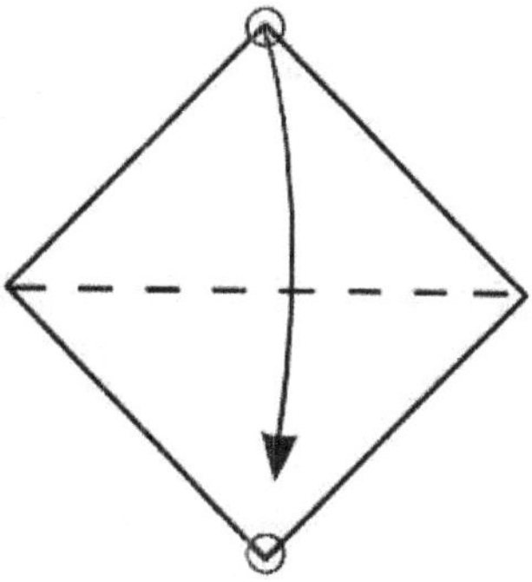
3. Fold the model to the marked point. 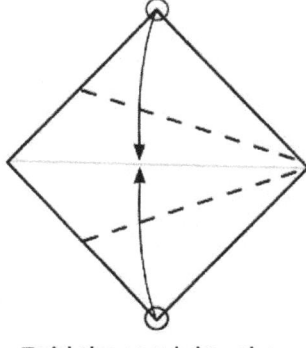
4. Fold back in the dotted lines.

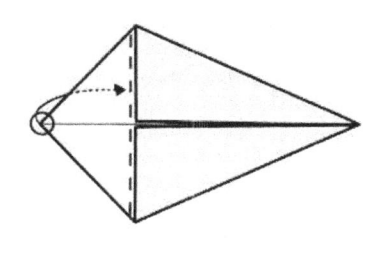

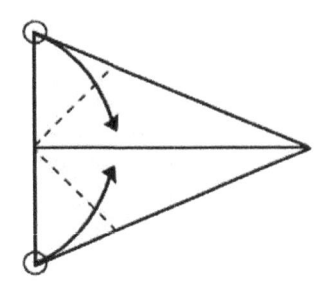

5 Fold in the dotted lines.

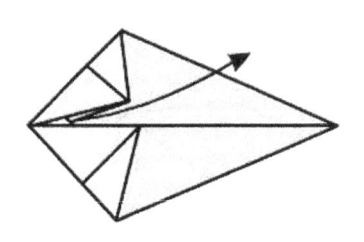

6 Pull out the pocket.

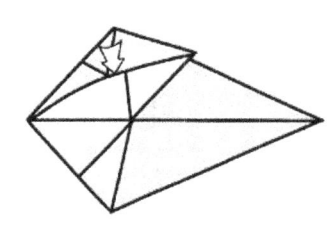

7 Squash fold the pocket.

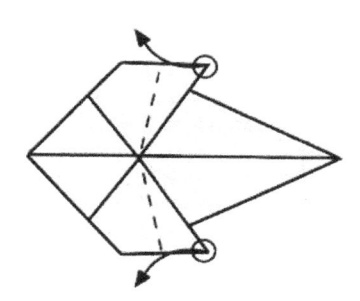

8 Fold in the dotted lines.

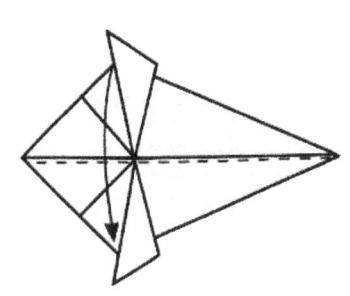

9 Fold in half.

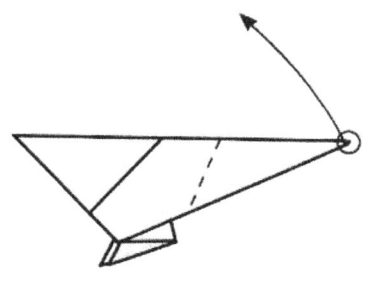

10 Pocket fold in the dotted lines.

100

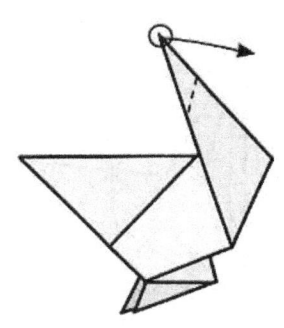

11 Pocket fold the head in the dotted lines.

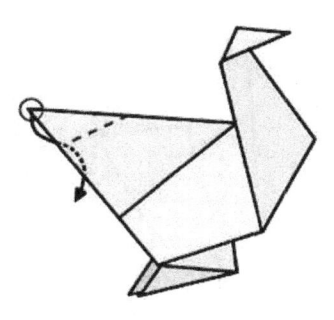

12 Pocket fold the tail in the dotted lines.

13 Fold in the dotted lines.

14 Finished chicken.

Camel

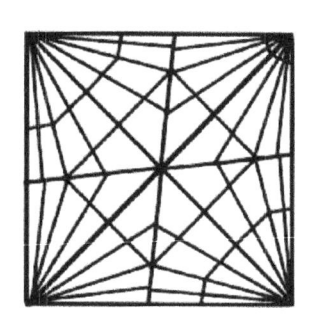

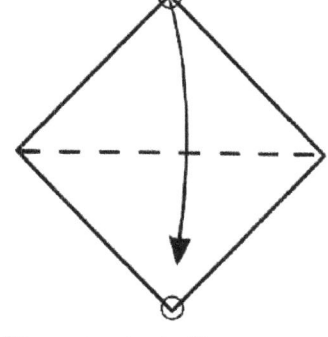

1. Start with the white side up.
2. Fold in half.
3. Fold the model to the marked point. 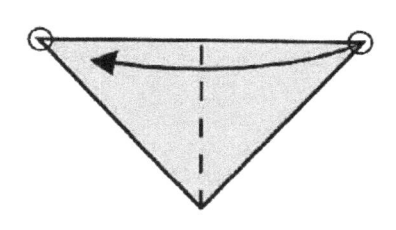 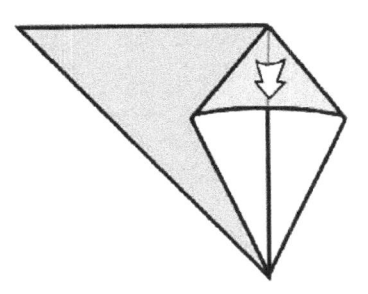
4. Squash fold the front layer.

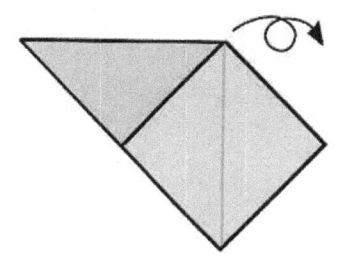

5 Turn the model over.

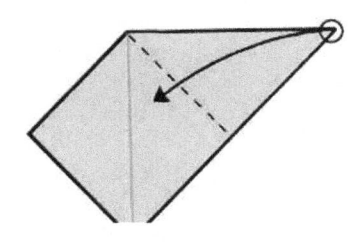

6 Squash fold the other side.

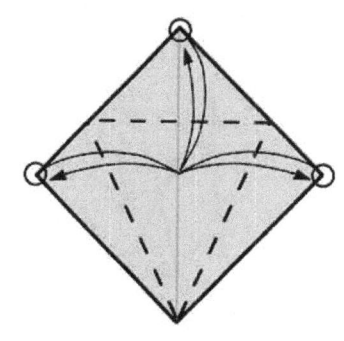

7 Fold and unfold the left, right and the top corners to the center.

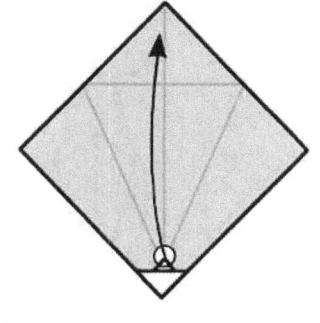

8 Lift the bottom corner up.

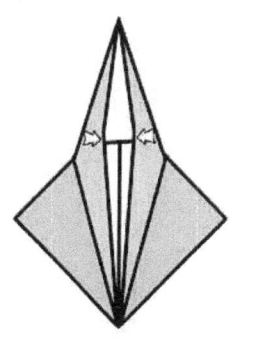

9 Squash fold the left and right sides.

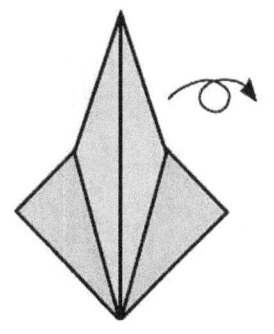

10 Turn the model over.

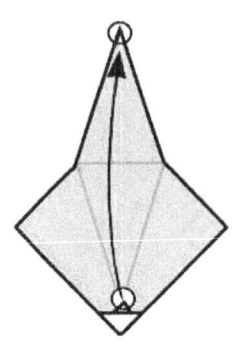

11 Lift the bottom corner up.

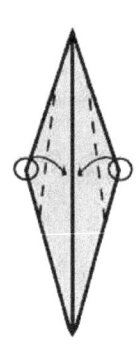

12 Fold the corners to the center.

13 Fold the bottom corners diagonally up turning them over.

14 Fold the right corner down doing an insert fold.

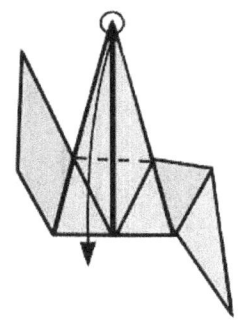

15 Fold the corners down to form the front legs.

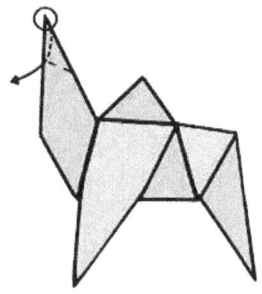

16 Squash fold down by separating the layers and pushing down the top.

17 Fold the corner inside. **18** Finished camel!

Rabbit

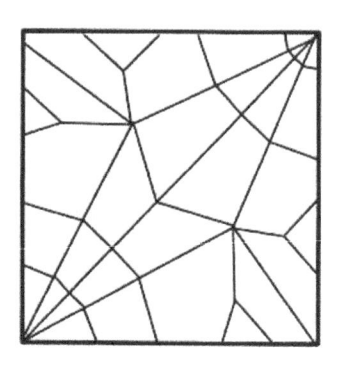

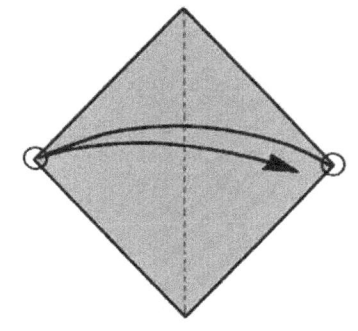

1. Start with the colored side up.
2. Fold and unfold in the half diagonally.
3. Fold the model to the marked point. 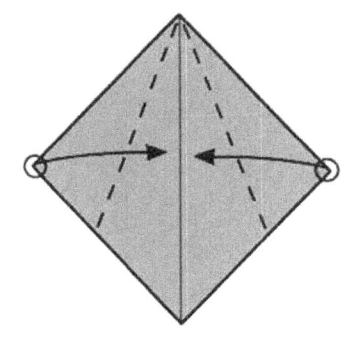 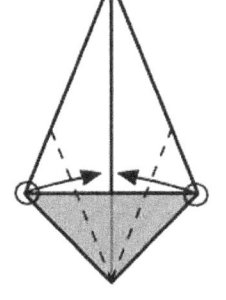
4. Fold the corners to the center.

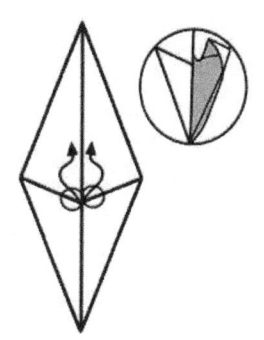

5 Open the pockets and squash fold according to the image.

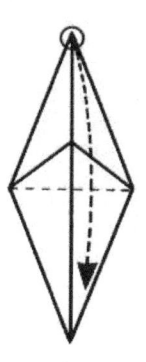

6 Fold back in the dotted lines.

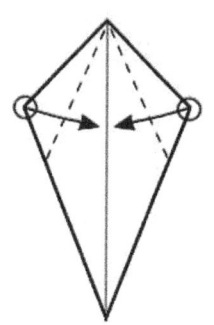

7 Fold the corners to the center.

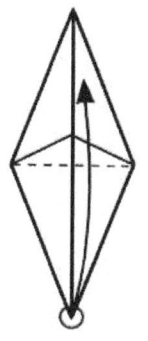

8 Fold up in the dotted line.

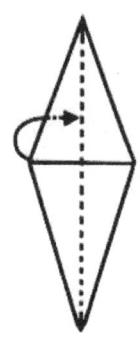

9 Fold in half.

10 Pocket fold to the marked point.

107

11 Pocket fold down in the dotted line.

12 Pocket fold to the marked point.

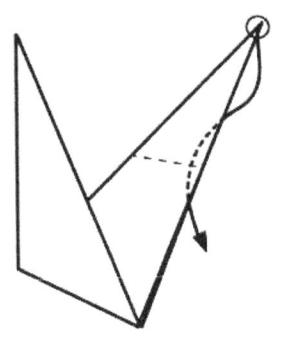

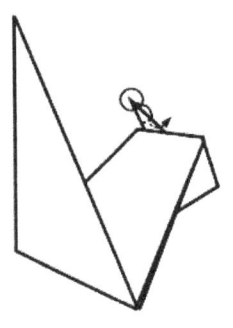

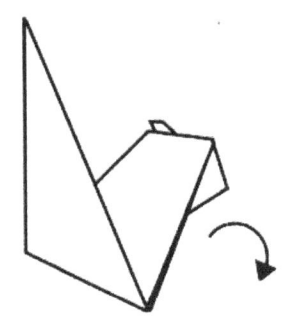

13 Fold inside.

14 Rotate the model.

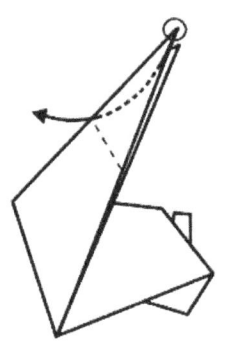

15 Pocket fold to form the head.

16 Fold inside in the dotted line.

17 Open the pockets to form the ears.

18 Finished Rabbit!

Sea Horse

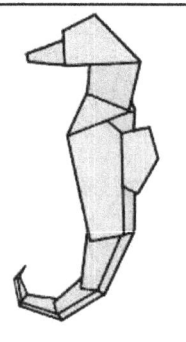

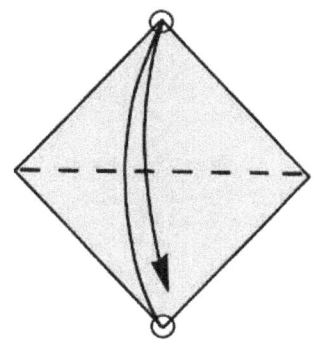

1. Start with the white side up.
2. Fold and unfold in the half diagonally.
3. Fold the corners to the center. 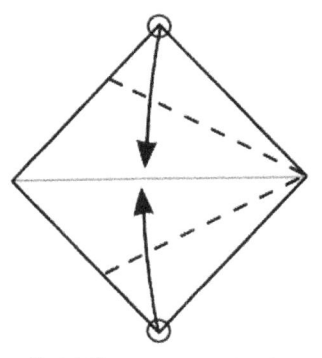 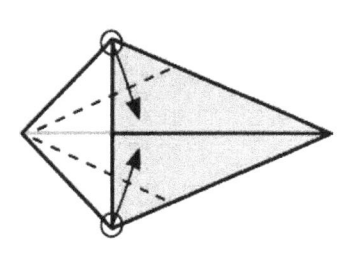
4. Fold in the dotted lines.

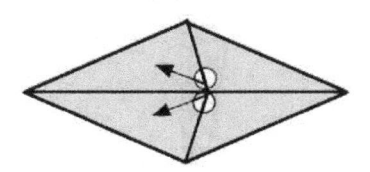

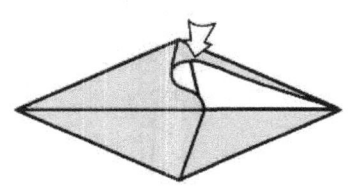

5 Open the pockets moving the corners to the marked point.

6 Flatten the pockets.

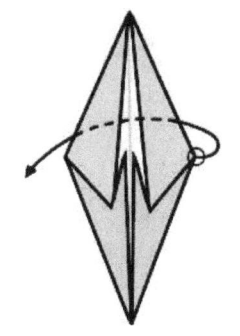

7 Fold in half.

8 Fold the flaps in the dotted lines.

9 Fold inside.

10 Fold the both layers inside.

11 Pocket fold in the dotted line.

12 Pocket fold forward.

13 Fold inside.

14 Do a step fold.

15 Step fold in the dotted lines.

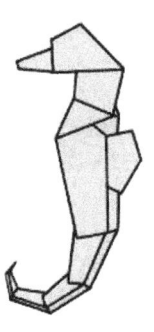

16 Finished Sea horse.

Cat

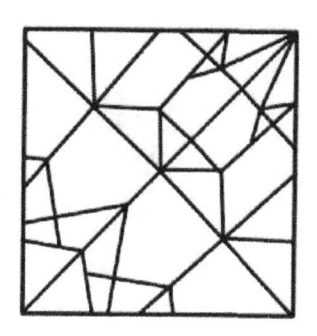

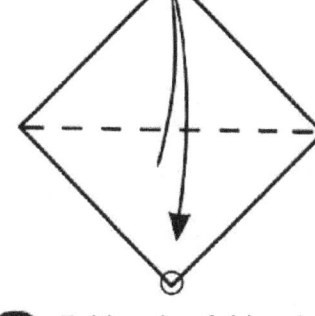

1 Start with the white side up.

2 Fold and unfold in the half diagonally.

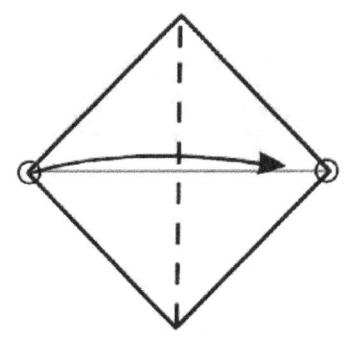

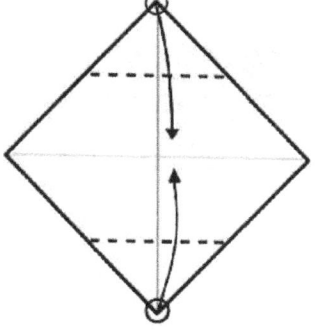

3 Fold and unfold in half.

4 Fold in the dotted lines.

5 Fold to the center.

6 Unfold the layers.

7 Fold in half.

8 Pocket fold lifting the marked corner up.

9 Fold the left, right and upper sides in the dotted lines and unfold.

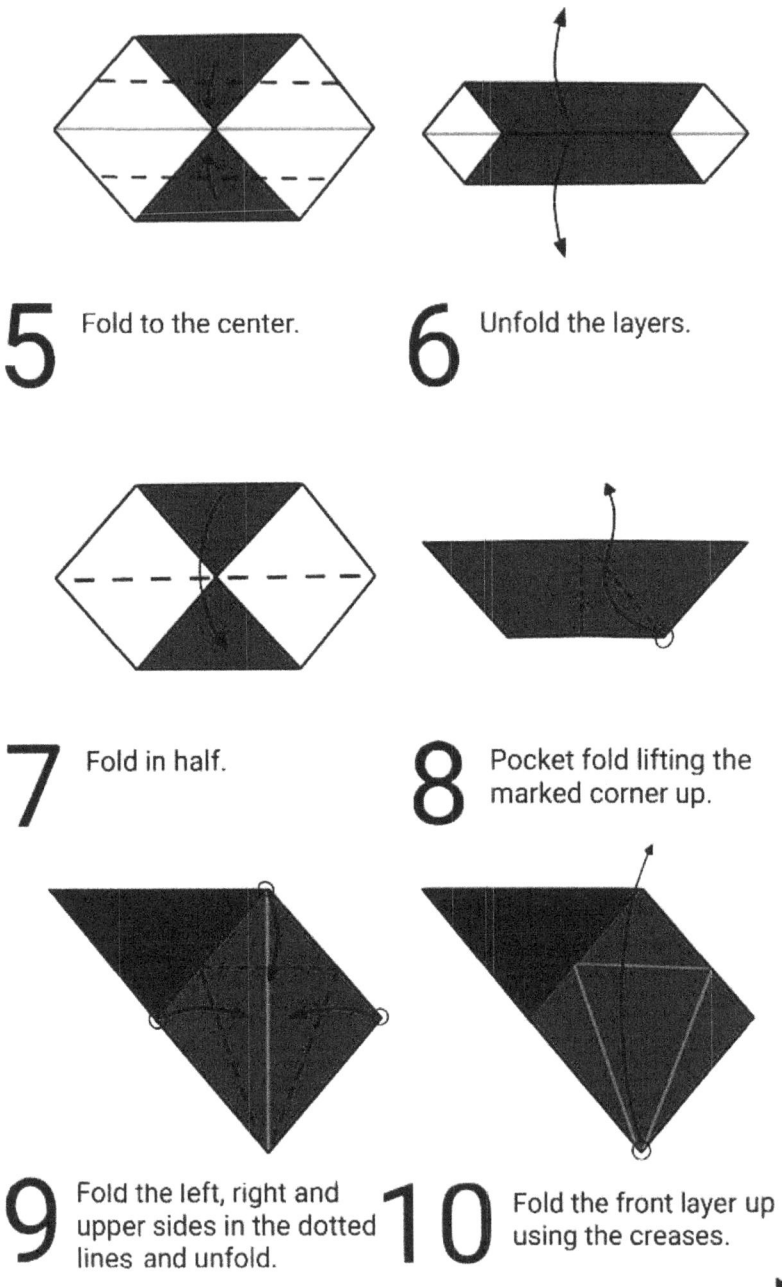

10 Fold the front layer up using the creases.

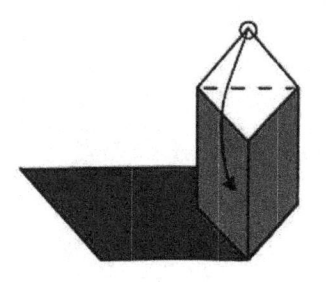

11 Fold down in the dotted line.

12 Step fold to form the ears.

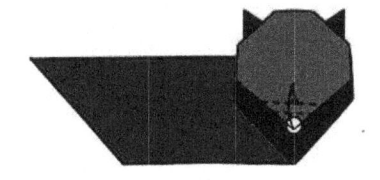

13 Fold up and then down to form the nose.

14 Fold and unfold in the dotted lines.

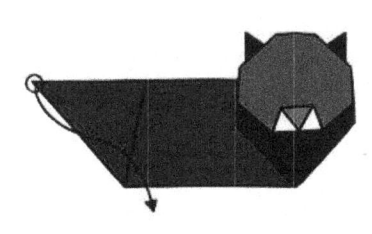

15 Do a pocket fold.

16 Pocket fold up to form the tail.

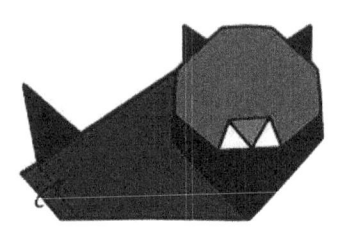

17 Fold inside in the dotted line.

18 Finished Cat!

Catfish

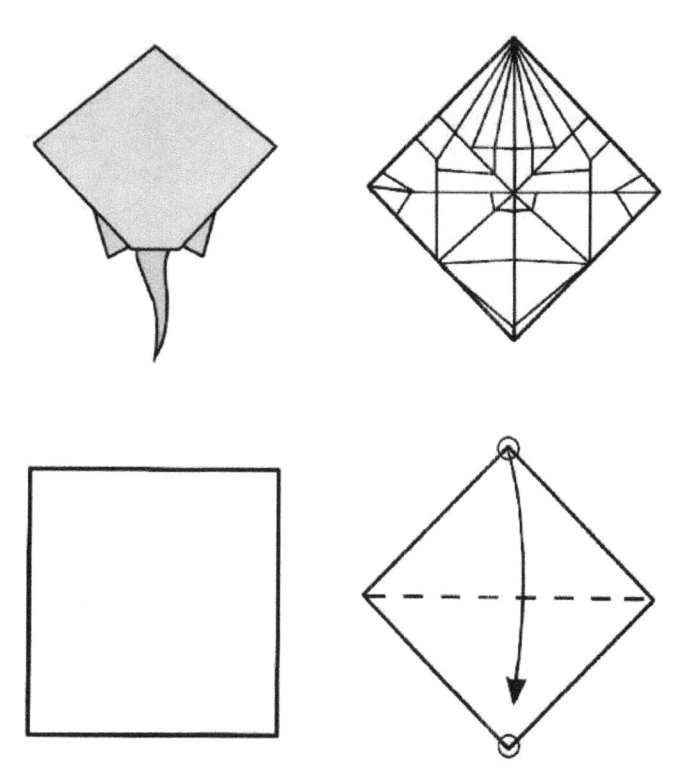

1. Start with the white side up.

2. Fold in half diagonally.

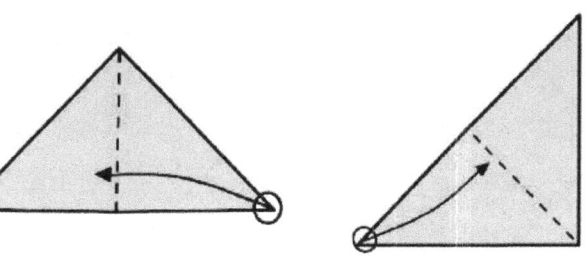

3. Fold in the dotted lines.

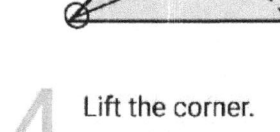

4. Lift the corner.

117

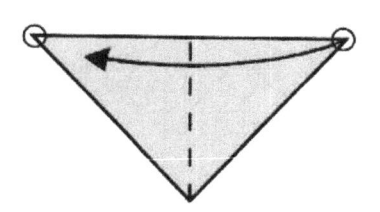

5 Fold in half.

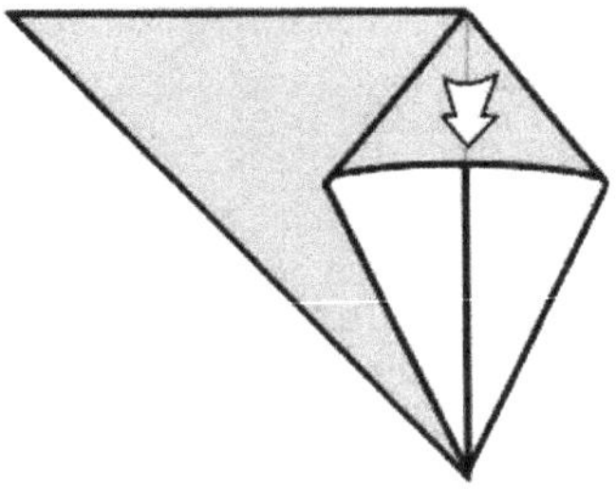

6 Do a squash fold.

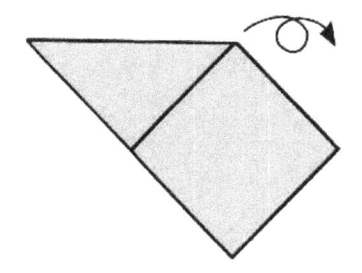

7 Turn the model over.

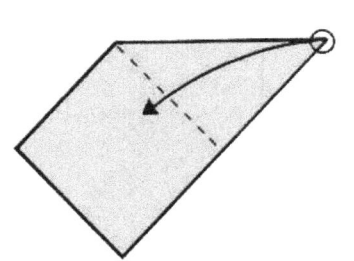

8 Squash fold the other side.

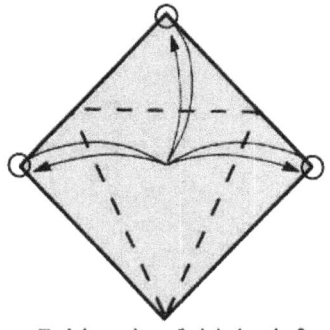

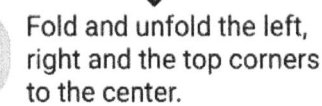

9 Fold and unfold the left, right and the top corners to the center.

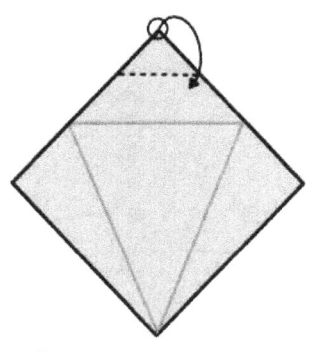

10 Fold in the dotted line.

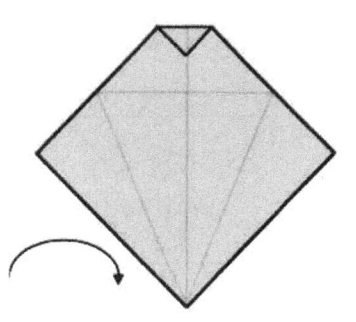

11 Turn the model over.

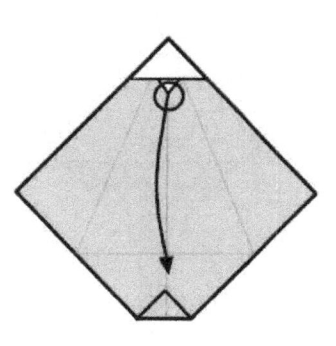

12 Fold the front layer down using the creases.

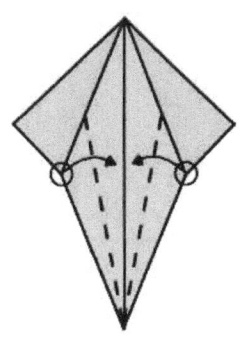

13 Fold the both sides to the center.

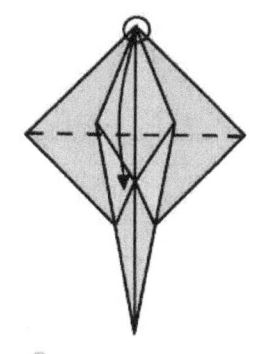

14 Fold in the dotted line.

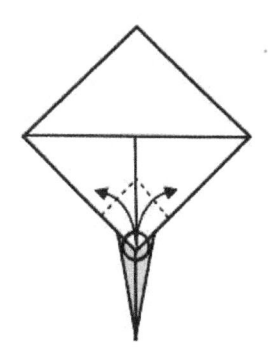

15 Fold diagonally up in the dotted lines.

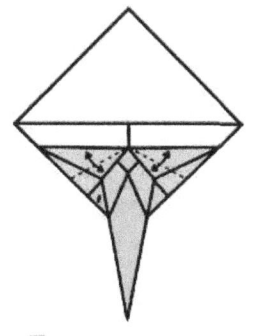

16 Fold and unfold in the dotted lines.

119

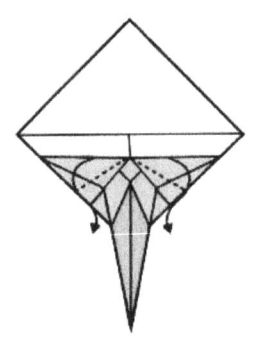

17 Fold down opening the pockets.

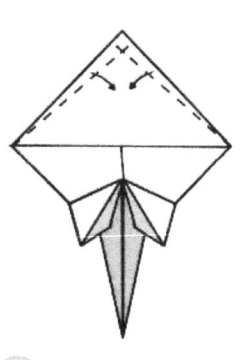

18 Fold inside to the marked point.

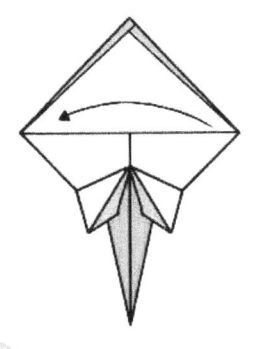

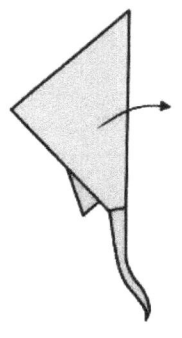

19 Fold in half.

20 Form the tail.

21 Unfold the model.

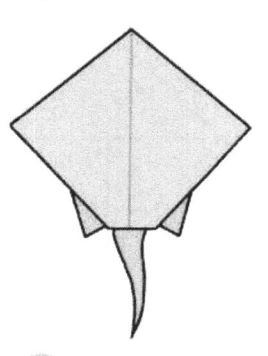

22 Finished Catfish!

Dog

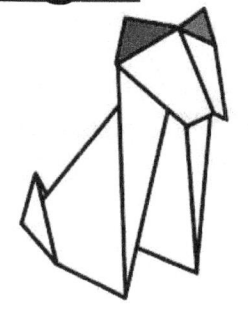

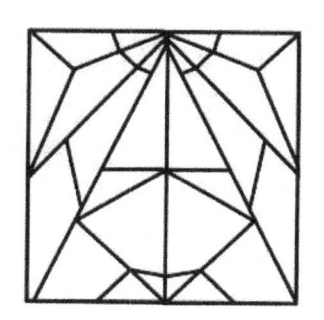

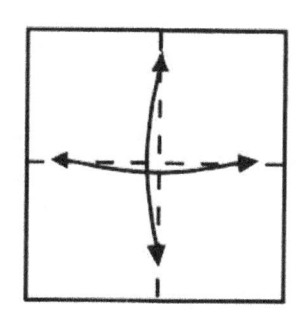

1 Start with the white side up.

2 Fold and unfold in the half

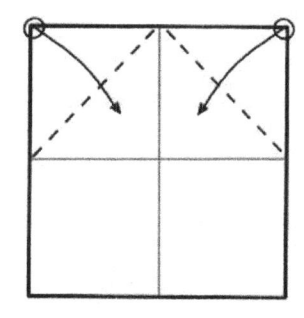

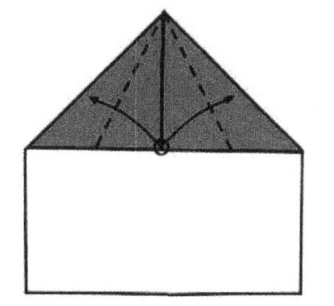

3 Fold the corners to the center.

4 Fold in the dotted lines.

121

5 Fold and unfold in the dotted lines.

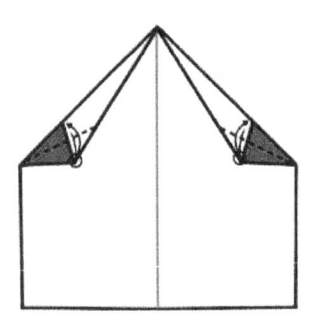

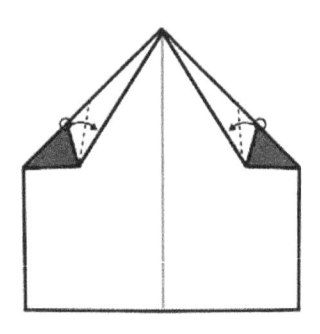

6 Fold inside to the marked point.

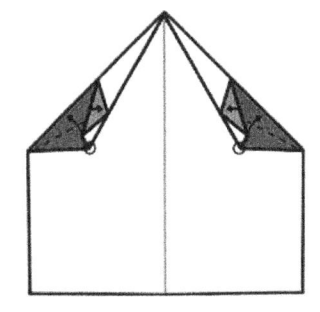

7 Slightly lift the triangle and fold in the dotted lines.

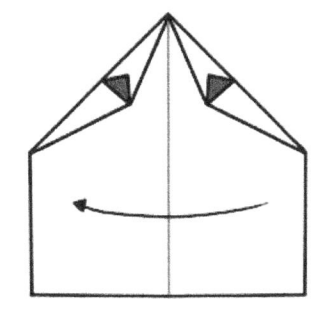

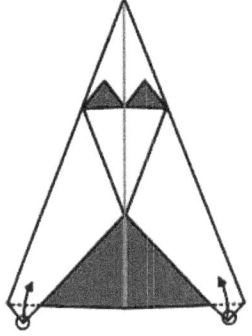

8 Fold in half.

9 Fold up in the dotted lines.

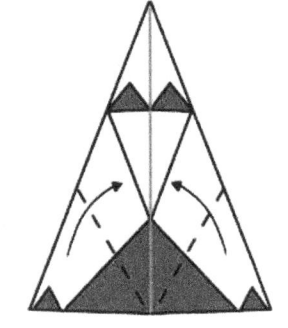

10 Fold inside.

11 Fold back in the dotted line.

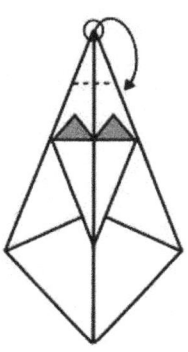

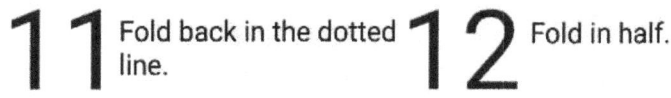

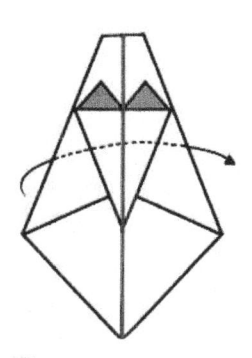

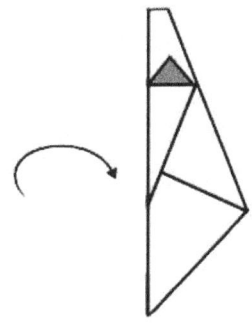

12 Fold in half.

13 Rotate the model.

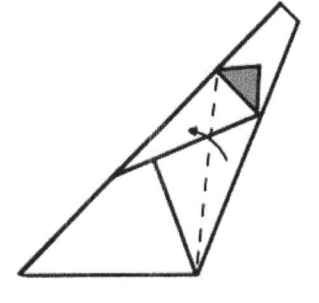

14 Fold the front layer in the dotted line.

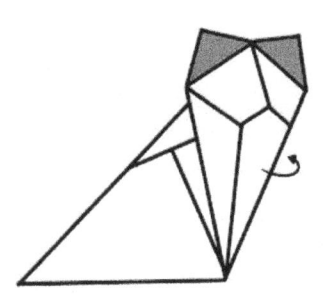

15 Fold the back layer backwards.

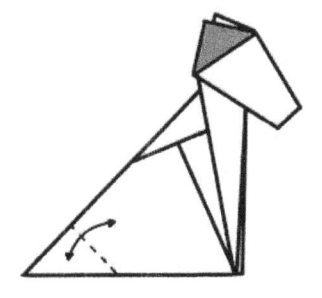

16 Fold and unfold in the dotted lines.

17 Pocket fold in the dotted line.

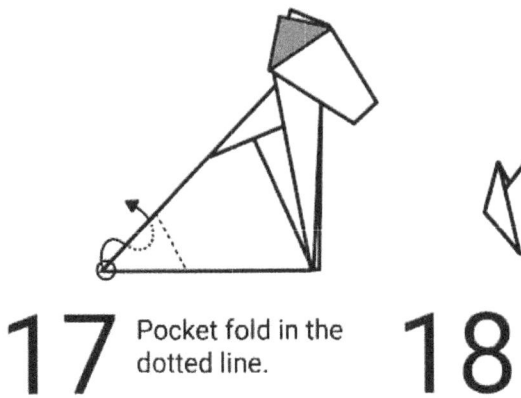

18 Finished dog!

Dinosaur

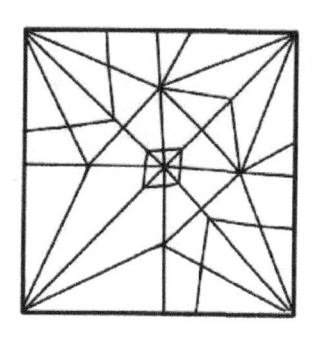

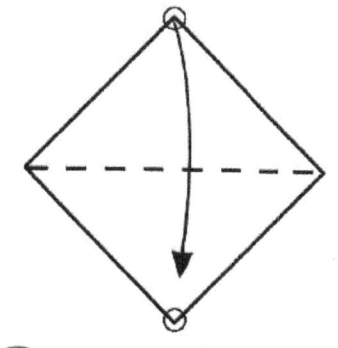

1 Start with the white side up.

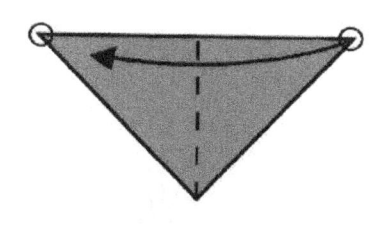

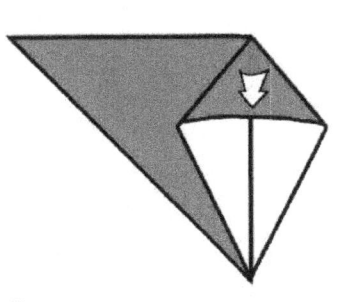

2 Fold in half.

3 Fold the corners to the center.

4 Fold in the dotted lines.

125

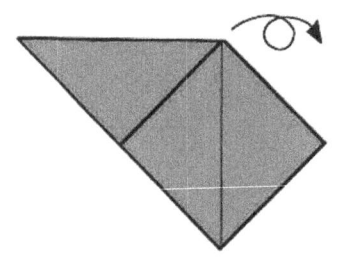

5 Turn the model over.

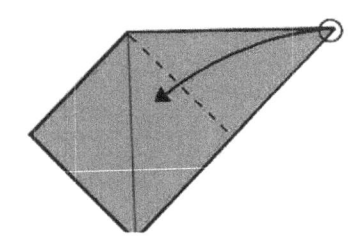

6 Squash fold the other side.

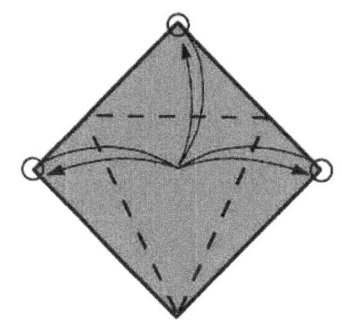

7 Fold and unfold the left, right and the top corners to the center.

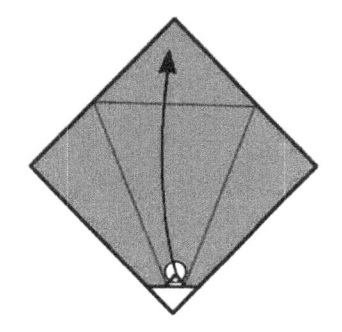

8 Lift the bottom corner up.

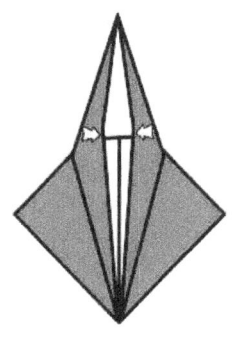

9 Squash fold the left and right sides.

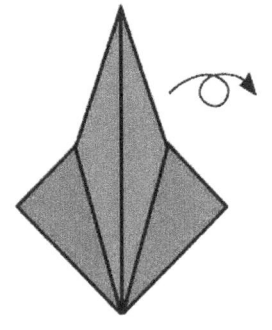

10 Turn the model over.

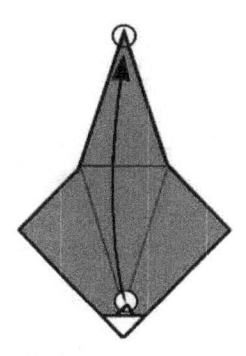

11 Lift the corner up using the creases.

12 Fold down in the dotted line.

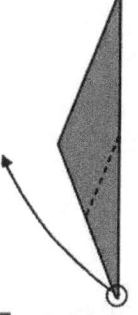

13 Fold in half.

14 Fold diagonally up to form the legs.

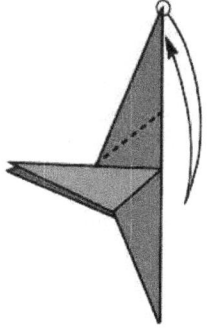

15 Fold and unfold in the dotted line.

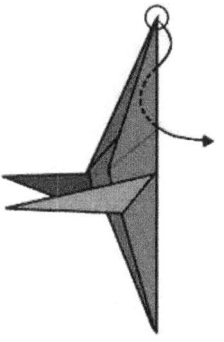

16 Pocket fold to form the neck.

17 Rotate the model.

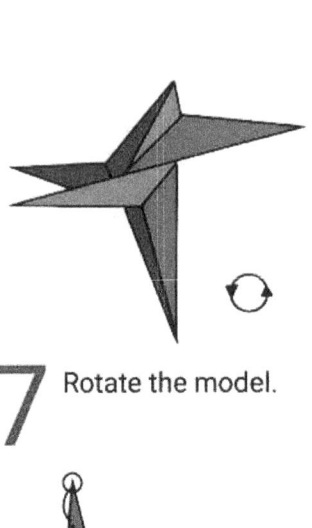

18 Fold and unfold in the dotted line.

19 Pocket fold in the dotted line.

20 Fold inside.

21 Do a pocket fold.

22 Fold and unfold in the dotted lines.

23 Do a pocket fold.

24 Finished dinosaur!

Scorpion

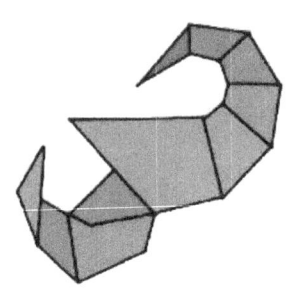

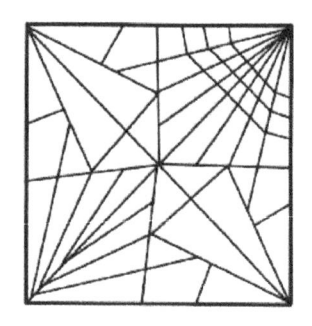

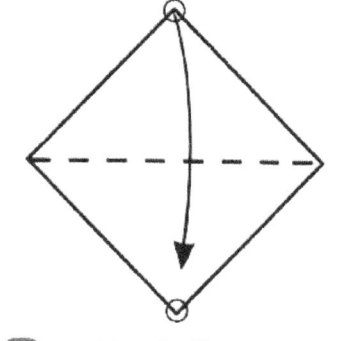

1. Start with the white side up.

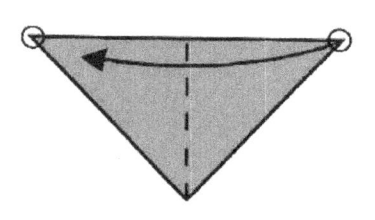

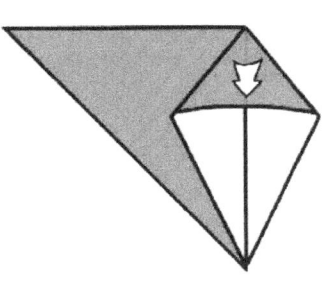

2. Fold in half.

3. Fold the corners to the center.

4. Fold in the dotted lines.

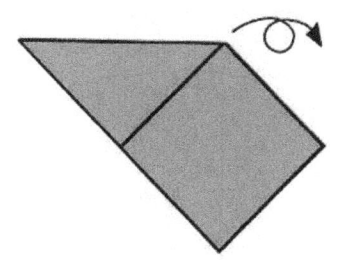

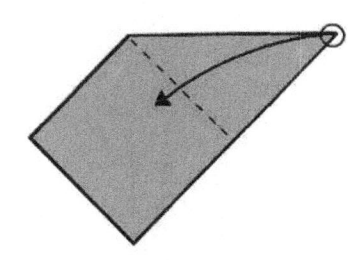

5 Turn the model over.

6 Squash fold the other side.

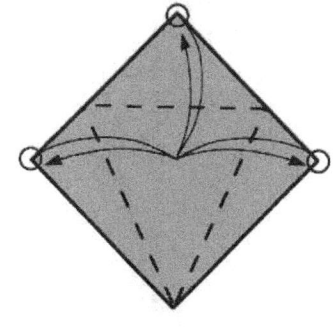

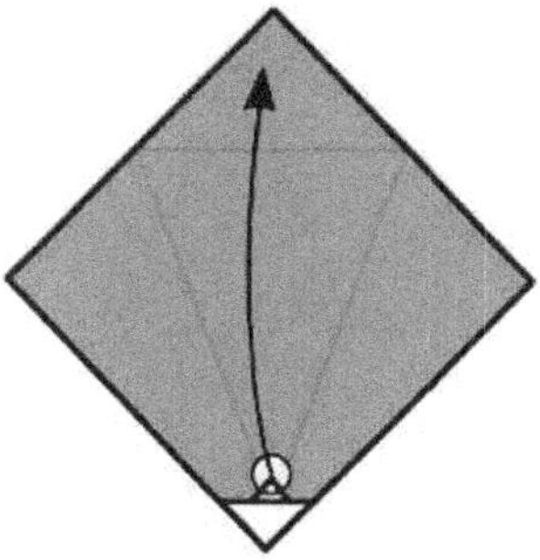

7 Fold and unfold the left, right and the top corners to the center.

8 Lift the bottom corner up.

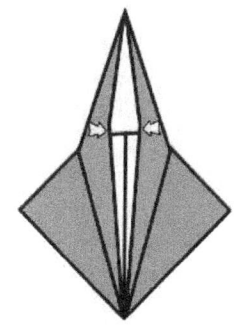

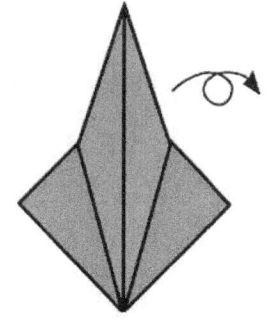

9 Squash fold the left and right sides.

10 Turn the model over.

11 Lift the corner up using the creases.

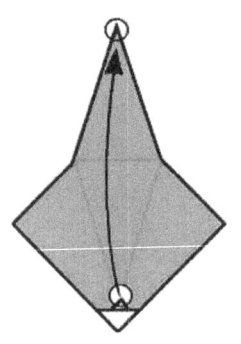

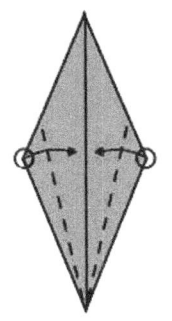

12 This is called bird base.

13 Fold to the center.

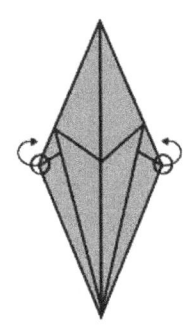

14 Do the same in the other side.

15 Fold the front right layer to the left and the back left layer to the right.

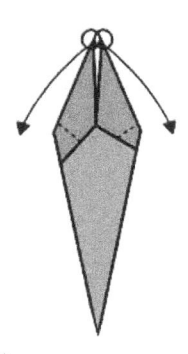

16 Fold in the dotted lines.

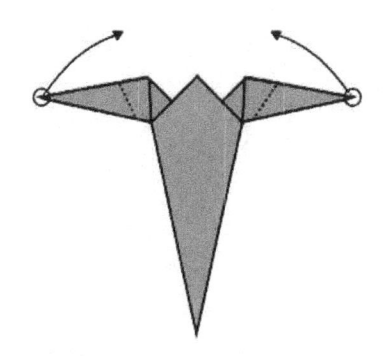

17 Fold up in the dotted lines.

18 Fold inside.

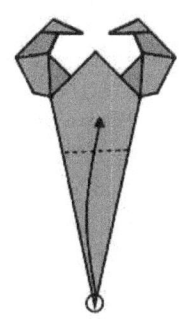

19 Fold the front layer up.

20 Fold down in the dotted line.

21 Fold up.

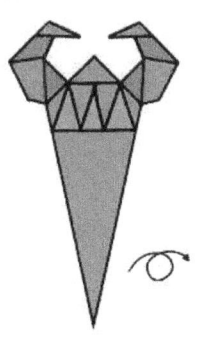

22 Turn over.

23 Do a step fold.

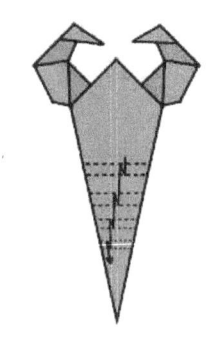

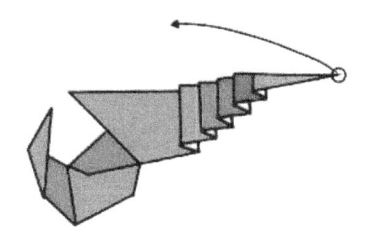

24 Fold in half.

25 Lift the tail to the marked point.

26 Finished scorpion!

Grasshoper

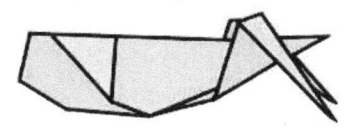

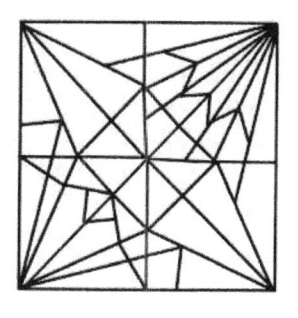

1. Start with the white side up.
2. Fold in the half diagonally. 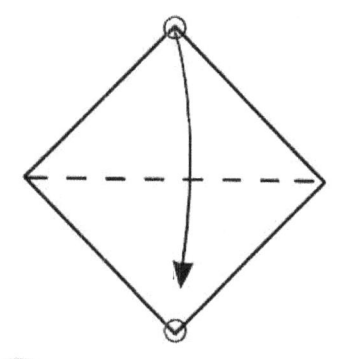
3. Fold the model to the marked point. 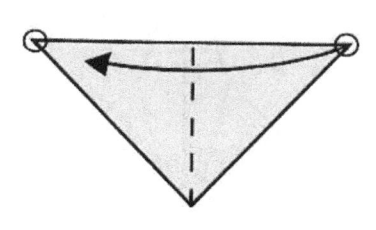
4. Squash fold the front layer. 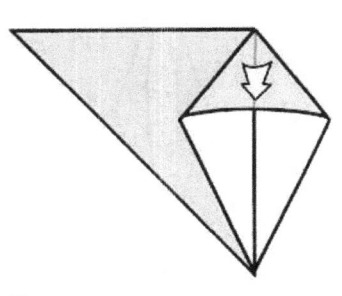

135

5. Turn the model over.

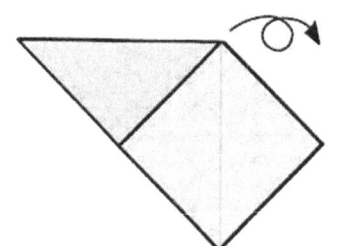

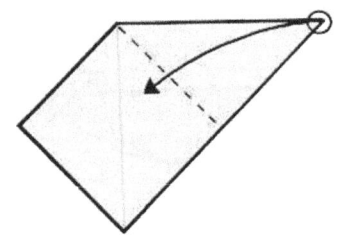

6. Squash fold the other side.

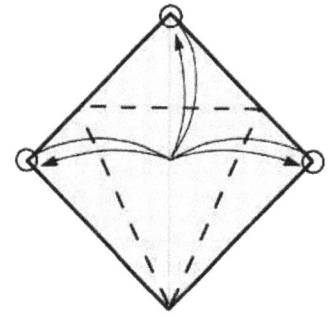

7. Fold and unfold the left, right and the top corners to the center.

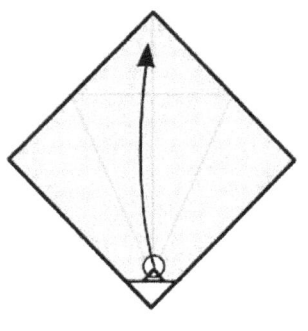

8. Lift the bottom corner up.

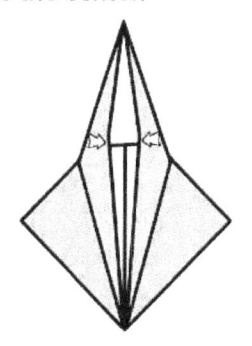

9. Squash fold the left and right sides.

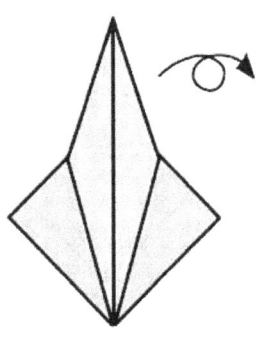

10. Turn the model over.

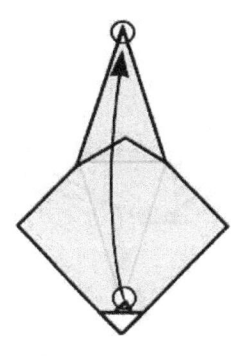

11 Lift the bottom corner up.

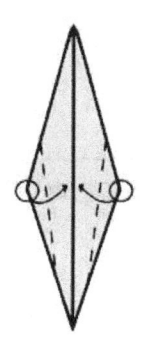

12 Fold the corners to the center.

13 Fold in the dotted line.

14 Fold backward in the dotted lines.

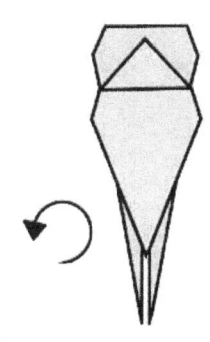

15 Turn the model around.

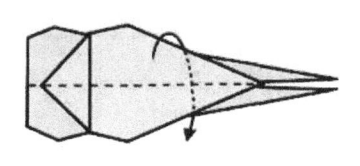

16 Fold in half.

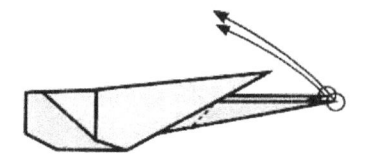

17 Lift the wings up.

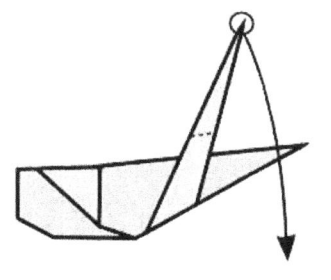

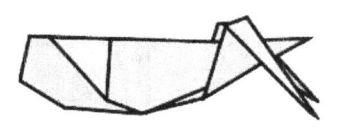

18 Fold the legs up in the dotted lines.

19 Fold down in the dotted lines.

20 Finished grasshopper!

Flapping Bird

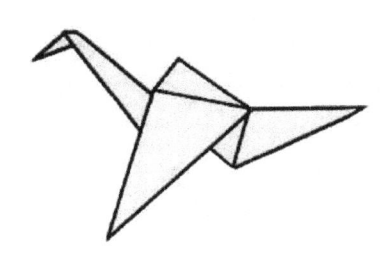

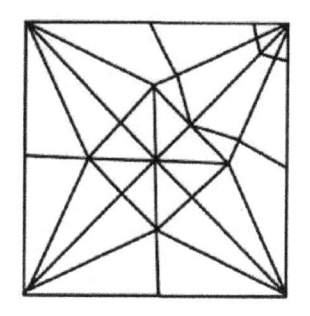

1. Start with the white side up.
2. Fold in half. 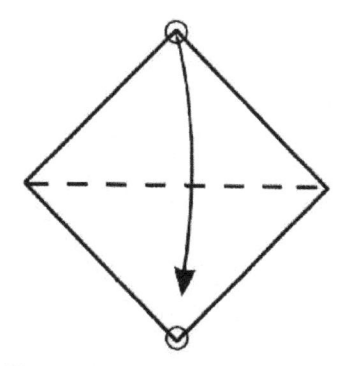
3. Fold the model to the marked point. 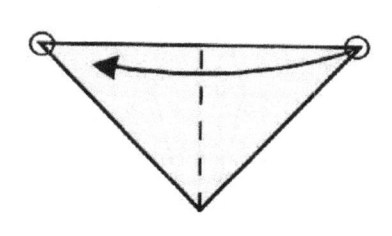
4. Squash fold the front layer.

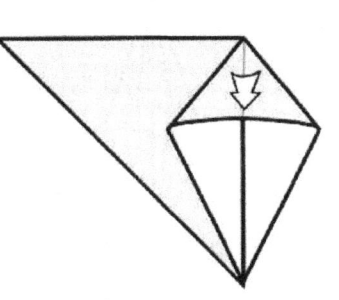

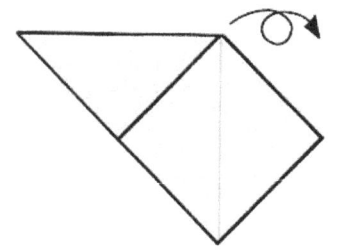

Turn the model over.

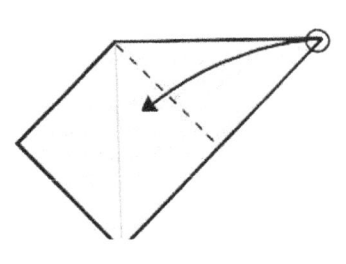

Squash fold the other side.

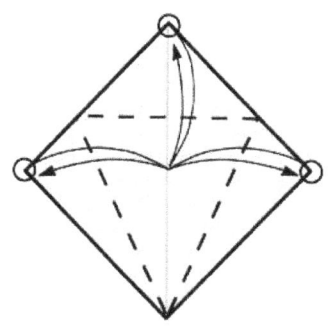

Fold and unfold the left, right and the top corners to the center.

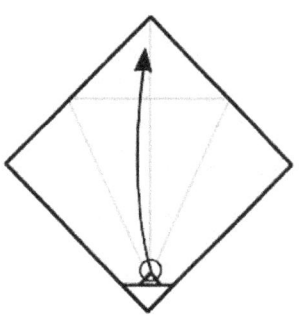

Lift the bottom corner up.

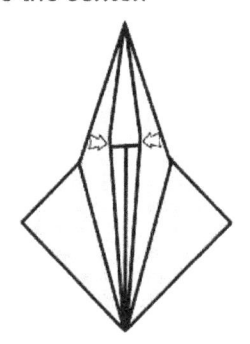

Squash fold the left and right sides.

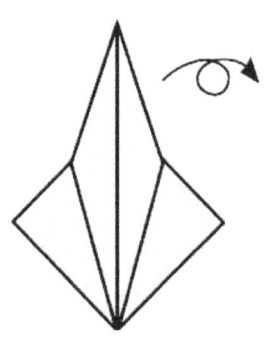

Turn the model over.

140

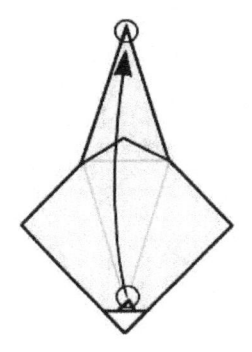

11. Lift the bottom corner up.

12. Pocket fold the front and back layers in the dotted line.

13. Pocket fold in the dotted lines.

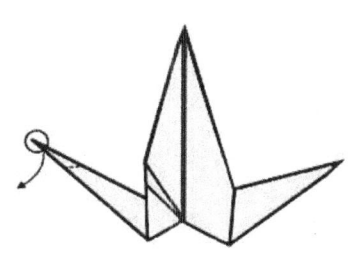

14. Pocket fold in the dotted lines.

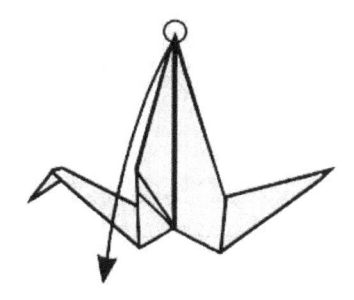

15. Fold the wings down.

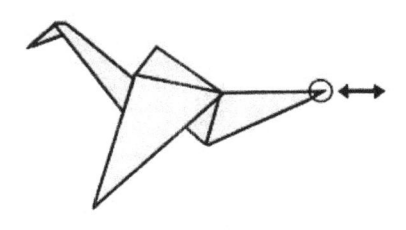

16. Finished Flapping bird! Pull the tail to flap the wings.

Elephant

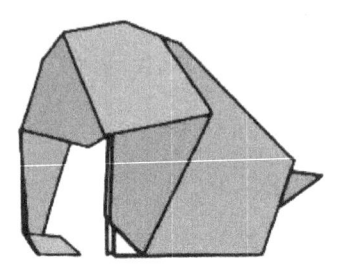

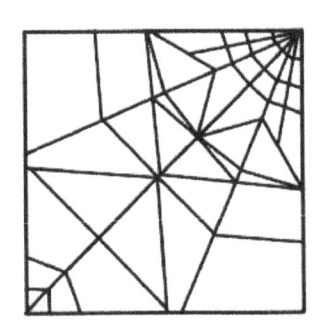

1 Start with the white side up.

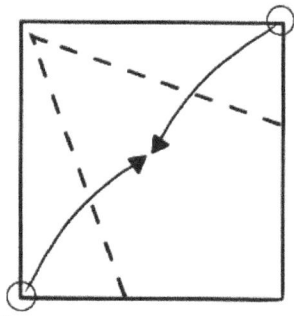

2 Fold the both sides to the center.

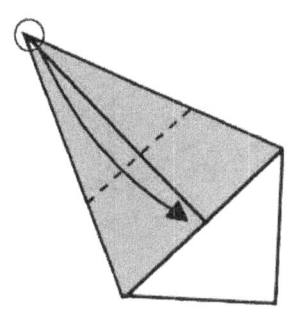

3 Fold down.

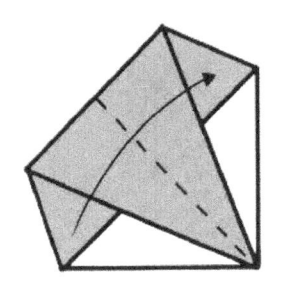

4 Fold in half.

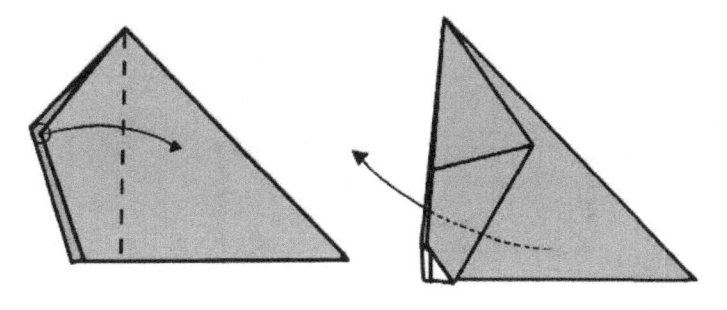

11 Fold the both sides in the dotted lines.

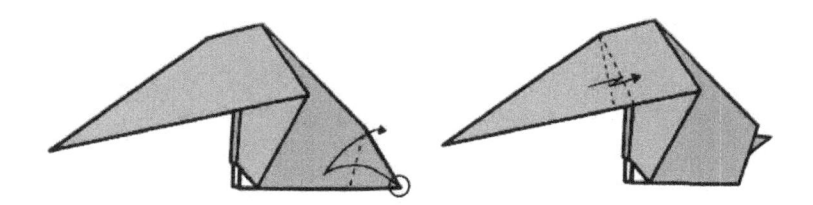

12 Pull out the inner layer.

13 Pocket fold and unfold to form the tail.

14 Do a step fold.

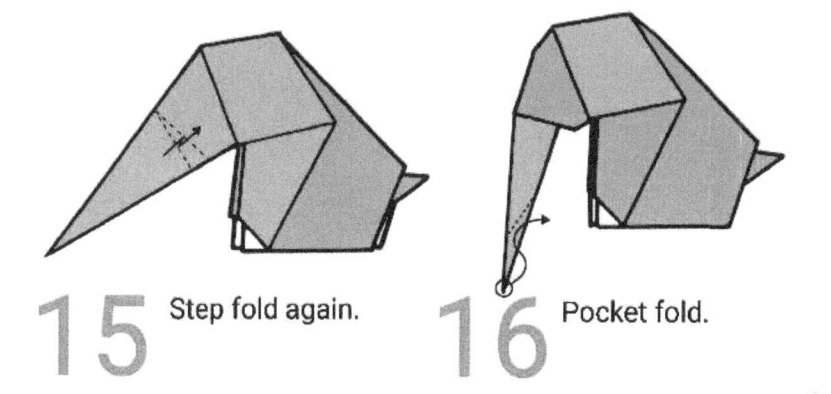

15 Step fold again.

16 Pocket fold.

17 Pocket fold.

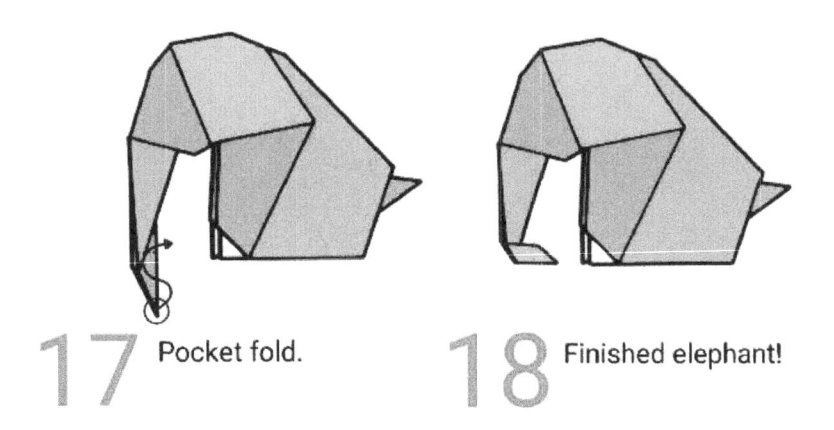

18 Finished elephant!

Owl

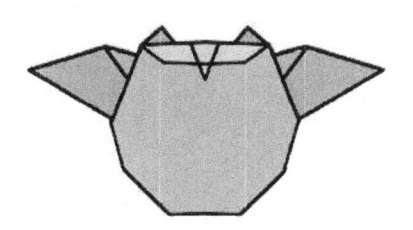

1. Start with the white side up.

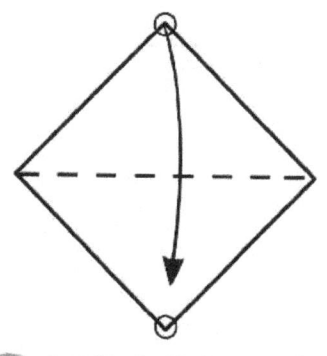

2. Fold in half diagonally.

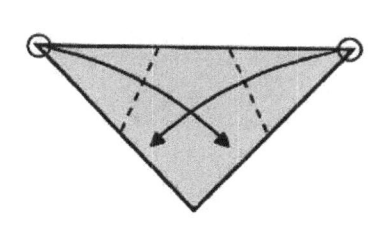

3. Fold the both sides in the dotted lines.

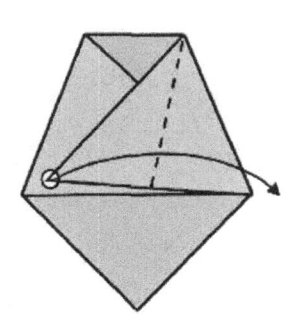

4. Fold to the marked point.

145

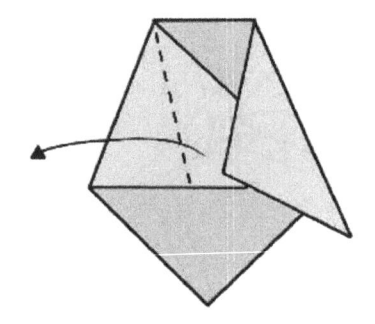

5 Fold the wing in the dotted line.

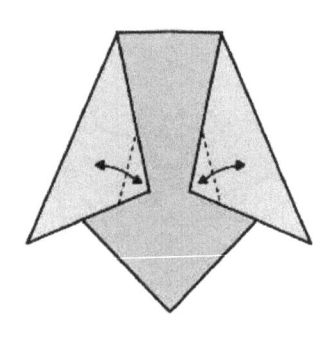

6 Fold and unfold in the dotted lines.

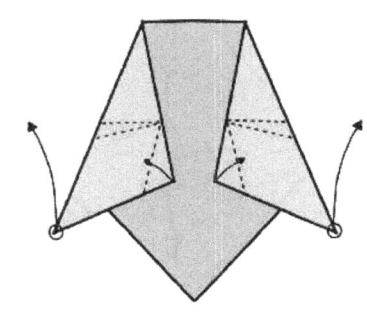

7 Fold the wings diagonally up folding the lower points inside.

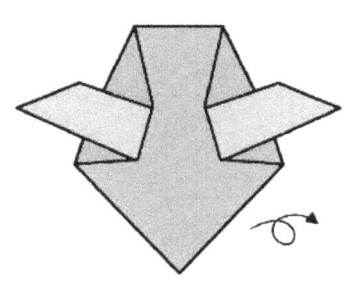

8 Turn the model over.

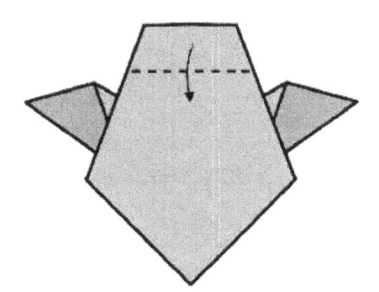

9 Fold down.

10 Fold inside.

146

11 Do a step fold.

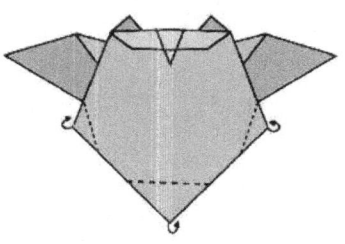

12 Fold the corners inside.

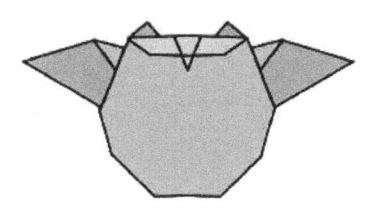

13 Finished owl!

Frog

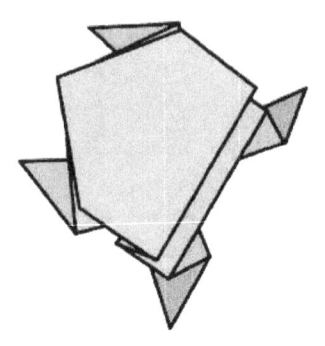

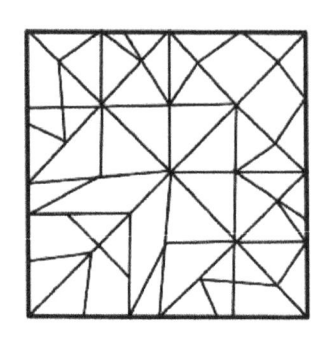

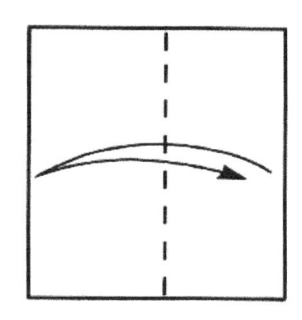

1. Start with the white side up.
2. Fold in the dotted line.
3. Fold in half. 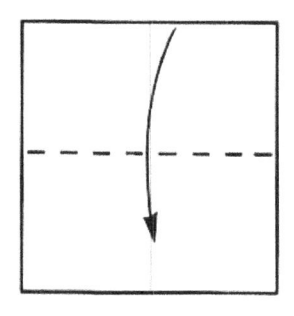 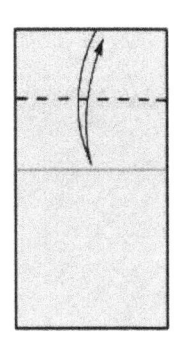
4. Fold to the center and unfold.

148

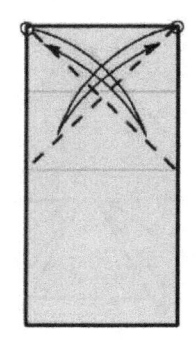

5 Fold and unfold in the dotted lines.

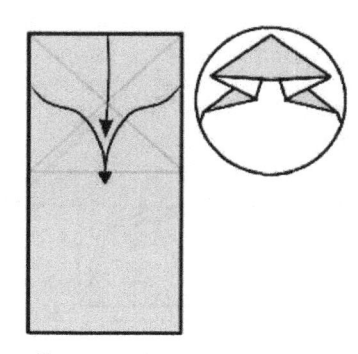

6 Pocket fold using the creases.

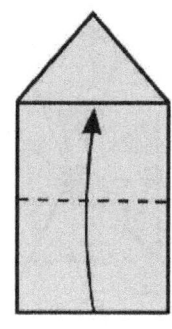

7 Fold up in the dotted line.

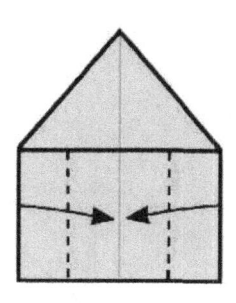

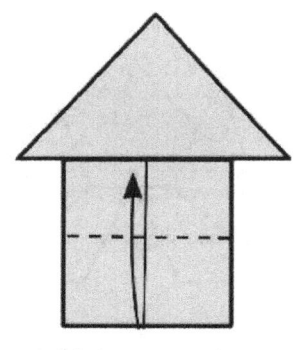

9 Fold the two sides to the center.

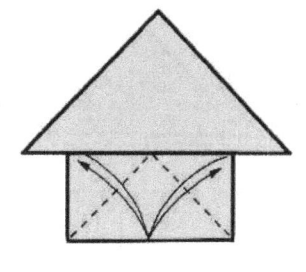

10 Fold and unfold in the dotted lines.

11 Open the pockets.

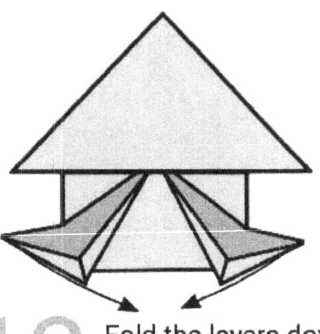

12 Fold the layers down connecting in the center.

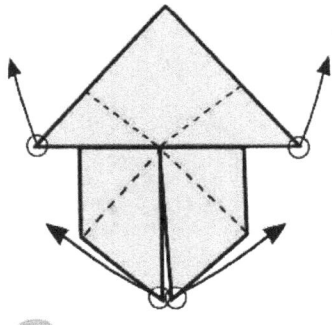

13 Fold up to form the legs.

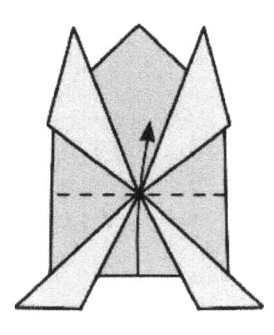

14 Fold in the dotted line.

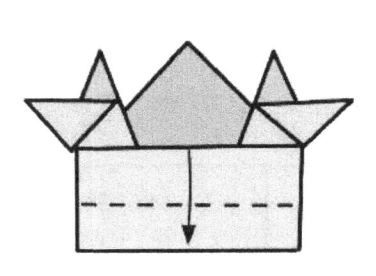

15 Unfold in the dotted line.

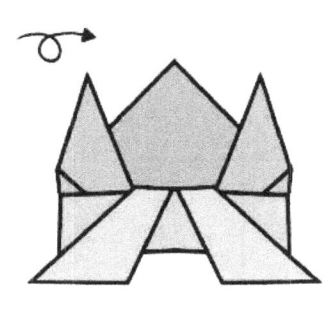

16 Turn over.

17 Finished frog!

Snake

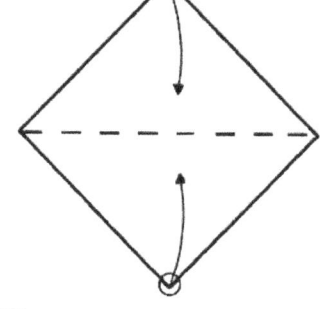

1. Start with the white side up.
2. Fold the corners to the center.
3. Fold in the dotted lines. 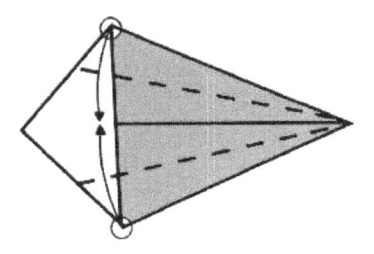 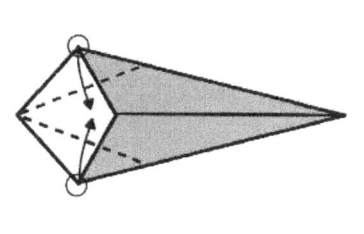
4. Fold to the marked point.

5 Turn the model over.

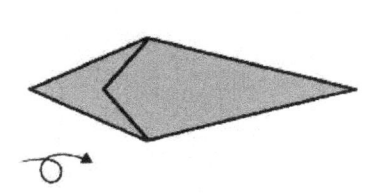

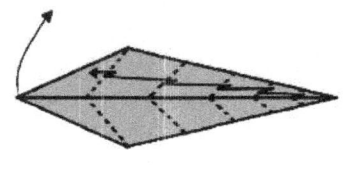

6 Do a step fold folding the left point up.

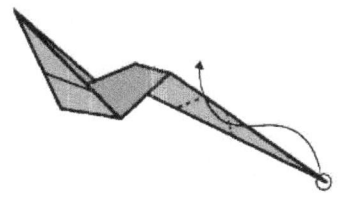

7 Pocket fold down.

8 Pocket fold up and down using the creases to form the tail.

9 Pocket fold the head and fold the point inside.

10 Finished Snake!

Leaf

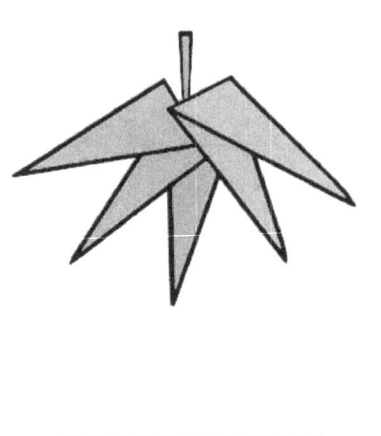

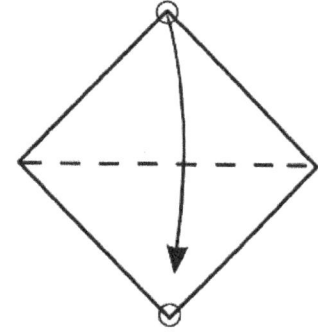

1. Start with the white side up.

2. Fold and unfold in the half diagonally.

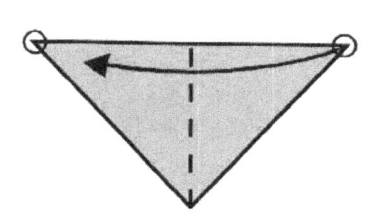

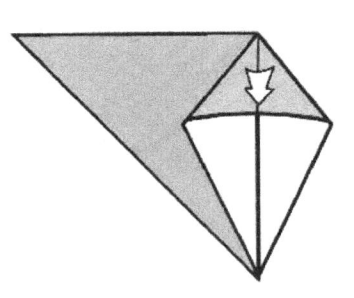

3. Fold the model to the marked point.

4. Squash fold the front layer.

154

5 Turn the model over.

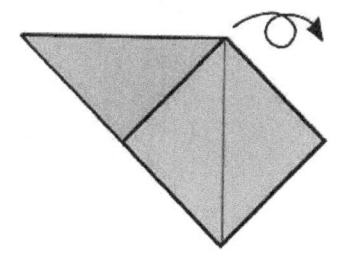

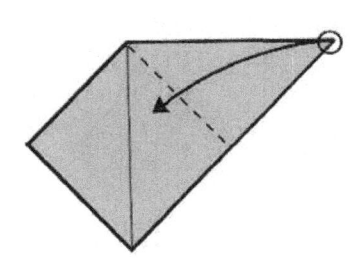

6 squash fold the other side.

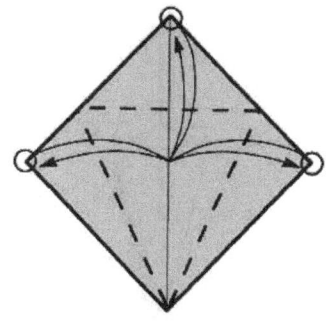

7 Fold and unfold the left, right and the top corners to the center.

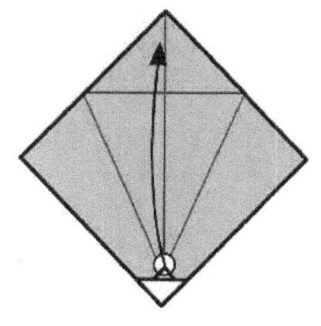

8 Lift the bottom corner up.

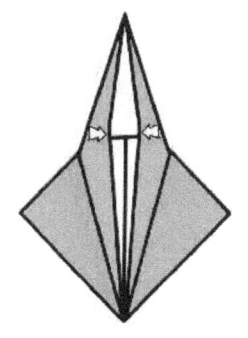

9 Squash fold the left and right sides.

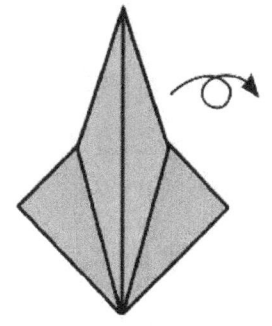

10 Turn the model over.

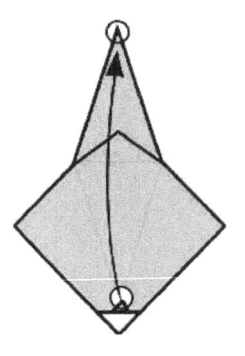

11. Lift the bottom corner up.

12. Fold the front layer forward and the back layer back.

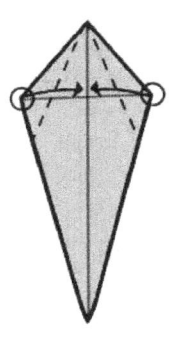

13. Fold the corners to the marked points.

14. Pocket fold the back layer to the marked point.

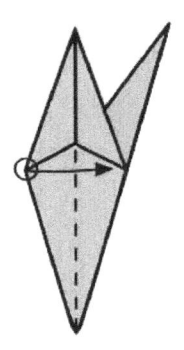

15. Fold the front left layer right.

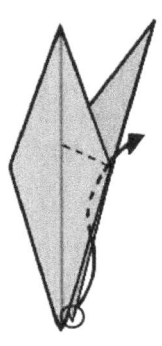

16. Pocket fold the back layer.

17 Fold in half.

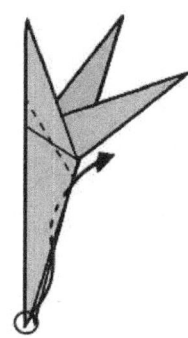

18 Pocket fold in the dotted lines.

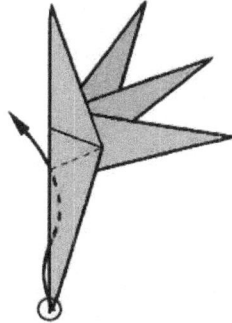

19 Pocket fold to the marked point.

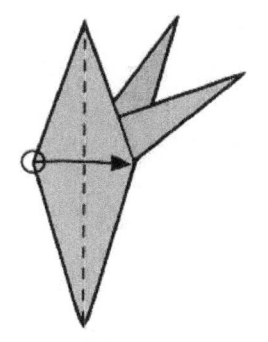

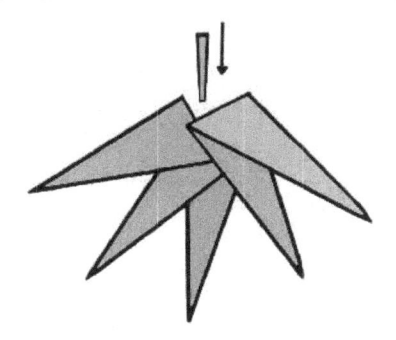

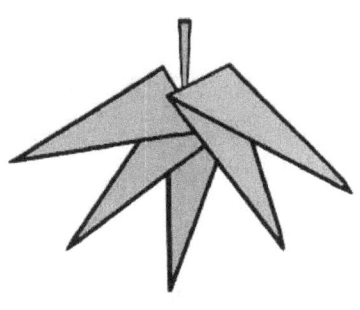

20 Turn over.

21 Add a stick.

22 Finished Leaf!

157

Swans

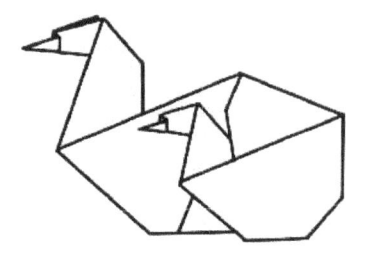

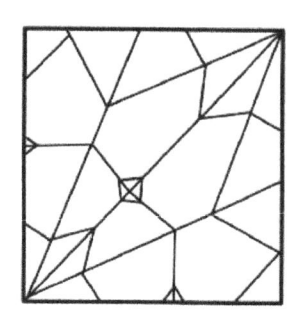

1. Start with the white side up.
2. Fold and unfold in the half diagonally. 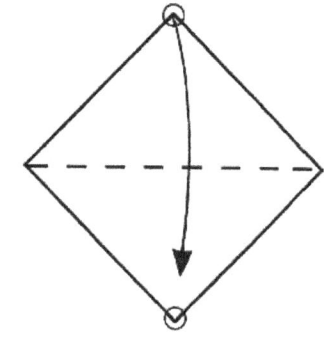
3. Fold the model to the marked point. 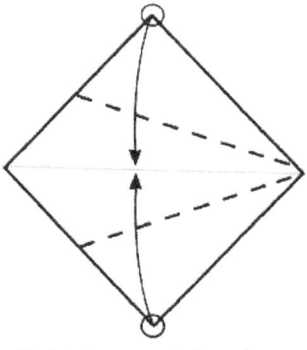
4. Fold back in the dotted lines.

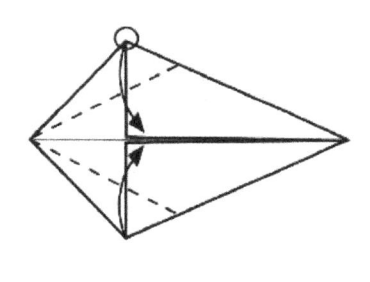

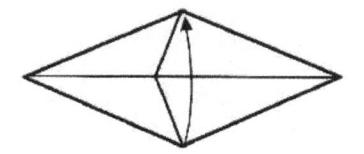

5 Fold in half.

6 Fold and unfold in the dotted lines.

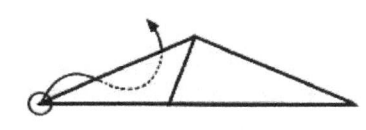

7 Pocket fold in the dotted line.

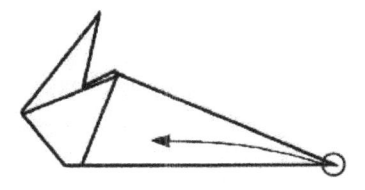

8 Fold in the dotted lines

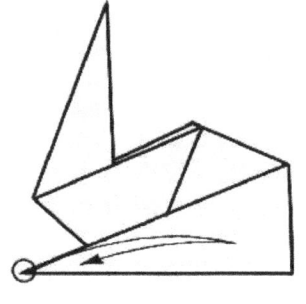

9 Fold back and unfold in the dotted line.

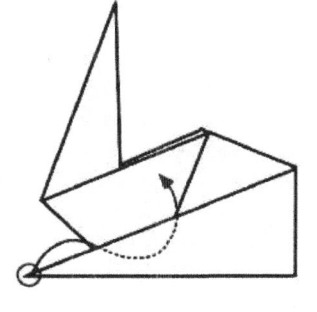

10 Pocket fold the tail up.

11 Fold to make a crease and unfold.

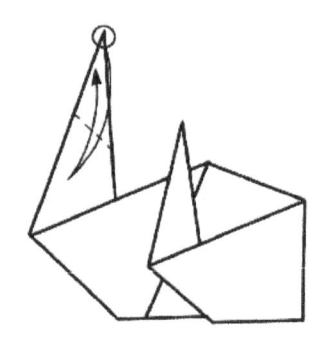

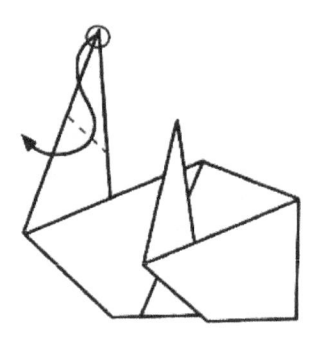

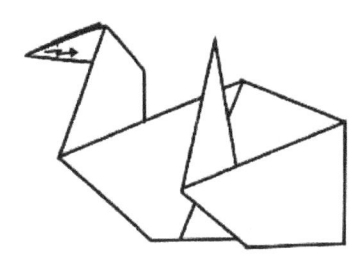

12 Pocket fold.

13 Step fold back.

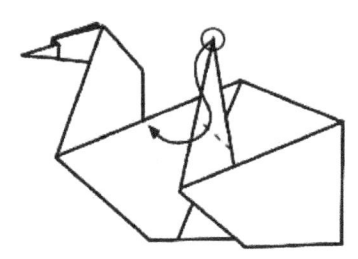

14 Pocket fold in dotted line.

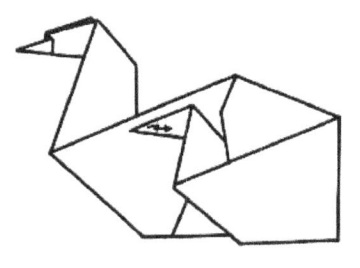

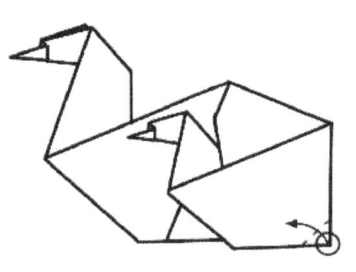

15 Step fold.

16 pocket fold inside.

160

17 Finished swans!

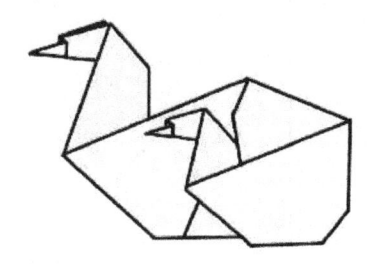

Prawn

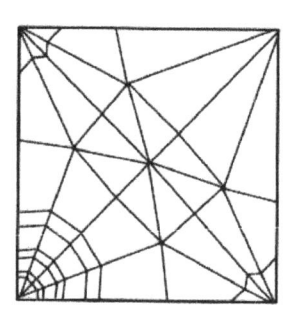

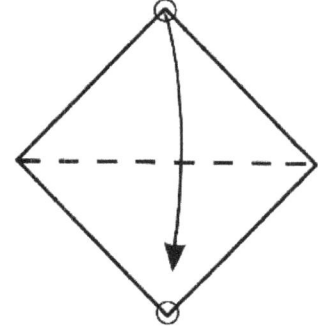

1. Start with the white side up.

2. Fold and unfold in the half diagonally.

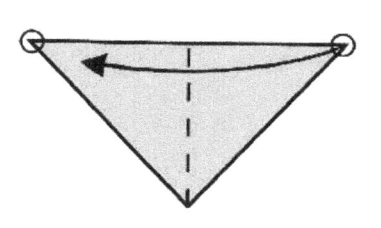

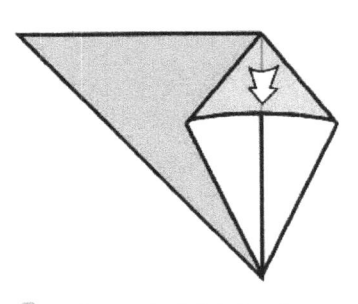

3. Fold the model to the marked point.

4. Squash fold the front layer.

162

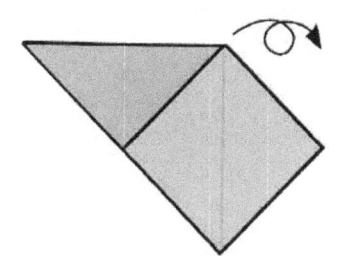

5 Turn the model over.

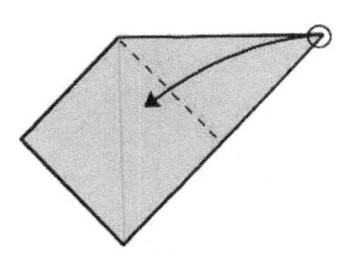

6 squash fold the other side.

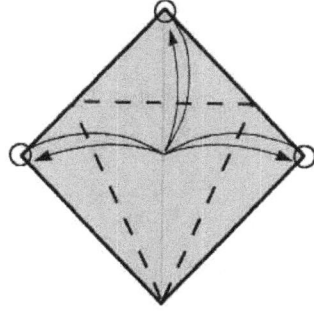

7 Fold and unfold the left, right and the top corners to the center.

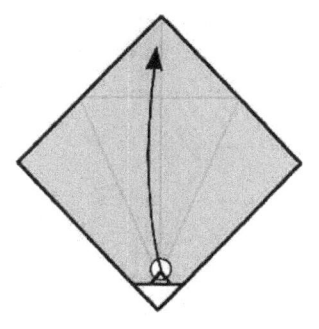

8 Lift the bottom corner up.

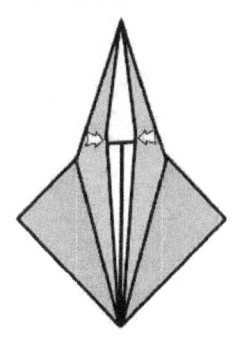

9 Squash fold the left and right sides.

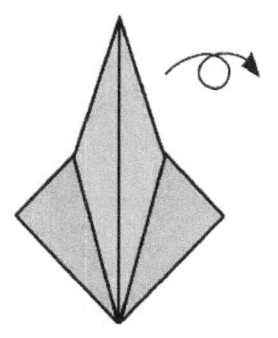

10 Turn the model over.

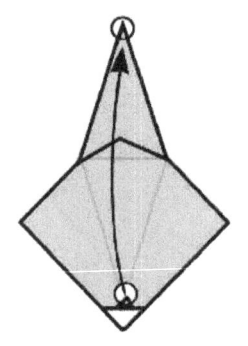

11 Lift the bottom corner up.

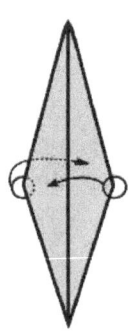

12 Fold the right front layer to the left and the left back layer to the right.

13 Step fold the front layer.

14 Cut and back layers fold backwards.

15 Front layers fold backwards.

16 Fold in half.

17 Finished prawn!

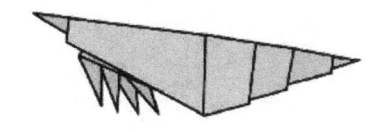

Duck

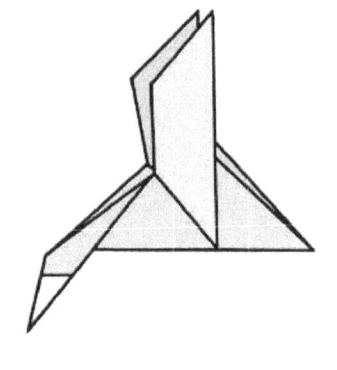

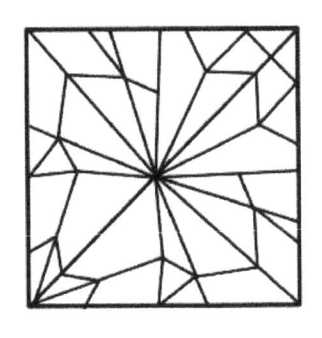

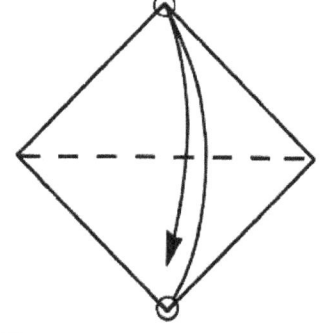

1. Start with the white side up.
2. Fold and unfold in the half diagonally.
3. Fold the point down. 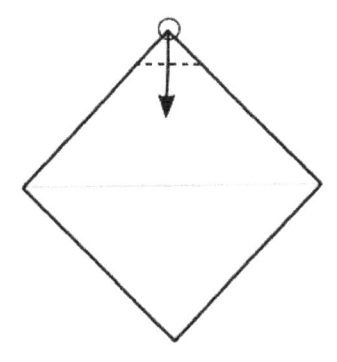 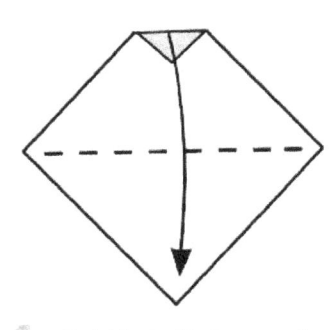
4. Fold in half diagonally.

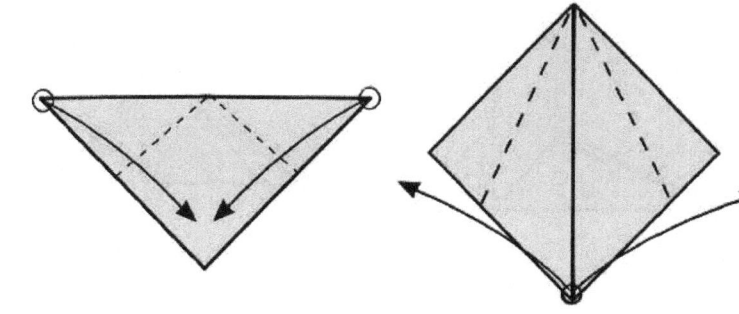

5 Fold both sides diagonally down.

6 Unfold in the dotted lines.

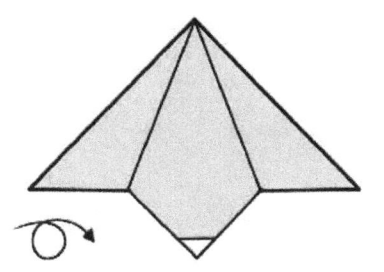

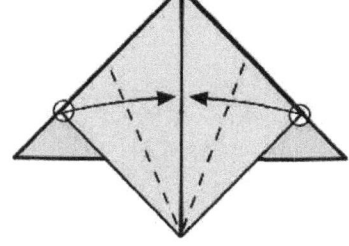

7 Turn the model over.

8 Fold both sides to the center.

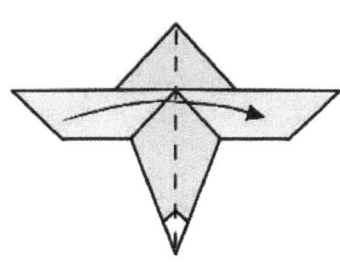

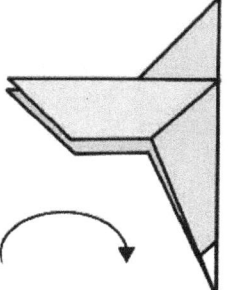

9 Fold in half.

10 Rotate the model.

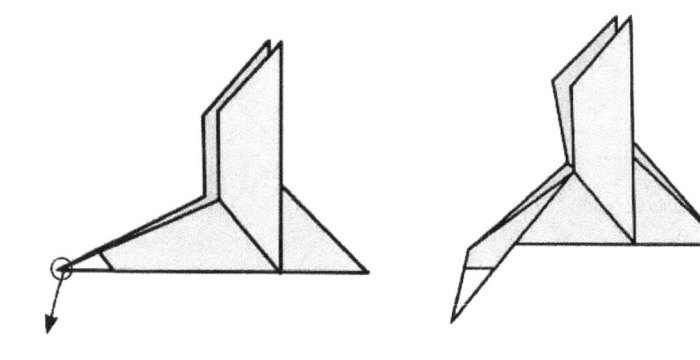

17 Pocket fold down to form the head.

18 Finished duck!

Penguin

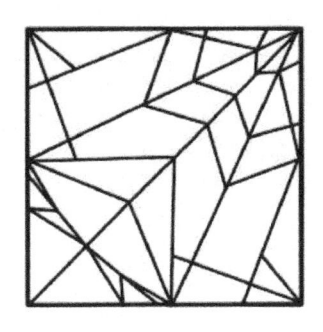

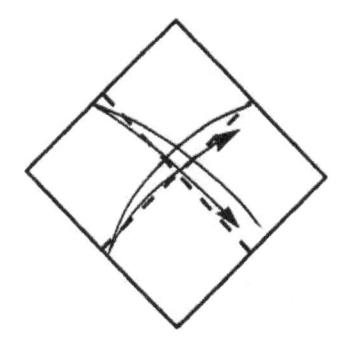

1. Start with the white side up.
2. Fold and unfold in the dotted lines.
3. Fold in half. 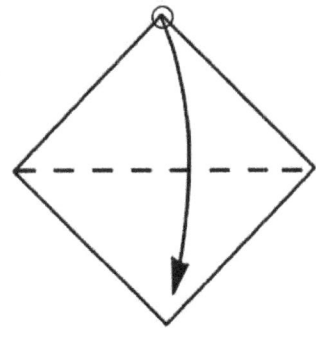 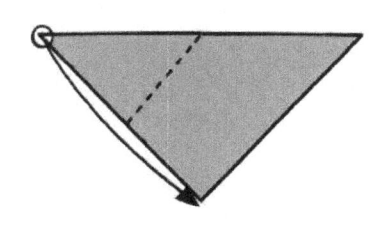
4. Do a pocket fold to the marked point.

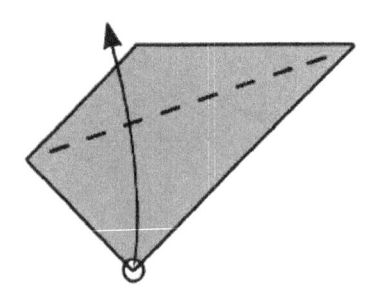

5 Fold the both sides up.

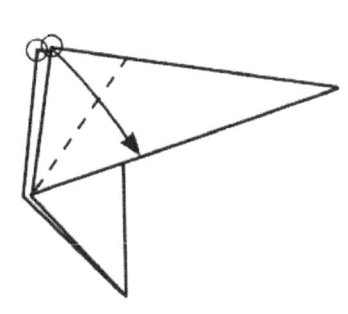

6 Fold down in the dotted lines.

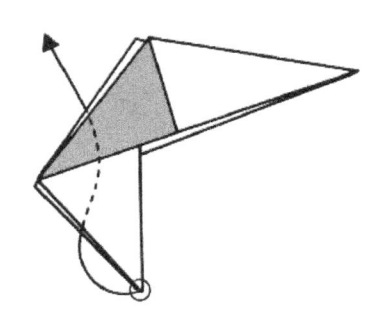

7 Do a pocket fold and rotate the model.

8 Fold and unfold to the marked point.

9 Do a step fold.

10 Fold diagonally up to form the legs.

170

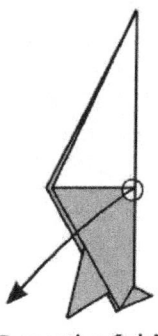

11 Open the fold.

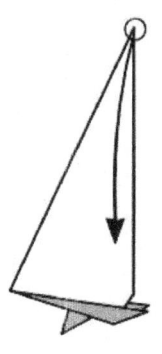

12 Fold down.

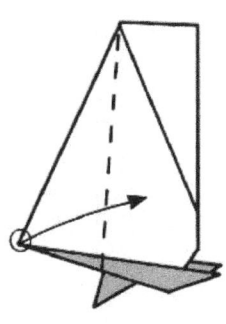

13 Fold in the dotted lines to form the wings.

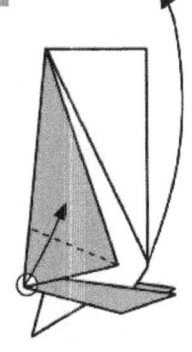

14 Fold inside and unfold the layer folded in the step 12.

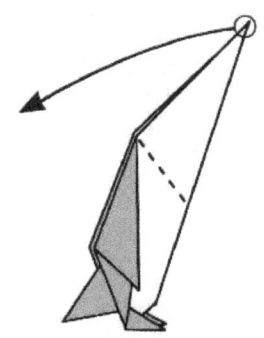

15 Fold diagonally down in the dotted line.

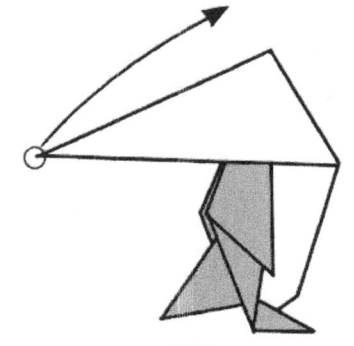

16 Unfold.

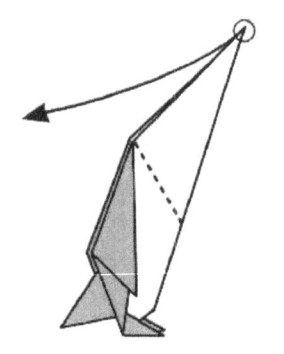

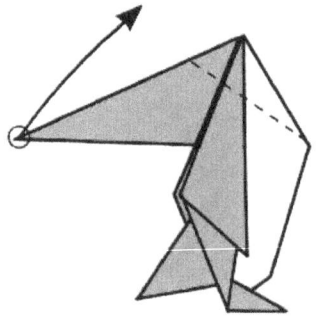

17 Fold diagonally down.

18 Fold in the dotted line.

19 Fold to the marked point.

20 Pocket fold to form the head.

21 Do a step fold.

22 Finished Penguin!

Snail

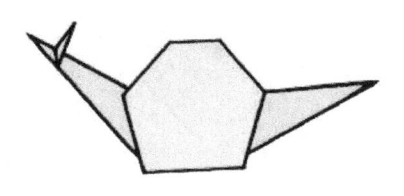

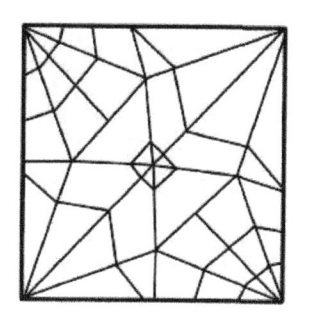

1. Start with the white side up.
2. Fold and unfold in the half diagonally. 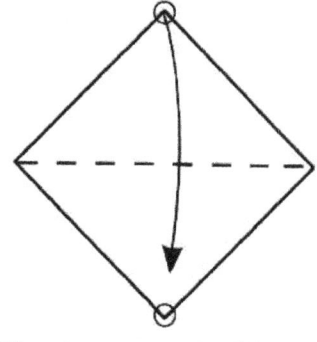
3. Fold the model to the marked point. 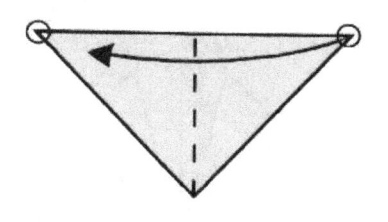
4. Squash fold the front layer.

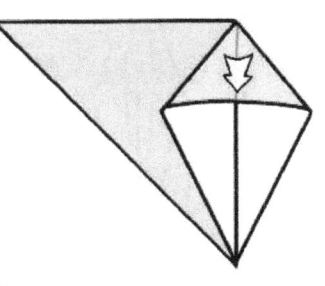

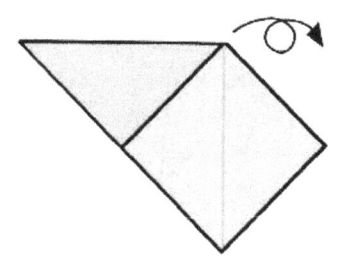

5. Turn the model over.

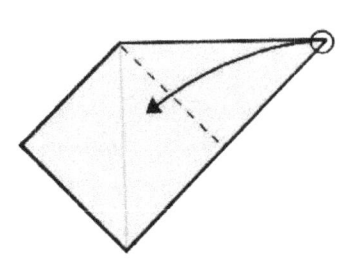

6. squash fold the other side.

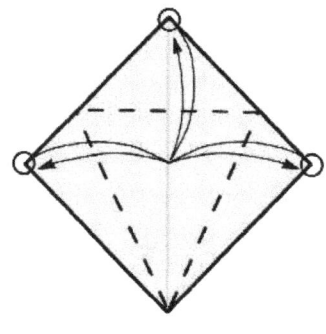

7. Fold and unfold the left, right and the top corners to the center.

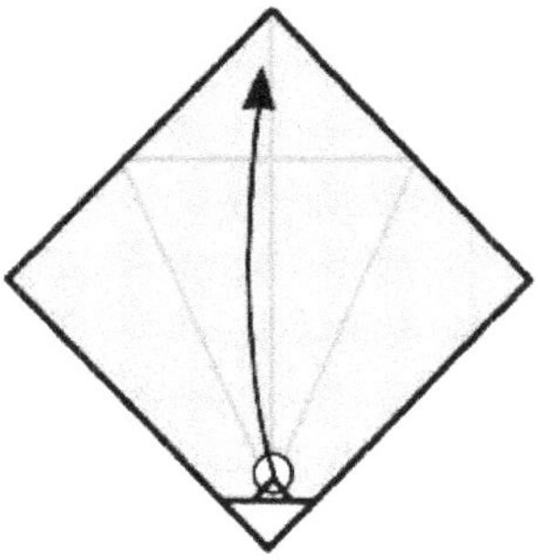

8. Lift the bottom corner up.

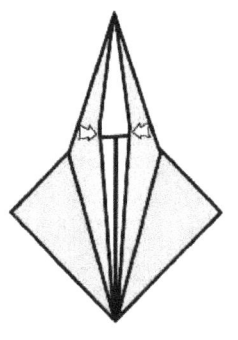

9. Squash fold the left and right sides.

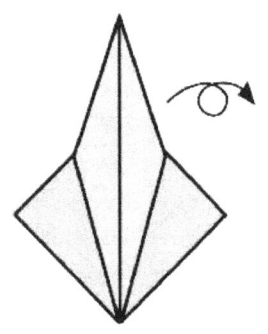

10. Turn the model over.

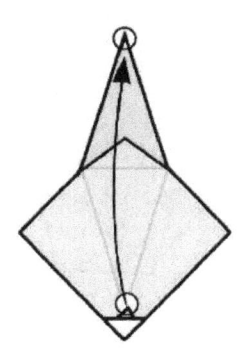

11 Lift the bottom corner up.

12 Fold the corners up and unfold.

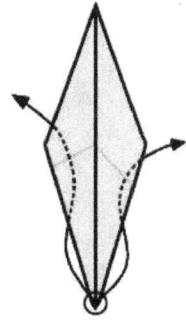

13 Pocket fold the left and right corners.

14 Fold down in dotted lines.

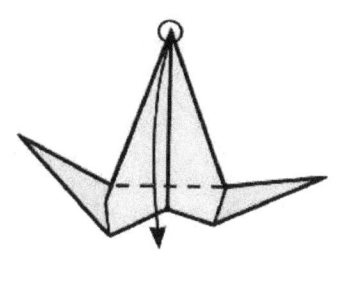

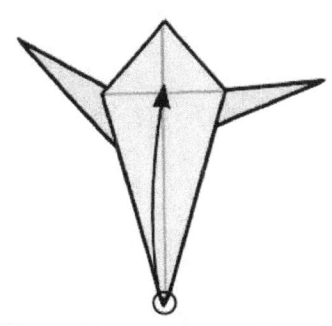

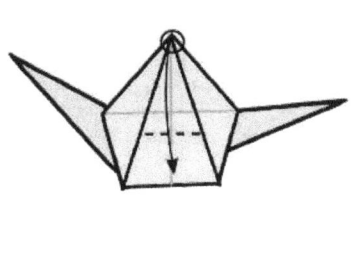

15 Fold up in dotted lines.

16 Fold down in the dotted lines.

17 Fold the layers inside.

18 Cut and separate the layers.

19 Fold the front layer back.

20 Fold the point back.

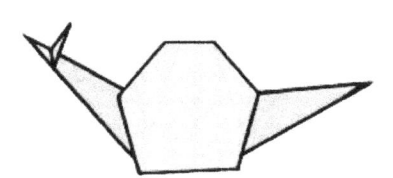

21 Finished Snail!

Crab

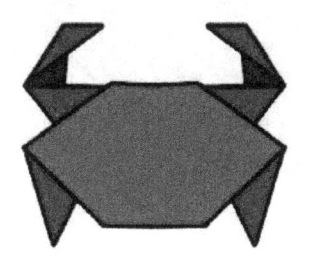

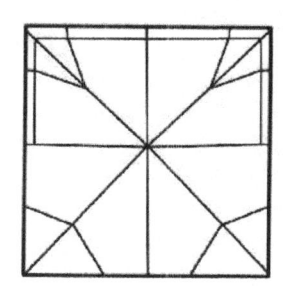

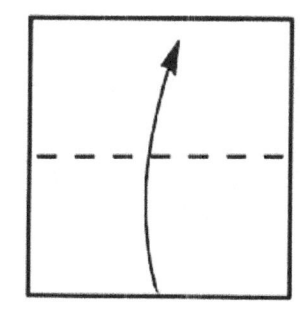

1. Start with the white side up.
2. Fold in half.
3. Fold in half. 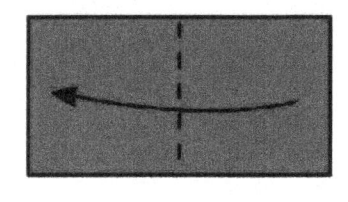 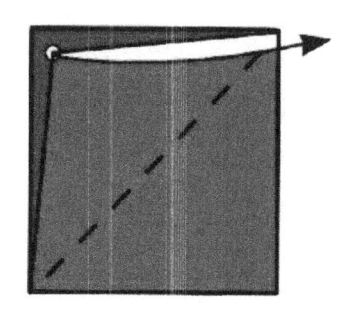
4. Open the pocket.

5 Do a squash fold.

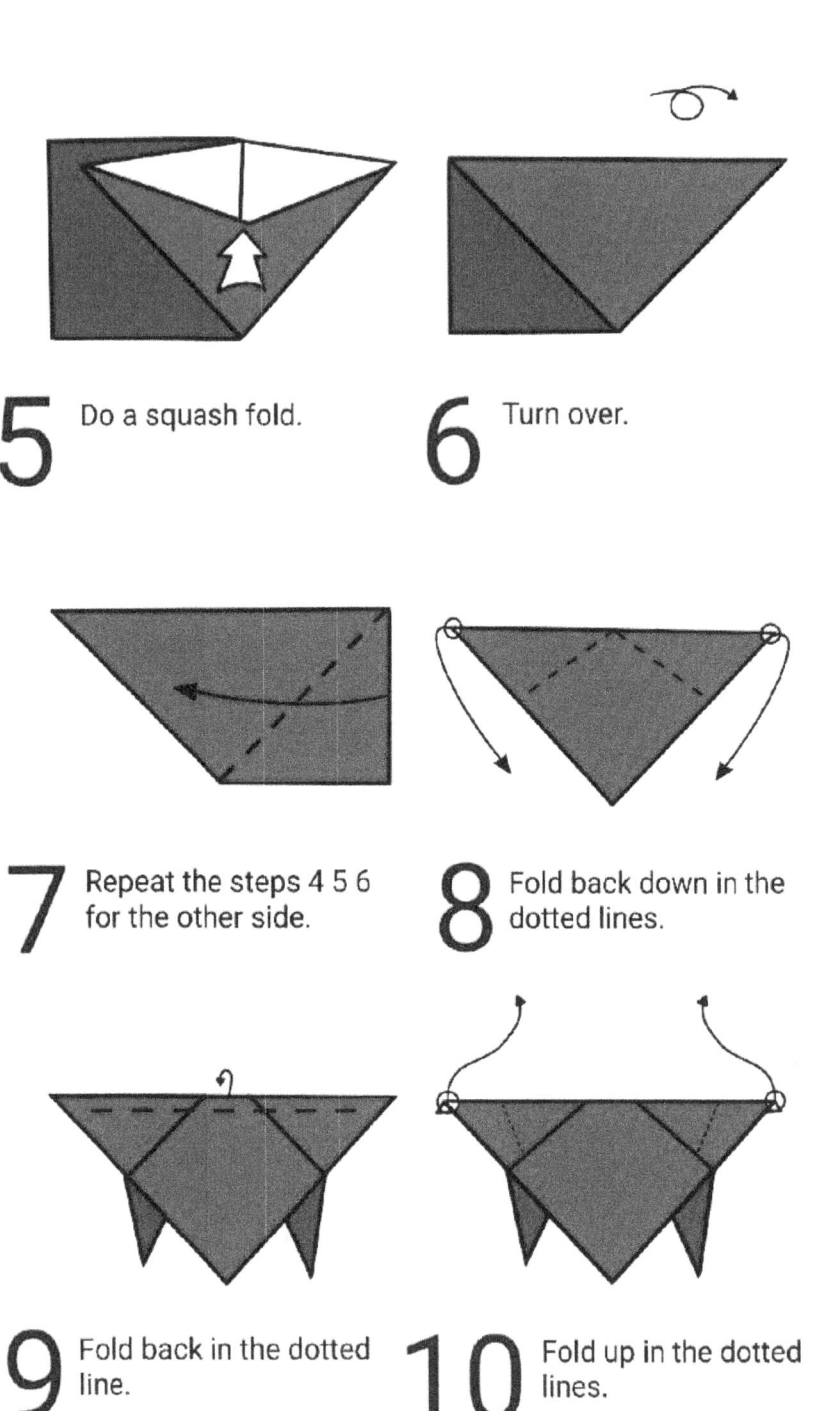

6 Turn over.

7 Repeat the steps 4 5 6 for the other side.

8 Fold back down in the dotted lines.

9 Fold back in the dotted line.

10 Fold up in the dotted lines.

11 Finished Crab!

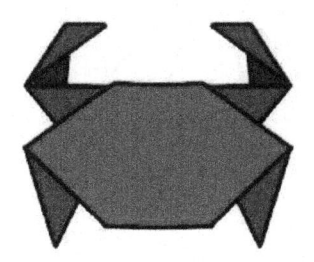

Eagle

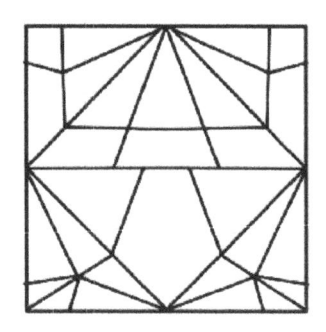

1 Start with the colored side up.

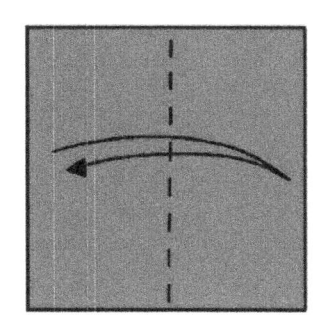

2 Fold and unfold in half.

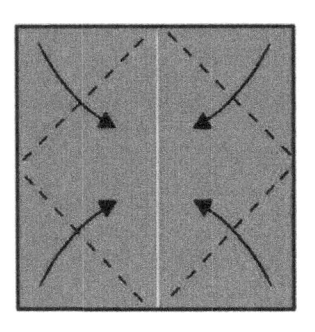

3 Fold the corners to the center.

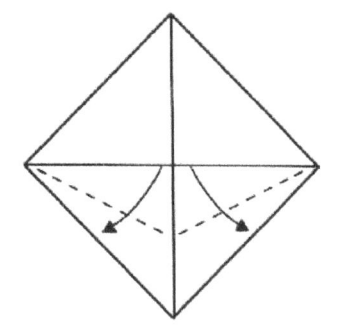

4 Fold in the dotted lines.

180

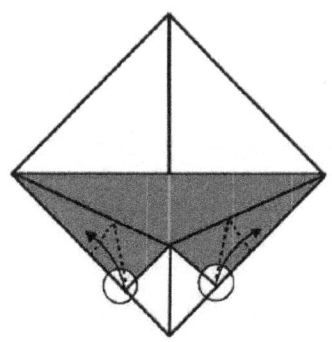

5 Pocket fold in the dotted lines.

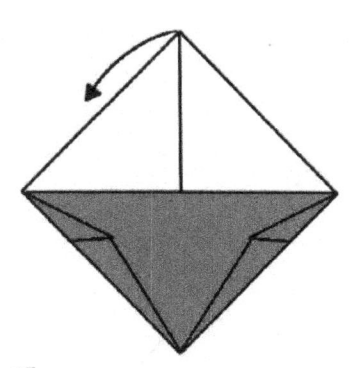

6 Fold behind.

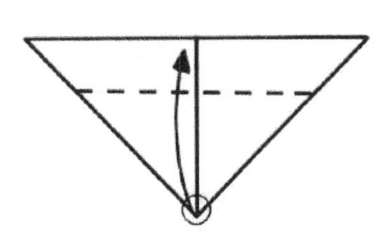

7 Fold up in the dotted line.

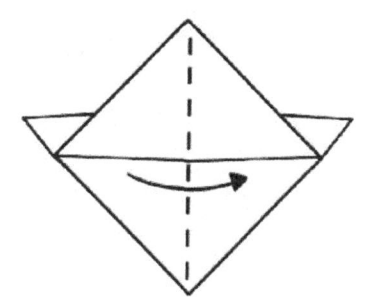

8 Fold in half.

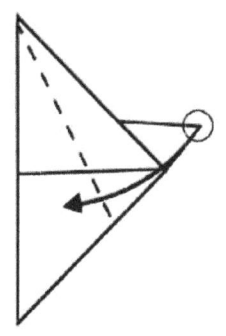

9 Fold in the dotted lines to form the wings.

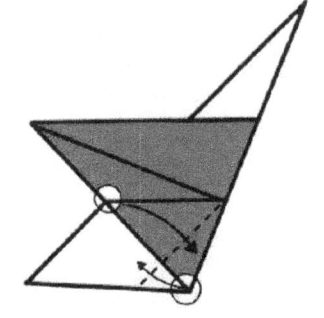

10 Fold in the dotted lines.

11 Fold inside.

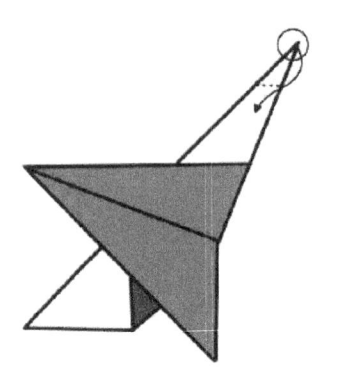

12 Fold the point to the right.

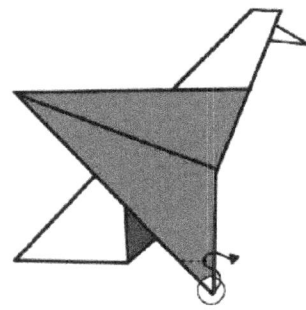

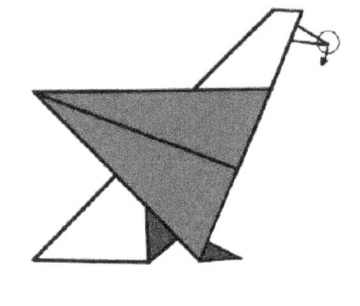

13 Pocket fold to the right.

14 Bend down.

15 Finished Eagle!

182

Jet

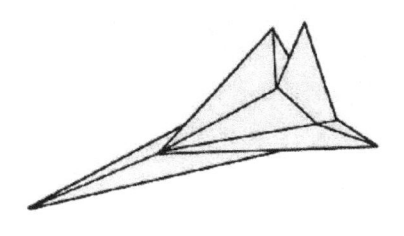

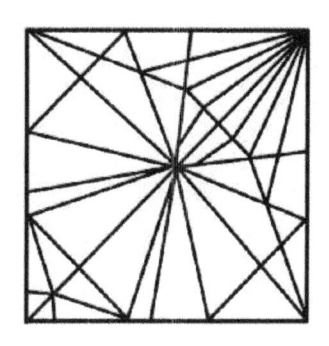

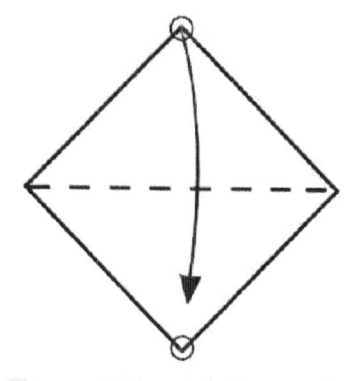

1. Start with the white side up.
2. Fold in half diagonally.
3. Fold the model to the marked point. 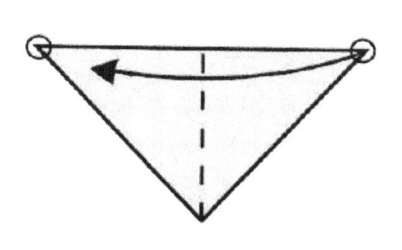 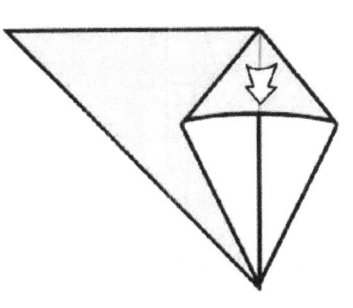
4. Squash fold the front layer.

183

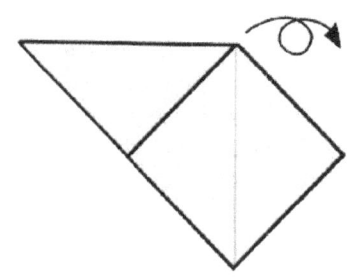

Turn the model over.

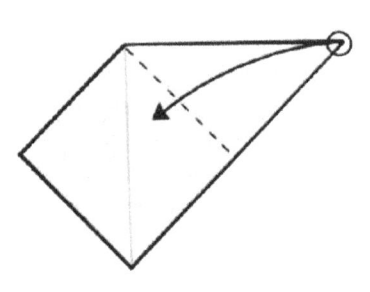

squash fold the other side.

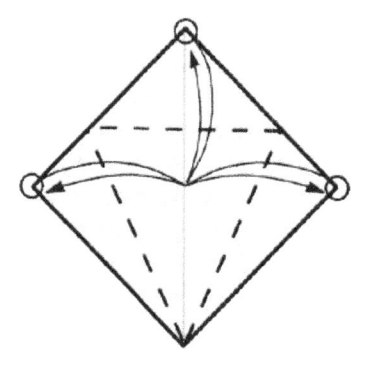

Fold and unfold the left, right and the top corners to the center.

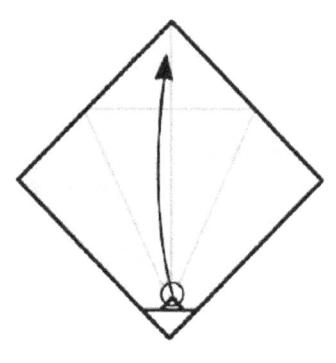

Lift the bottom corner up.

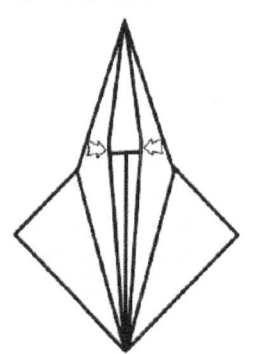

Squash fold the left and right sides.

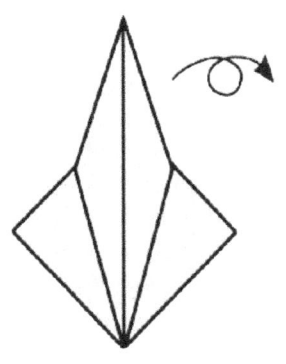

Turn the model over.

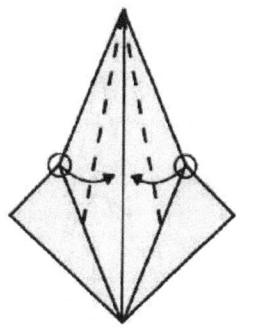

11. Fold inside in the dotted lines.

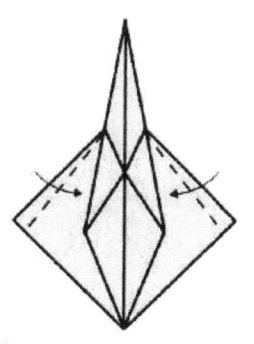

12. Fold in the dotted lines.

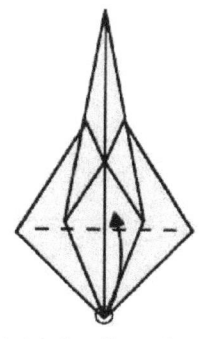

13. Fold the front layer up.

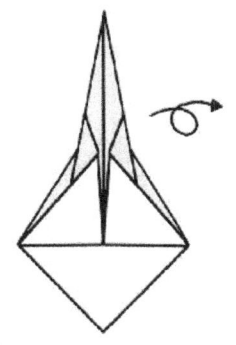

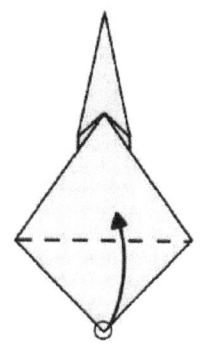

14. Turn over.

15. Fold up.

16. Fold down in the dotted line.

185

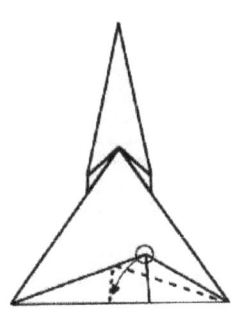

Pocket fold in the dotted lines.

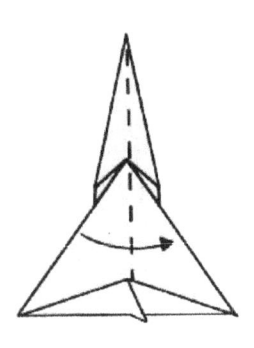

Fold in half.

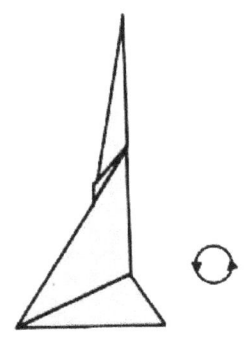

Rotate.

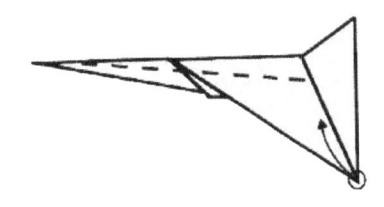

Fold up in the dotted lines.

Finished Jet!

Sheep

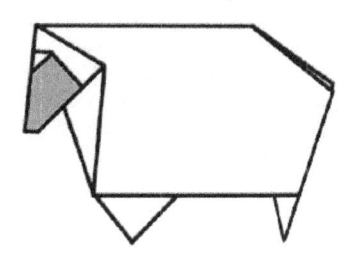

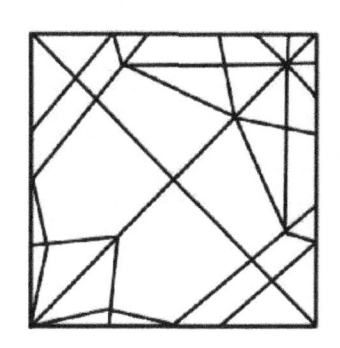

1. Start with the white side up.
2. Fold in the dotted line. 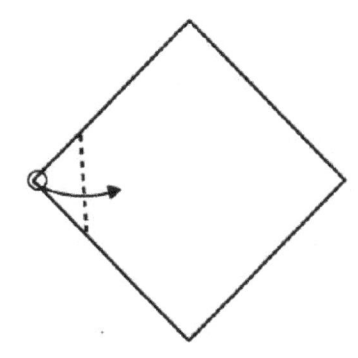
3. Turn over. 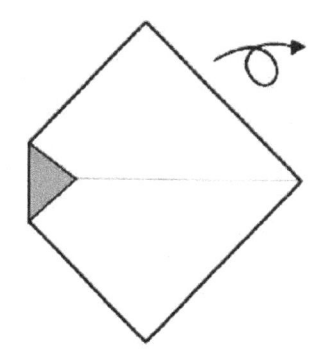
4. Fold to the center. 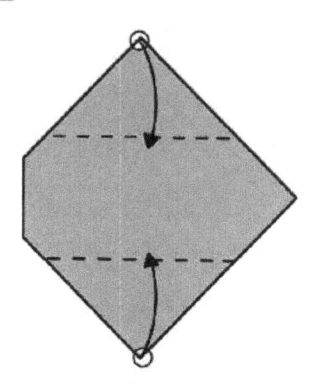

187

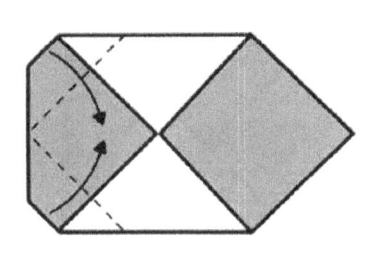

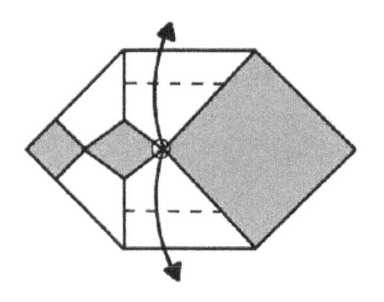

5 Fold inside in the dotted lines.

6 Unfold in the dotted lines.

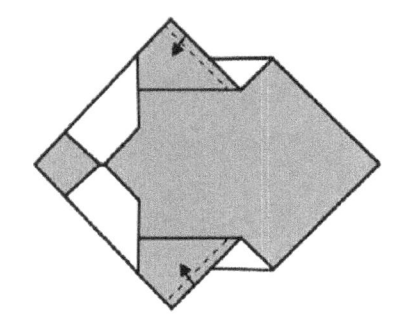

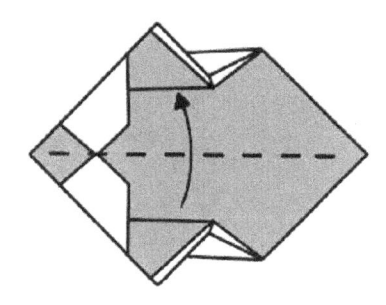

7 Fold inside.

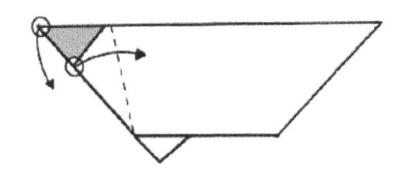

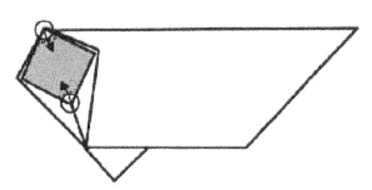

8 Fold in half.

9 Open the pocket and fold the colored part down.

10 Fold in the dotted lines.

188

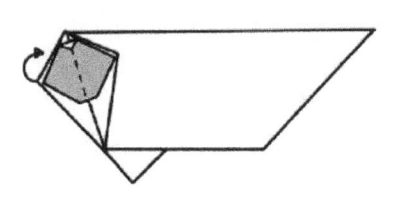

11 Fold back the left side.

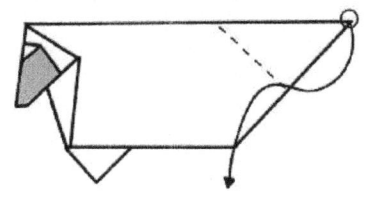

12 Pocket fold in the dotted line.

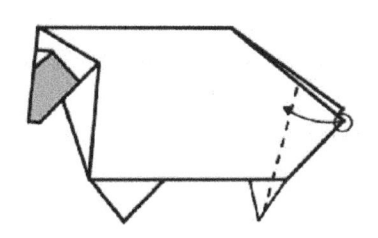

13 Fold inside.

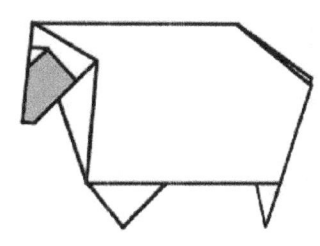

14 Finished sheep!

Flower

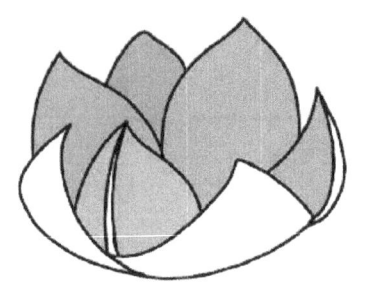

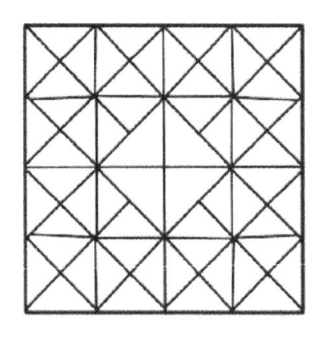

1. Start with the white side up.
2. Fold and unfold in the dotted lines. 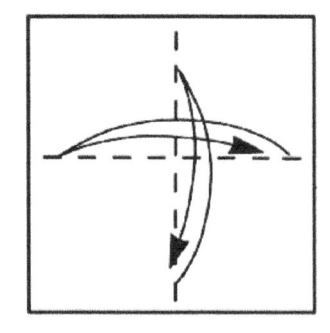
3. Fold inside. 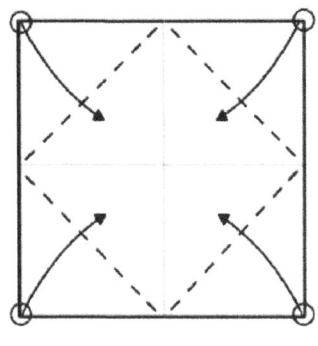
4. Fold inside. 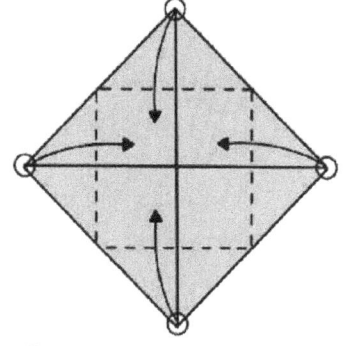

190

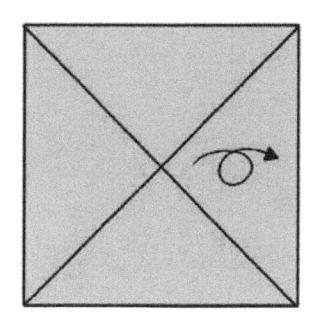

5 Turn over.

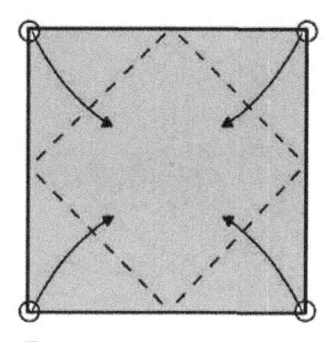

6 Fold in the dotted lines.

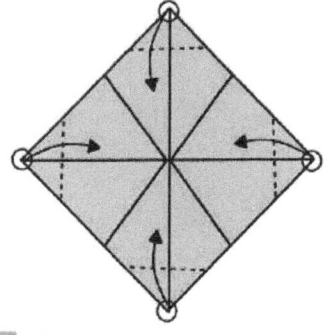

7 Fold the corners inside.

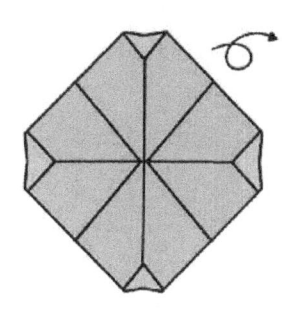

8 Turn over.

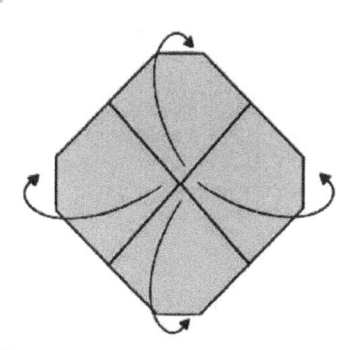

9 Open the front layers.

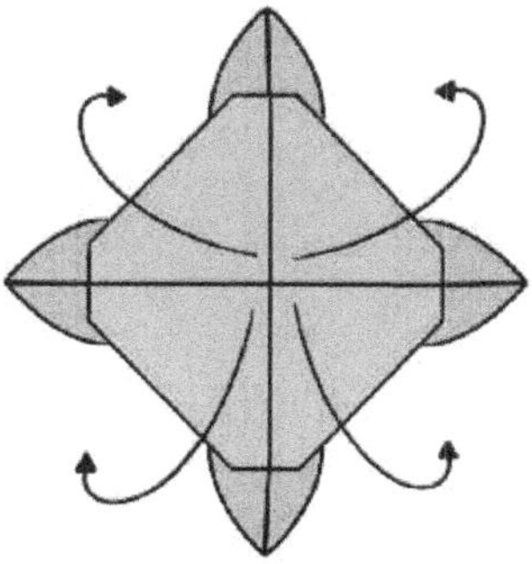

10 Unfold and form the leaves.

11 Finished flower.

Spaceplane

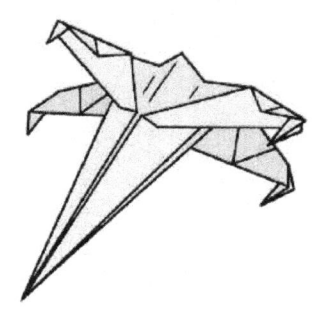

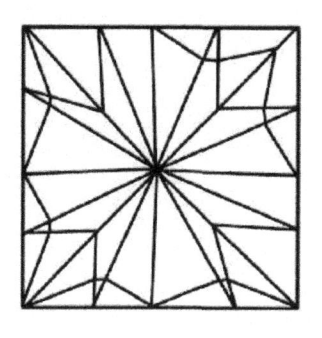

1. Start with the white side up.
2. Fold in half. 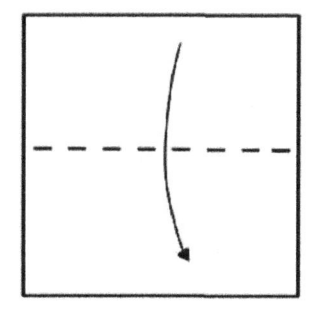
3. Fold in half. 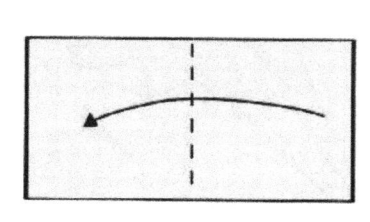
4. Do a pocket fold opening the front layer.

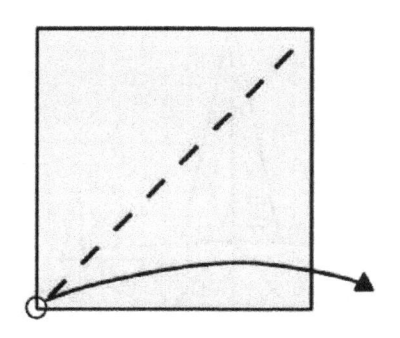

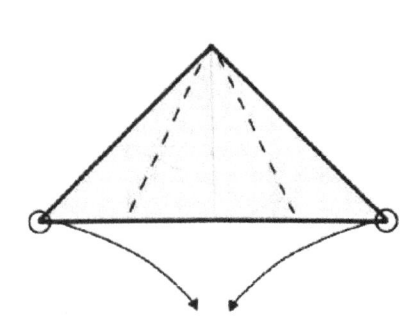

Fold down.

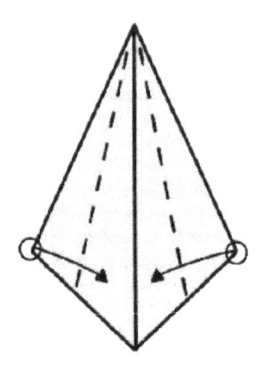

Fold to the center.

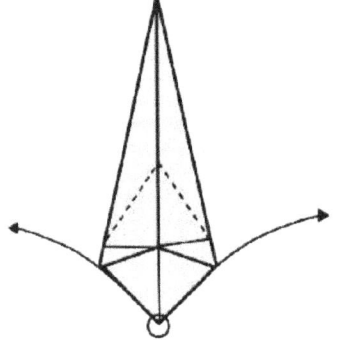

Unfold to the marked points.

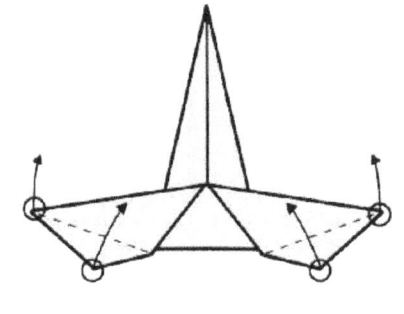

Fold the bottom parts of the wings and points up.

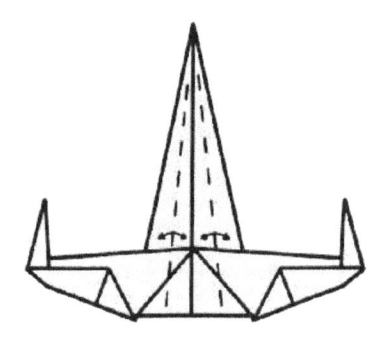

Fold and unfold in the dotted lines.

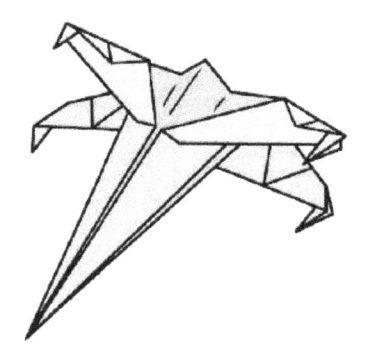

finished spaceplane!

Dress

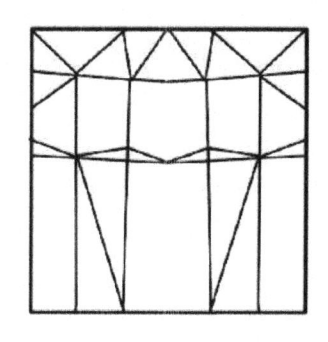

1. Start with the colored side up.
2. Fold and unfold in the dotted lines. 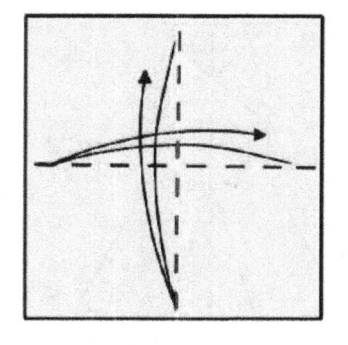
3. Step fold in the dotted lines. 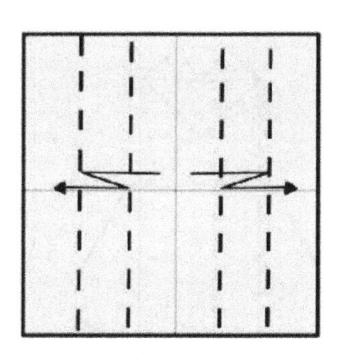
4. Step fold.

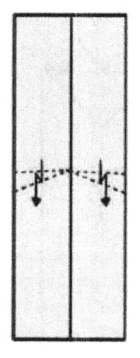

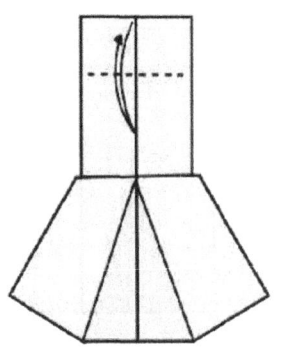

Fold to the marked point and unfold.

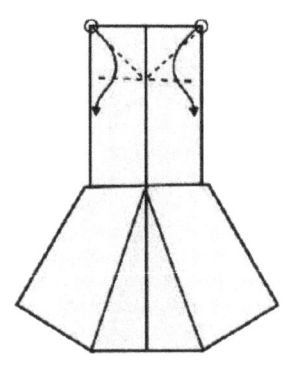

Pocket fold the front layer.

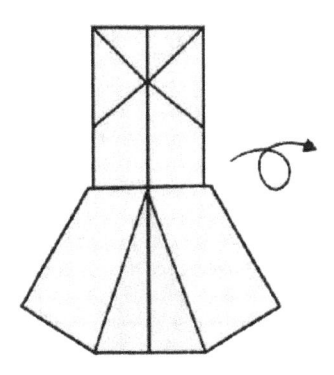

Turn over.

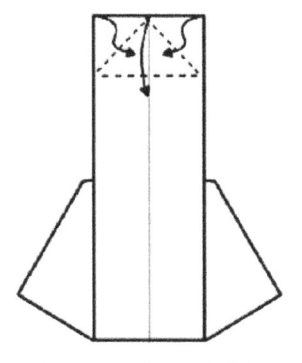

Do a pocket fold.

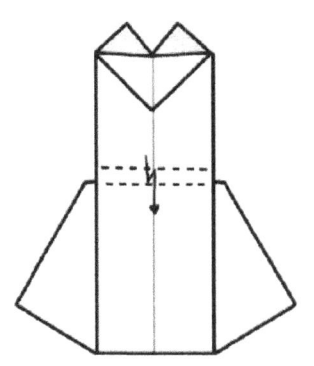

Step fold in the dotted lines.

Fold inside.

196

Fold inside.

Turn over.

Do a pocket fold.

Finished Dress!

Flying dragon

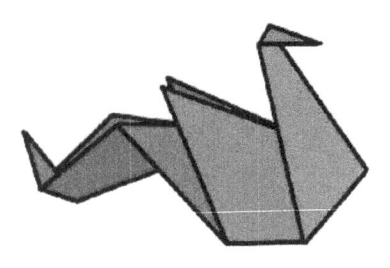

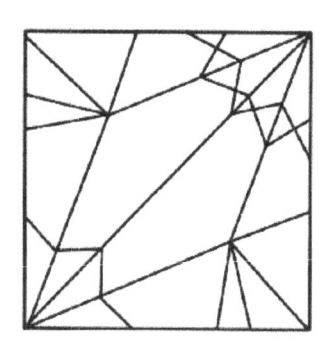

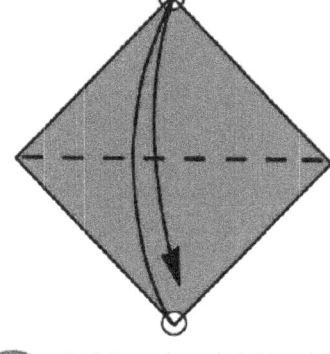

1. Start with the white side up.

2. Fold and unfold in the half diagonally.

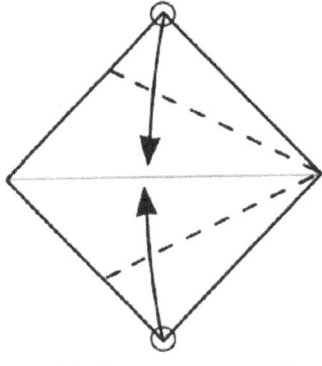

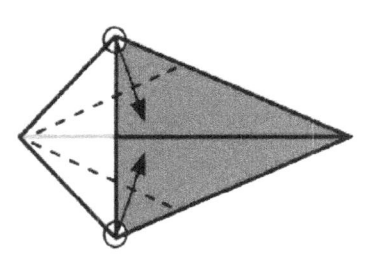

3. Fold the corners to the center.

4. Fold in the dotted lines.

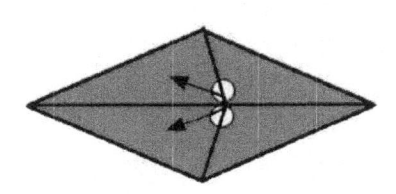

5 Open the pockets moving the corners to the marked point.

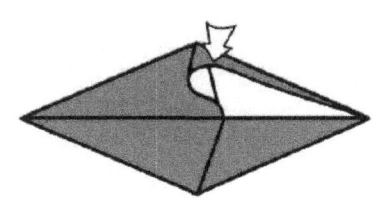

6 Flatten the pockets.

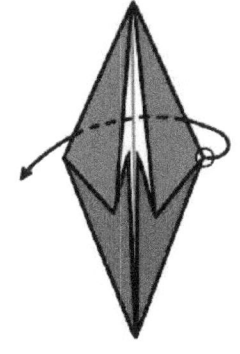

7 Fold in half.

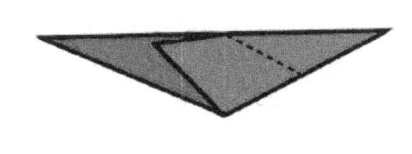

8 Do a pocket fold.

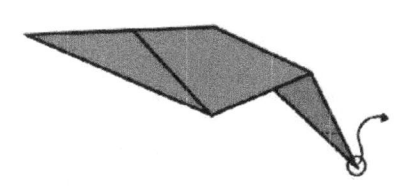

9 Pocket fold the point.

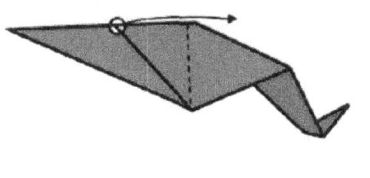

10 Fold to the right in the dotted line.

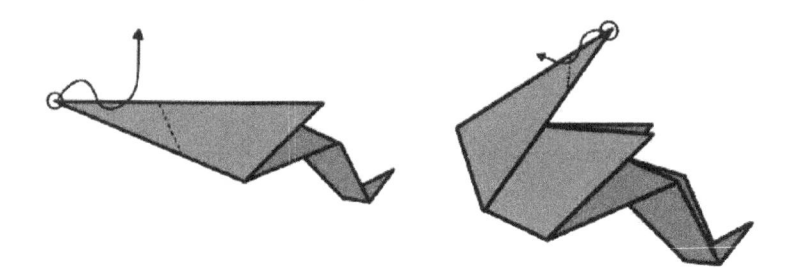

11 Pocket fold in the dotted line.

12 Pocket fold to form the head.

13 Finished flying dragon!

Bear

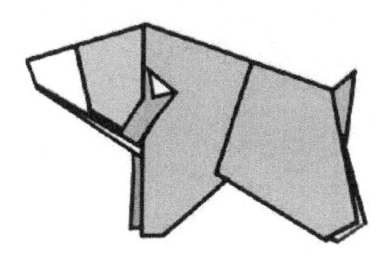

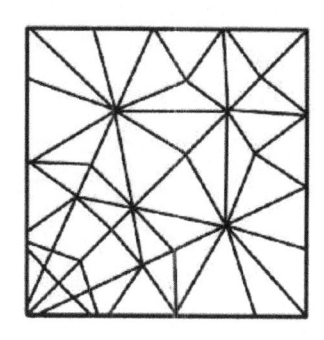

1. Start with the white side up.
2. Fold and unfold in the half diagonally. 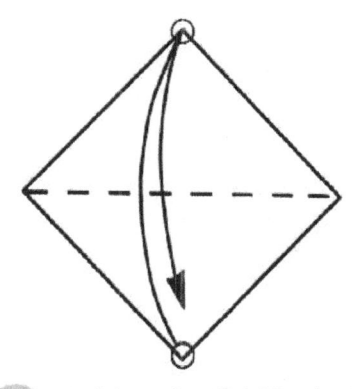
3. Fold the corners to the center. 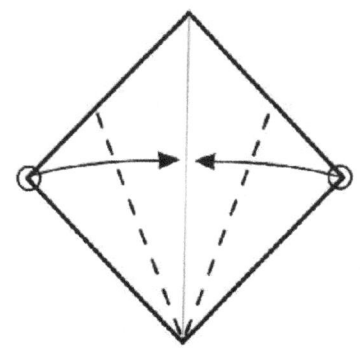
4. Fold to the marked point and unfold. 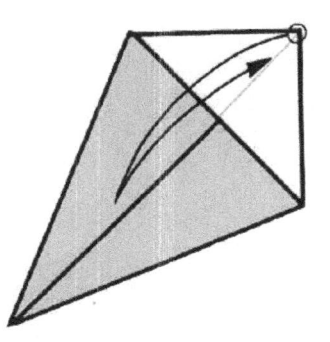

201

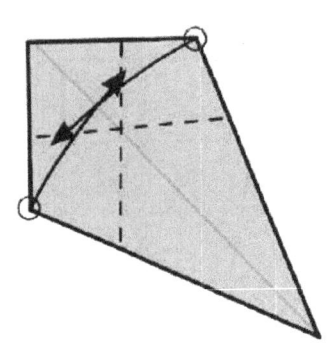

5 Pocket fold to form the tail.

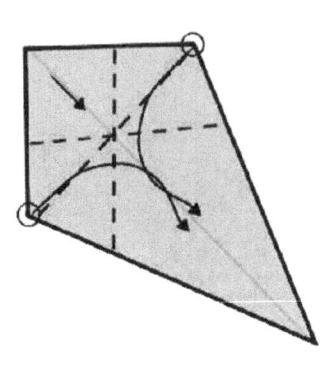

6 Fold in the dotted line.

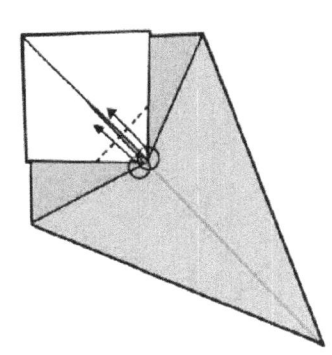

7 Fold to the marked point and unfold the point to form the ears.

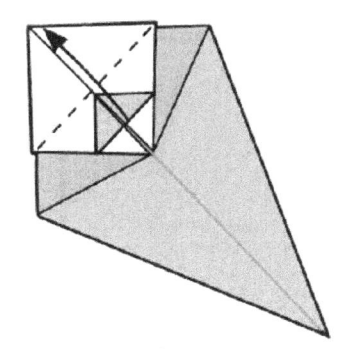

8 Pocket fold inside.

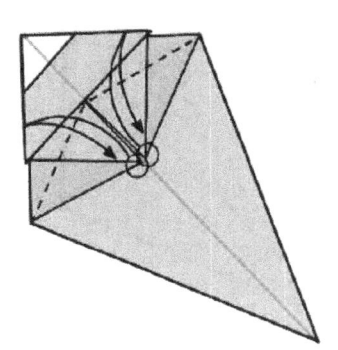

9 Finished bear!

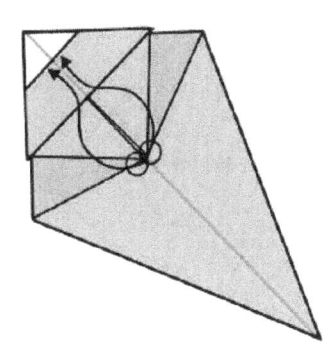

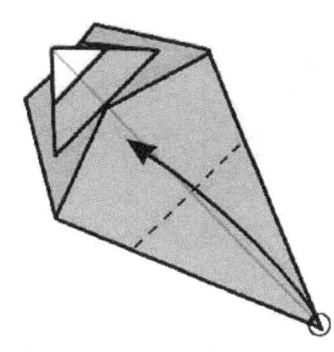

11 Pocket fold to form the tail.

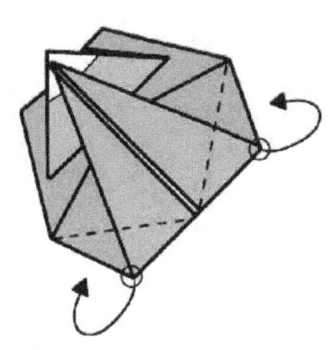

12 Fold in the dotted line.

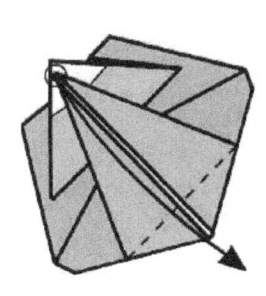

13 Fold to the marked point and unfold the point to form the ears.

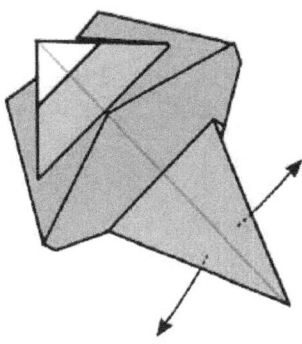

14 Pocket fold inside.

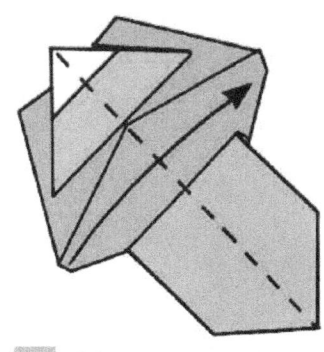

15 Finished bear!

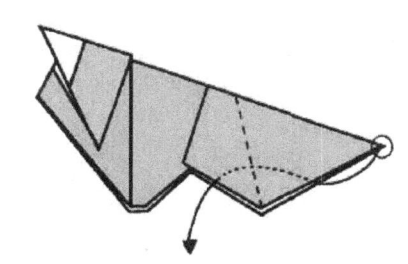

16

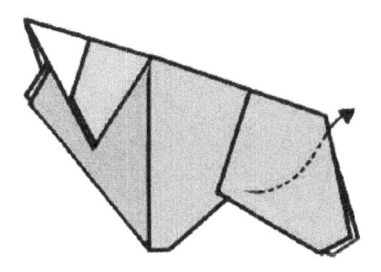

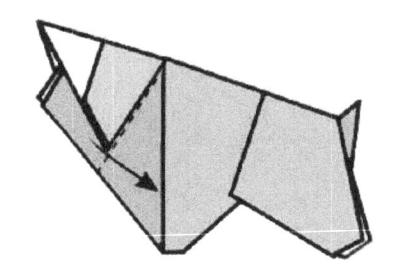

17 Pocket fold to form the tail.

18 Fold in the dotted line.

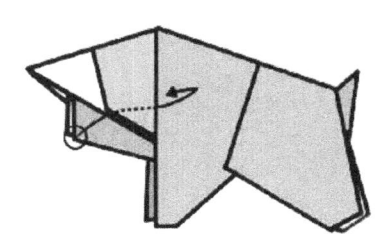

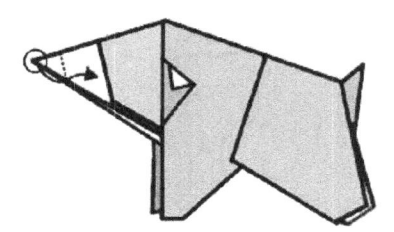

19 Fold to the marked point and unfold the point to form the ears.

20 Pocket fold inside.

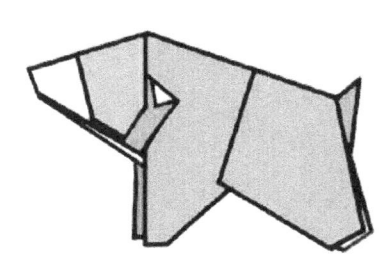

21 Finished bear!

204

Swallow

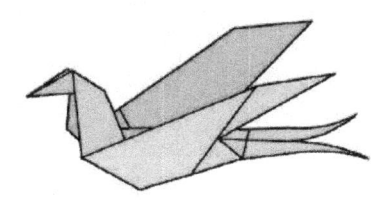

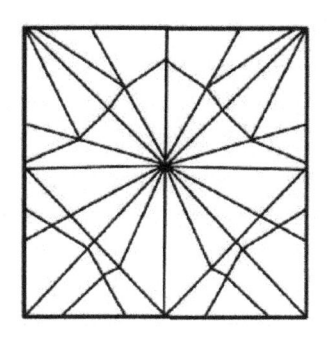

1. Start with the white side up.
2. Fold in half. 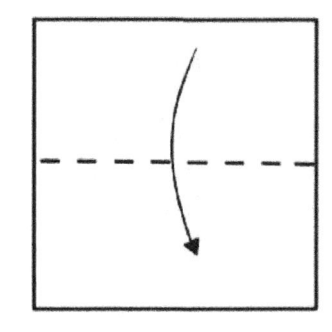
3. Fold to the left. 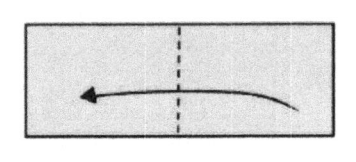
4. Pocket fold to the marked point. 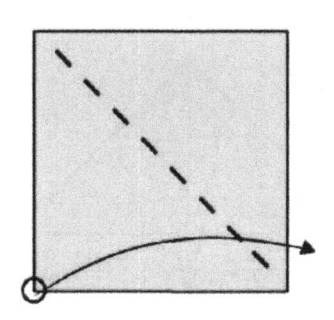

205

5. Pocket fold the other side.

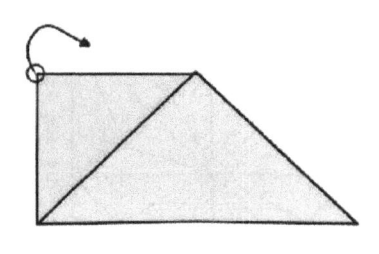

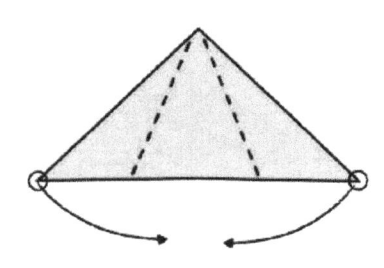

6. Fold down in the dotted lines.

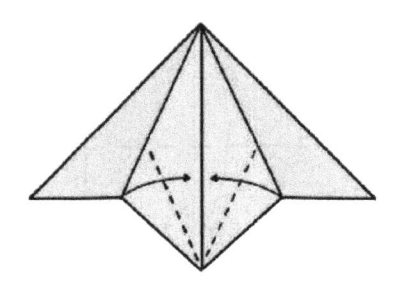

7. Fold to the center.

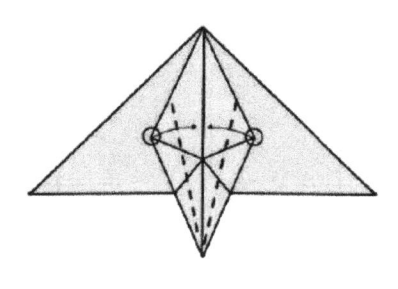

8. Fold to the center.

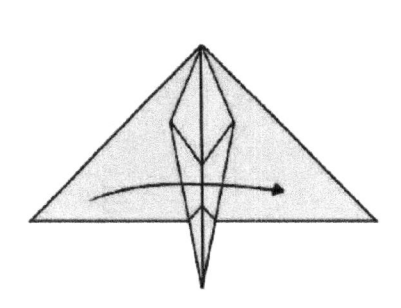

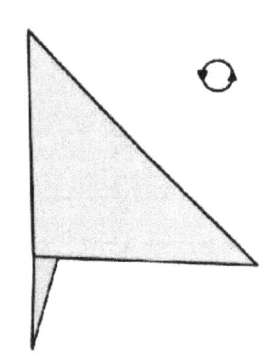

9. Fold in half.

10. Rotate the model.

206

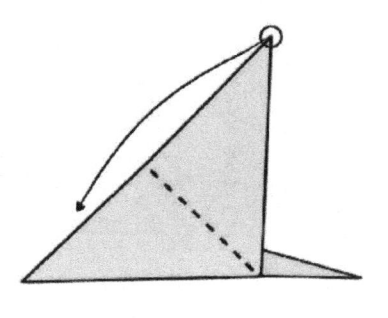

11 Fold down in the dotted line.

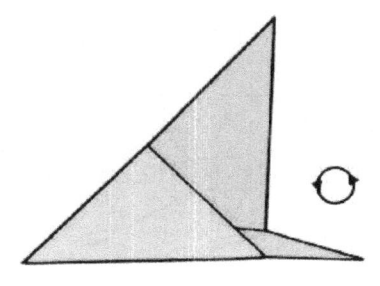

12 Rotate the model l.

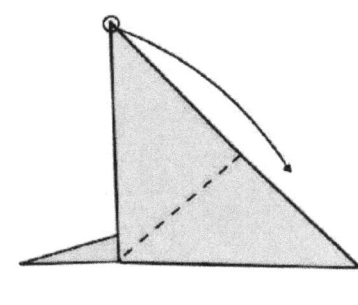

13 Fold down.

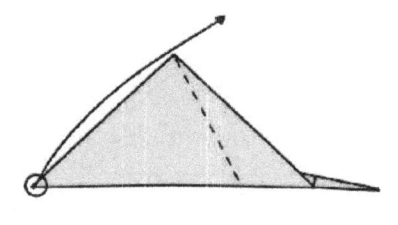

14 Fold diagonally up.

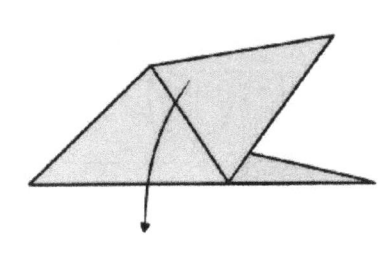

15 Fold the wing down.

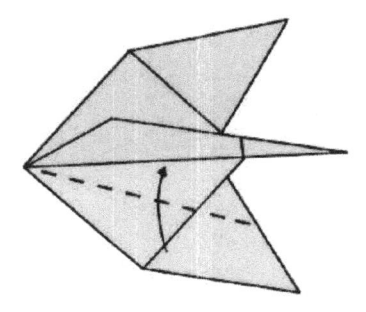

16 Fold up in the dotted line.

17 Fold the wing up.

18 Rotate the model.

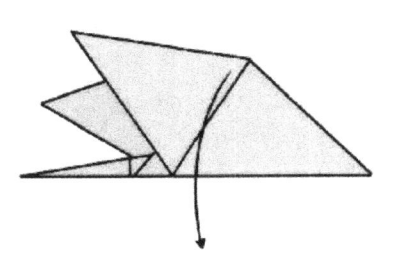

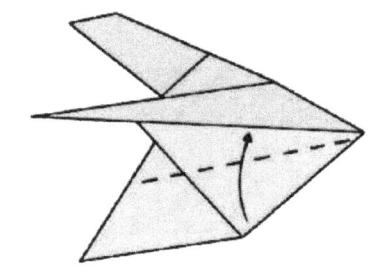

19 Fold down.

20 Fold up in the dotted line.

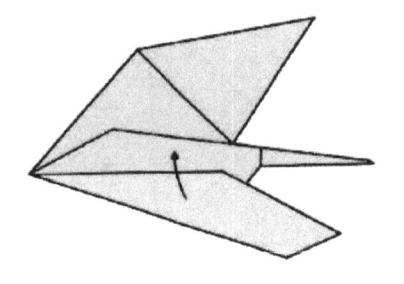

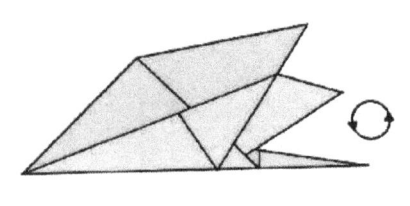

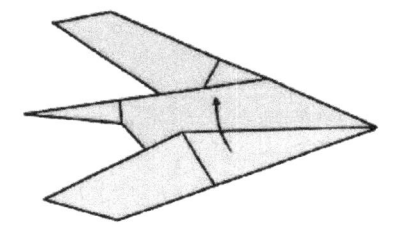

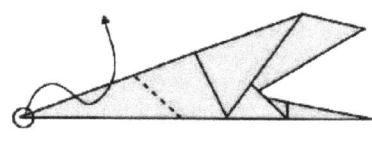

21 Fold the wing up.

22 Do a pocket fold.

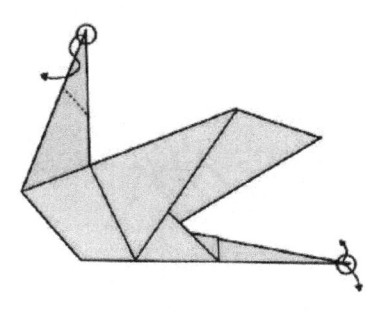

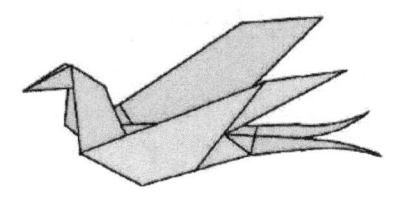

23 Pocket fold the head and separate the feathers.

24 Finished swallow!

Toucan

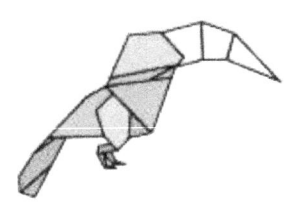

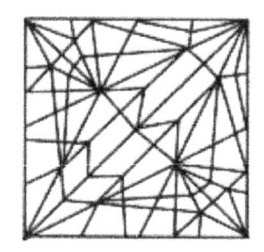

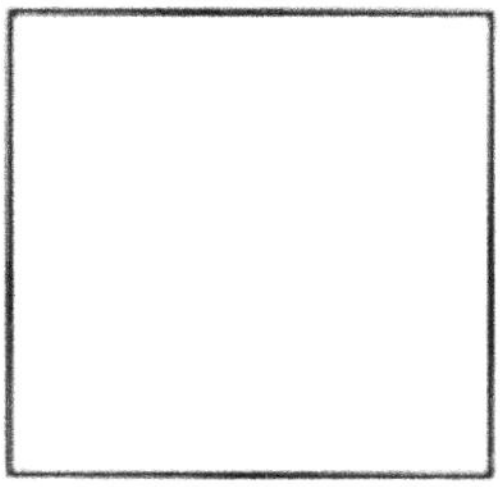

1. Start with the white side up.
2. Fold and unfold in the half diagonally. 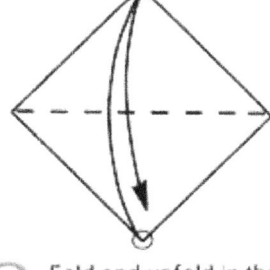
3. Fold the corners to the center. 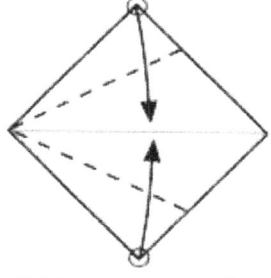
4. Fold in the dotted lines. 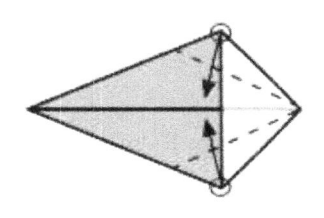

210

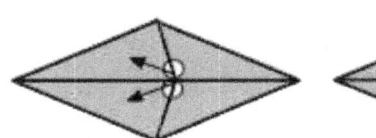

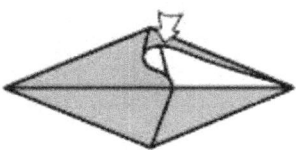

5 Open the pockets moving the corners to the marked points.

6 Flatten the pockets.

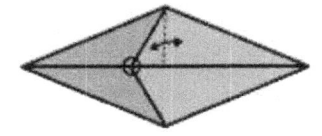

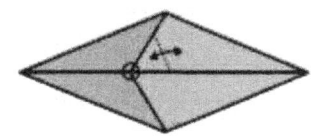

7 Fold and unfold in the dotted line.

8 Fold and unfold in the dotted line.

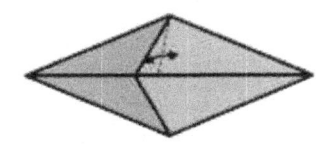

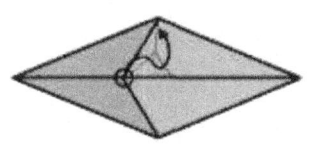

9 Fold and unfold in the dotted line.

10 Pocket fold and repeat the steps 7, 8, 9, 10 for the other side.

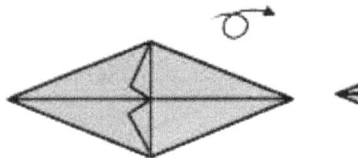

11 Turn over.

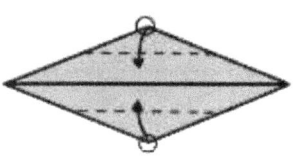

12 Fold into the center.

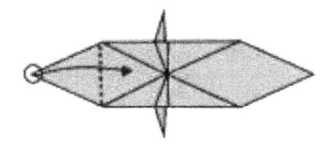

13 Fold to the right.

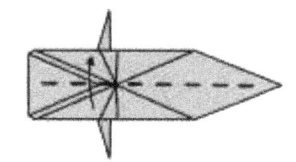

14 Fold in half.

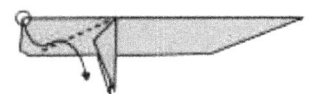

15 Pocket fold down.

16 Fold in the dotted lines.

17 Fold the leg to the left.

18 Fold the point into the right.

19 Fold up in the dotted lines.

20 Pocket fold up.

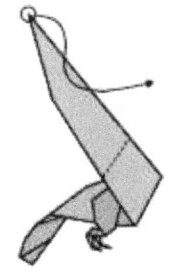

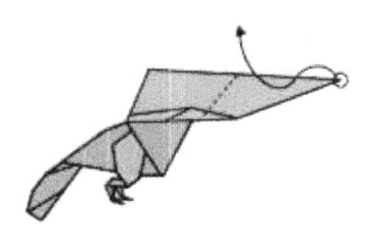

21 Do a pocket fold.

22 Pocket fold up.

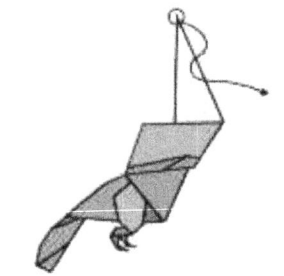

23 Pocket fold to the right.

24 Step fold in the dotted lines.

25 Finished toucan!

Star

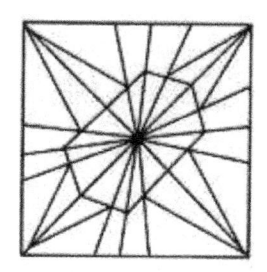

1. Start with the white side up.
2. Fold and unfold in the dotted lines. 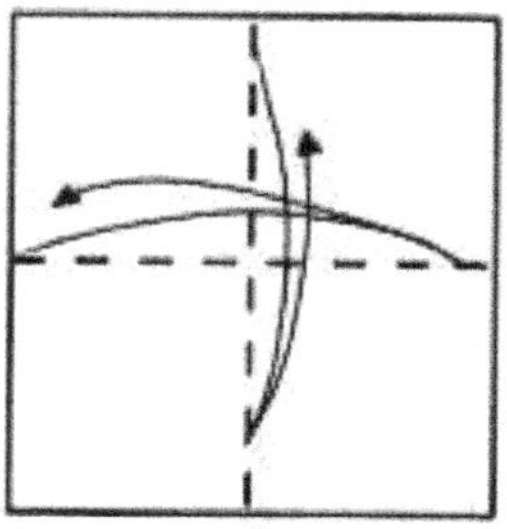
3. Fold and unfold in the dotted lines. 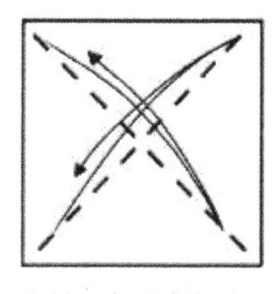
4. Do a pocket fold. 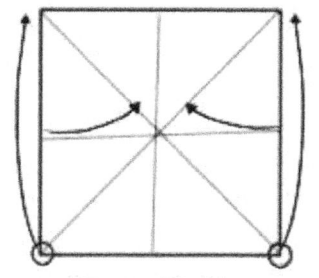

215

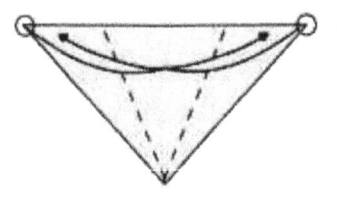

Fold the left and right sides to the center and unfold.

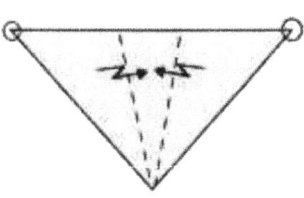

Step fold in the dotted lines.

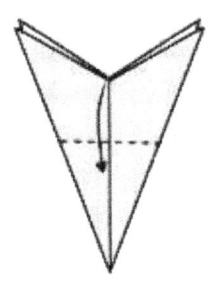

Fold down.

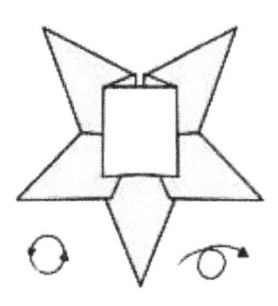

Rotate the model and turn it over.

Finished star!

Koala

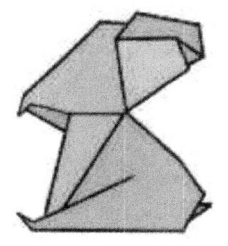

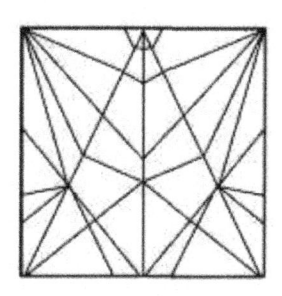

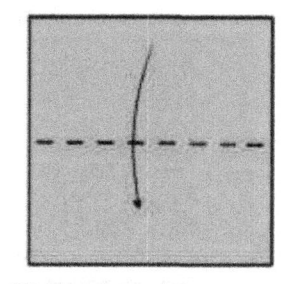

1. Start with the colored side up.
2. Fold in half.
3. Fold up in the dotted line. 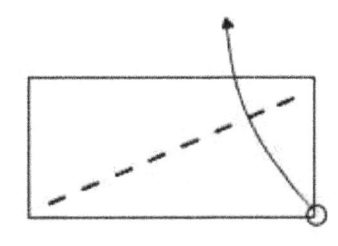 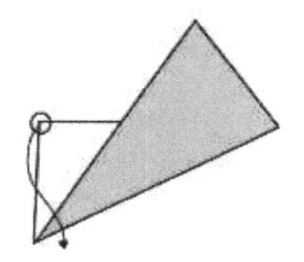
4. Pocket fold inside.

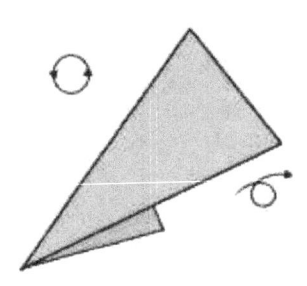

5 Rotate the model and turn it over.

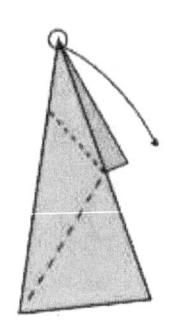

6 Fold diagonally down to form the ears and front legs.

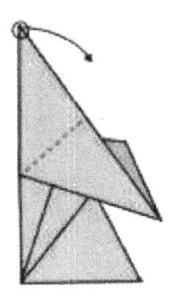

7 Fold back.

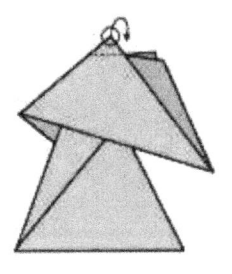

8 Fold inside.

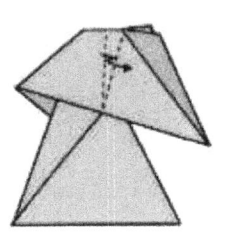

9 Do a step fold.

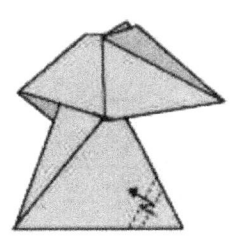

10 Step fold to form the tail.

11 Pocket fold the ears.

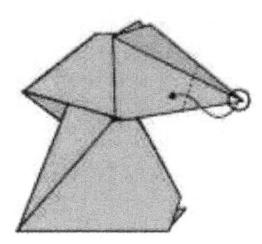

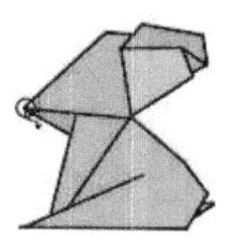

12 Fold the nose down.

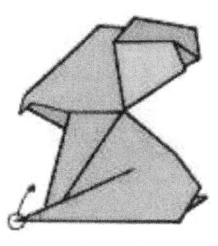

13 Fold up.

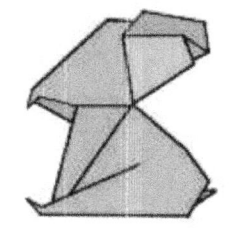

14 Finished Koala!

Bunny

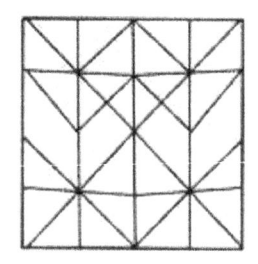

1. Start with the white side up.
2. Fold to the center. 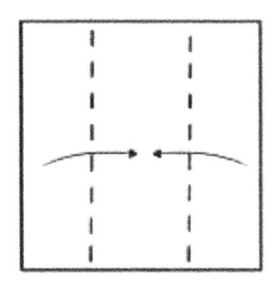
3. Pocket fold the 4 sides. 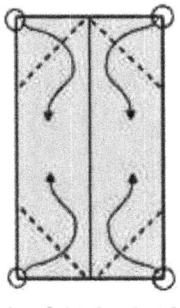
4. Turn over.

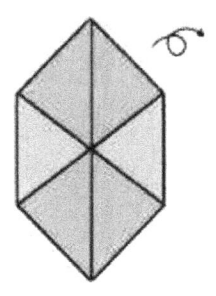

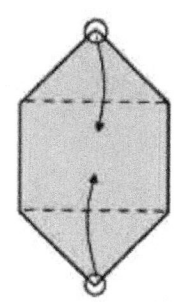

5 Fold in the dotted lines.

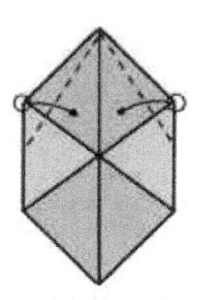

6 Fold back in the dotted lines.

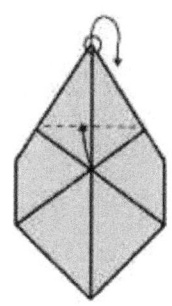

7 Fold back.

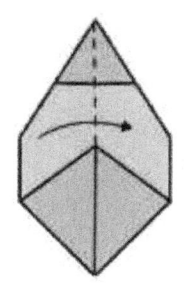

8 Fold in half.

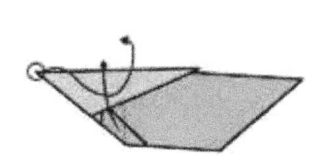

9 Lift the head up doing a pocket fold and fold the point inside.

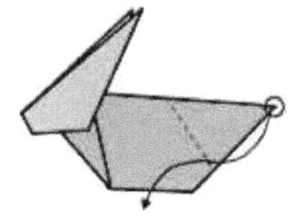

10 Pocket fold to form the legs.

221

11 Finished bunny!

Boat

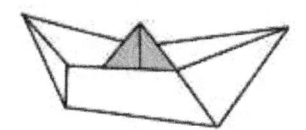

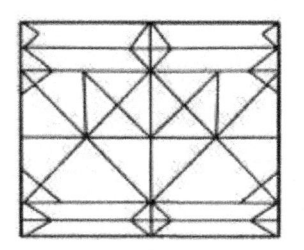

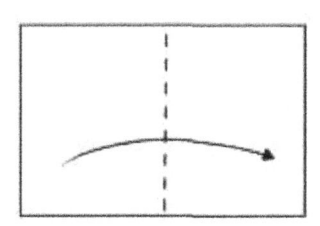

1. Start with the white side up.
2. Fold in half.
3. Rotate the model. 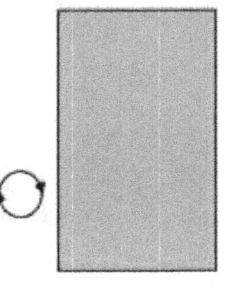 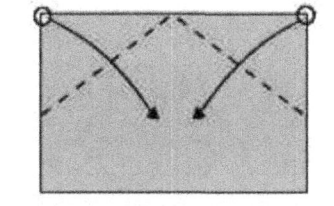
4. Fold the corners to the center.

5 Fold up.

6 Fold to the marked point.

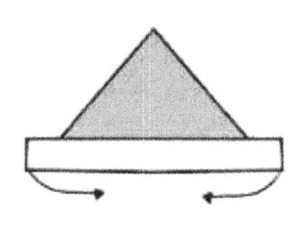

7 Open the pocket.

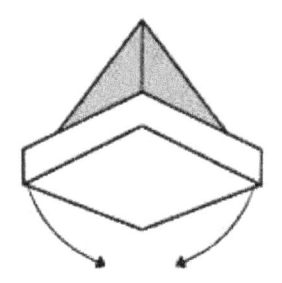

8 Fold the corners down to meet each other.

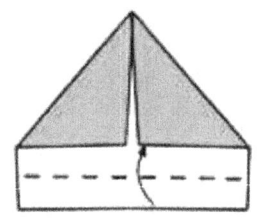

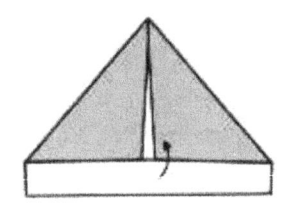

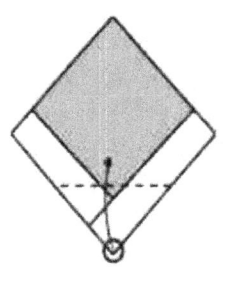

9 Fold up in the dotted line.

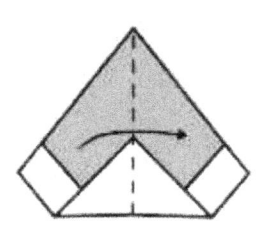

10 Fold in half.

224

11 Fold up.

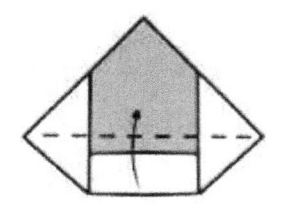

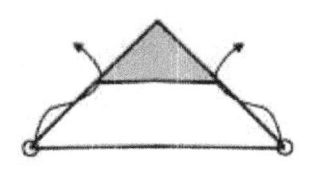

12 Pull out the inner corners to form a boat.

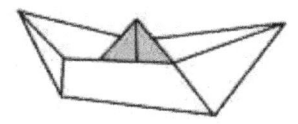

13 Finished boat!

Dolphin

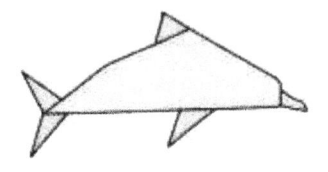

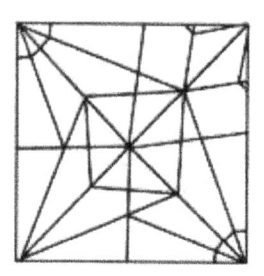

1. Start with the white side up.
2. Fold in half diagonally. 
3. Fold in half diagonally. 
4. Pocket fold down in the dotted lines.

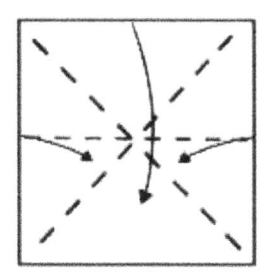

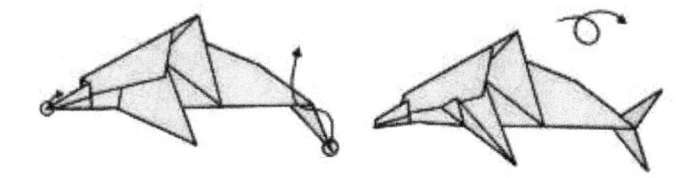

11 Pocket fold the inner layer up.

12 Turn over.

13 Finished dolphin!

Sea dog

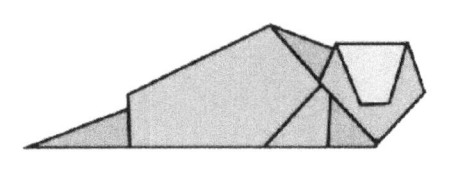

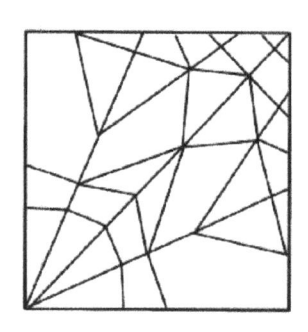

1. Start with the white side up.

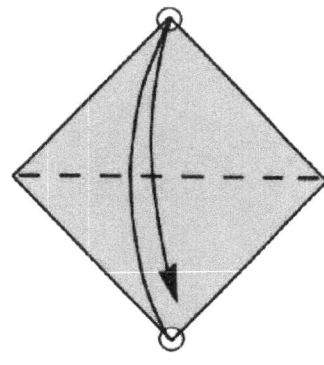

2. Fold and unfold in the half diagonally.

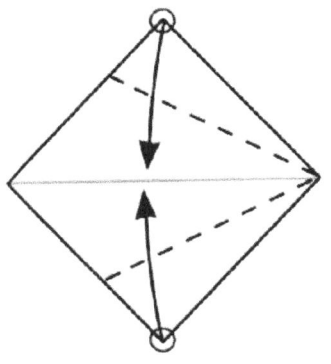

3. Fold the corners to the center.

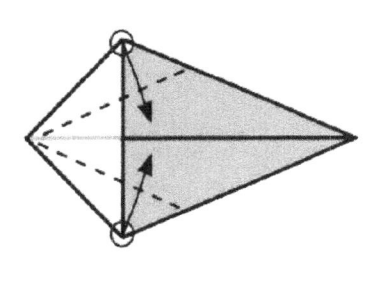

4. Fold in the dotted lines.

228

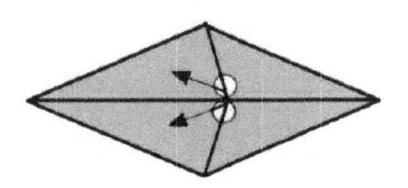

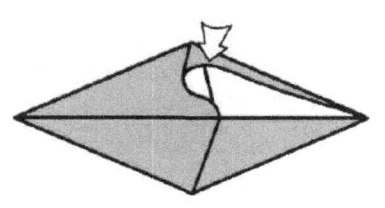

5 Open the pockets moving the corners to the marked point.

6 Flatten the pockets.

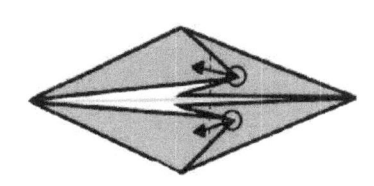

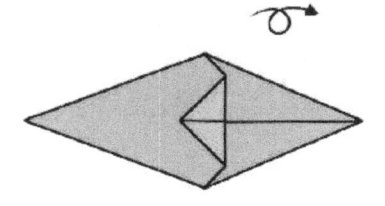

7 Fold the corners up.

8 Turn over.

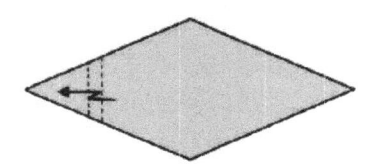

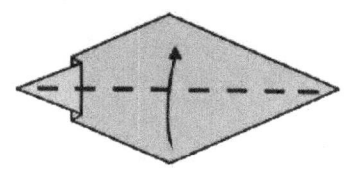

9 Do a step fold.

10 Fold in half.

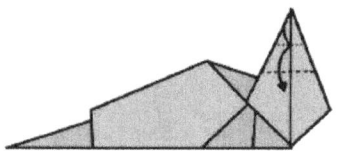

11 Pocket fold opening the layers.

12 Fold in the dotted lines.

13 Finished sea dog!

Ostrich

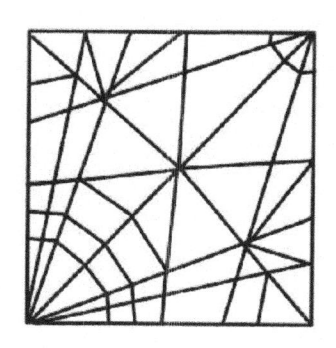

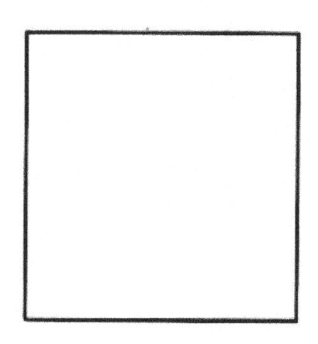

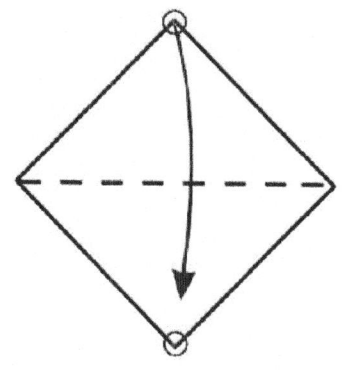

1 Start with the white side up.

2 Fold in the half diagonally.

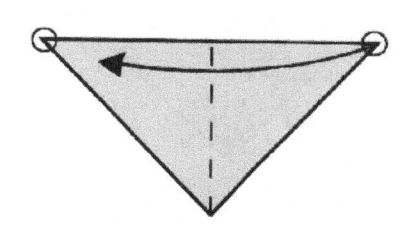

3 Fold the model to the marked point.

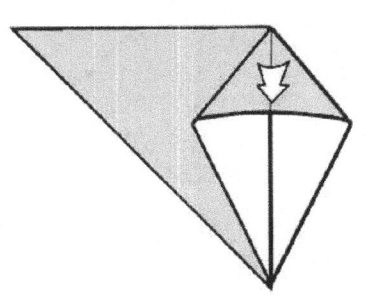

4 Squash fold the front layer.

5 Turn the model over.

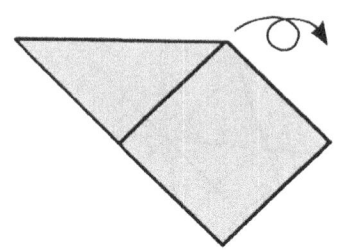

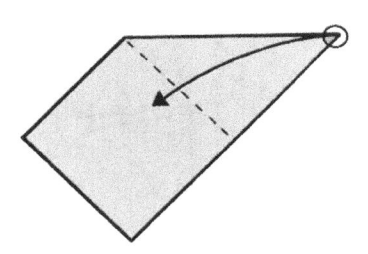

6 squash fold the other side.

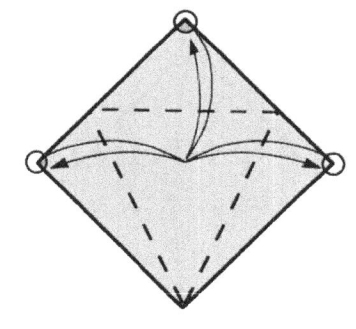

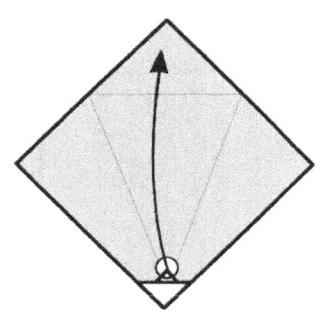

7 Fold and unfold the left, right and the top corners to the center.

8 Lift the bottom corner up.

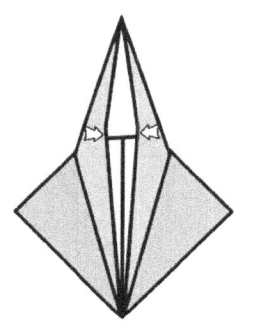

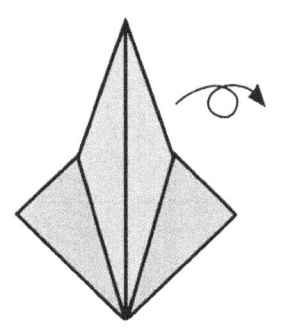

9 Squash fold the left and right sides.

10 Turn the model over.

11 Lift the corner up using the creases.

12 this is called bird base.

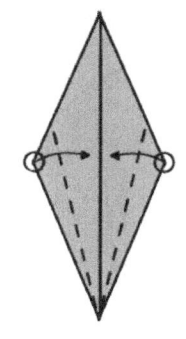

13 Fold to the center.

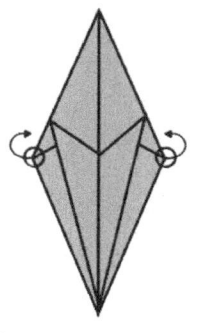

14 Do the same in the other side.

15 Fold inside.

16 Do a pocket fold in the dotted line.

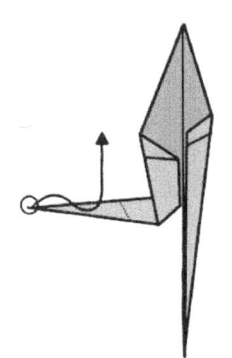

17 Pocket fold up to form the neck.

18 Do a pocket fold.

19 Fold the wings diagonally down and fold the legs.

20 Finished ostrich!

Blowfish

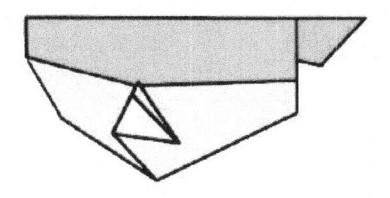

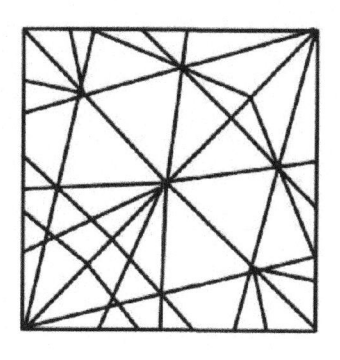

1. Start with the colored side up.

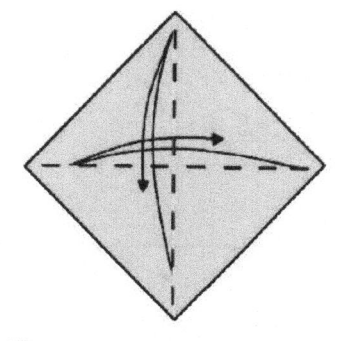

2. Fold and unfold in the dotted lines.

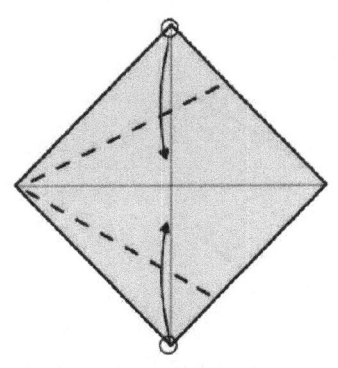

3. Fold to the middle line.

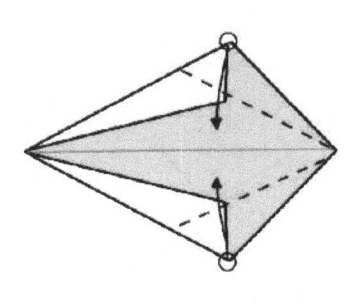

4. Fold in the dotted lines.

235

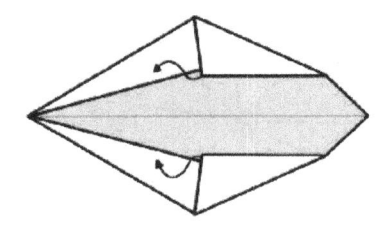

5. Pull out the inner layers.

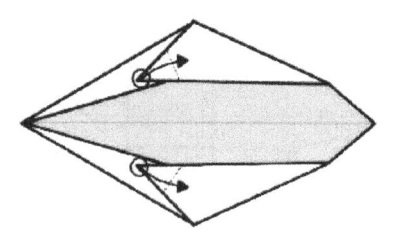

6. Fold to the right.

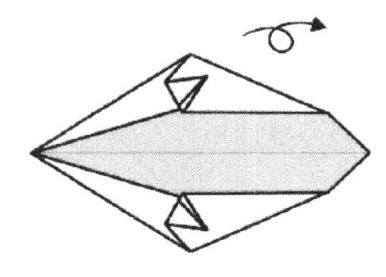

7. Turn over.

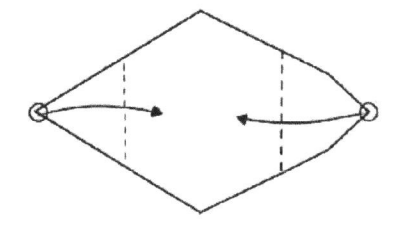

8. Fold in the dotted lines.

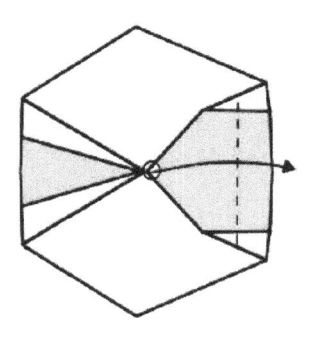

9. Fold to the right.

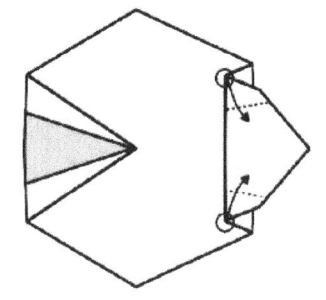

10. Fold inside in the dotted lines.

11 Fold in half.

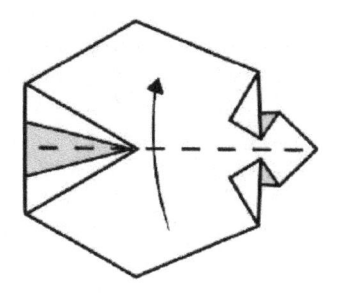

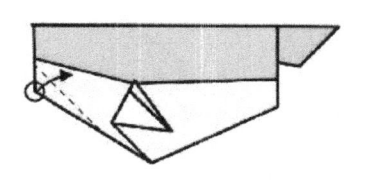

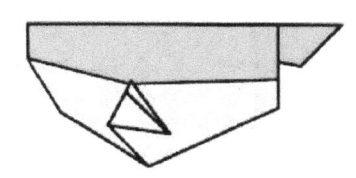

12 Fold inside.

13 Finished blowfish!

Shooting star

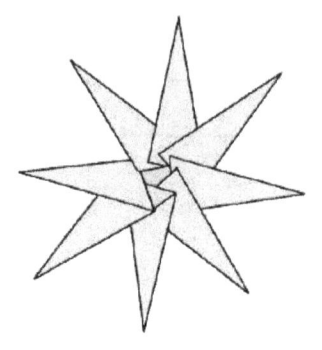

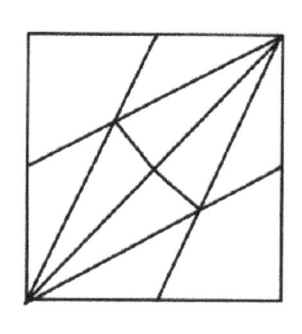

1 Start with the white side up.

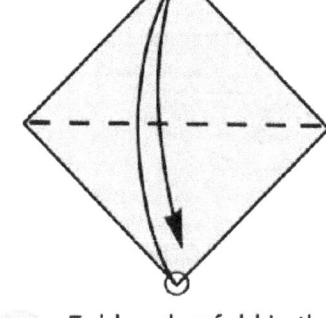

2 Fold and unfold in the half diagonally.

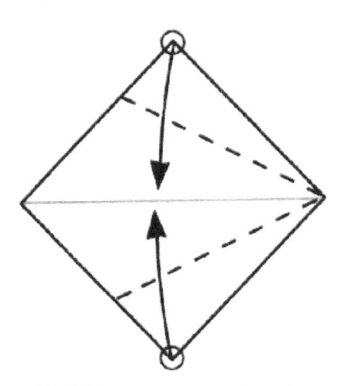

3 Fold the corners to the center.

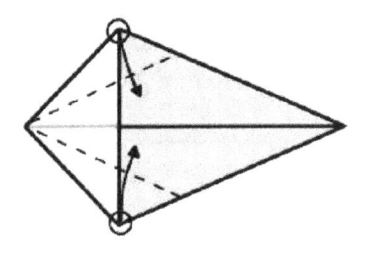

4 Fold the corners to the center.

238

5 Fold back.

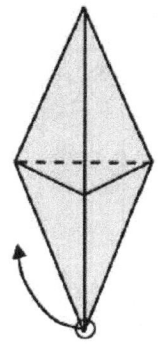

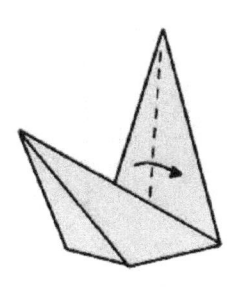

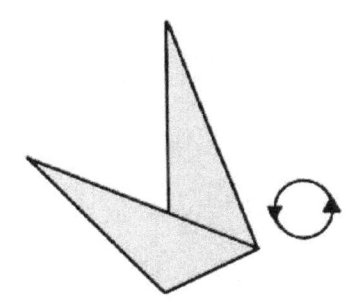

6 Fold in half.

7 Rotate the model.

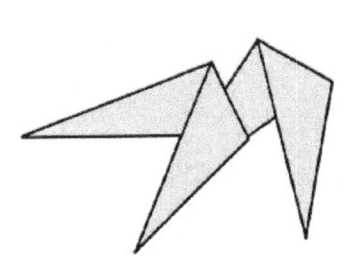

8 Repeat the steps 1-7.

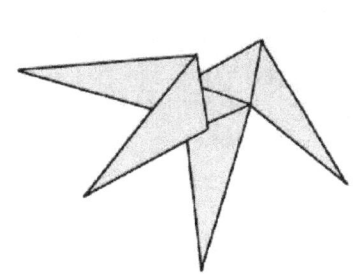

9 Connect the pieces together.

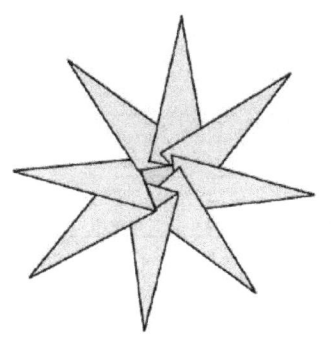

10 Finished shooting star!

239

Platypus

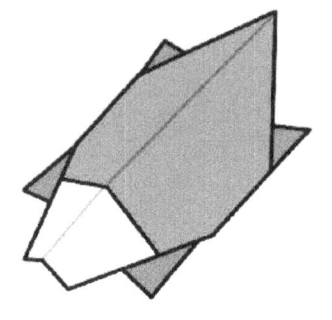

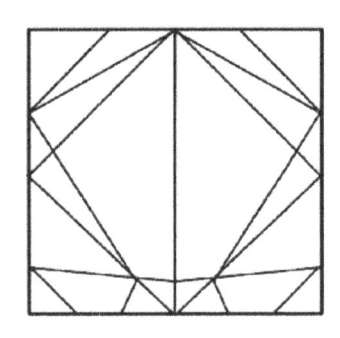

1. Start with the colored side up.

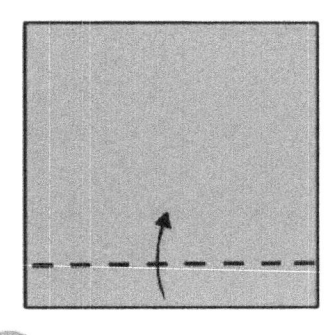

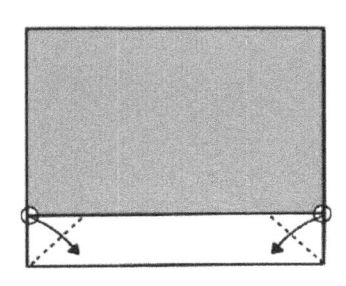

2. Fold up.

3. Fold in the dotted lines.

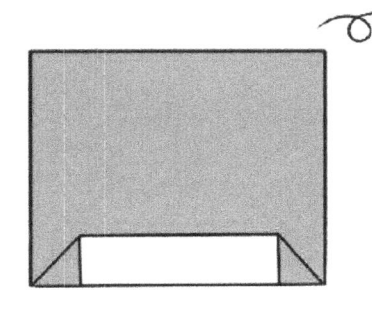

4. Turn over.

240

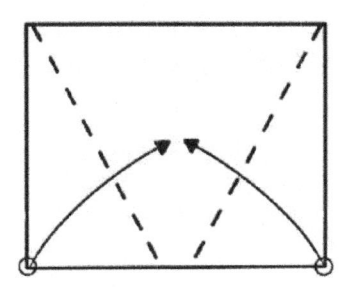

5 Fold in the dotted lines.

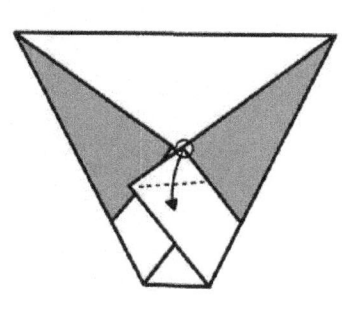

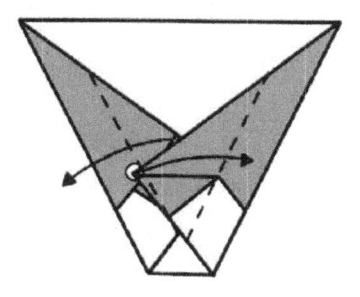

6 Fold down.

7 Fold out in the dotted lines.

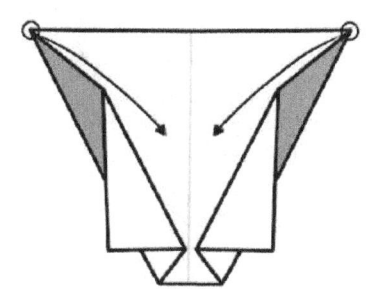

8 Fold to the center.

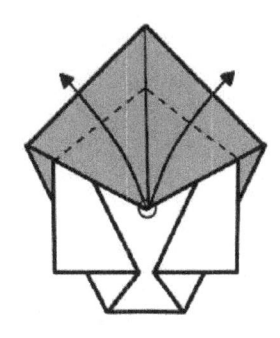

9 Fold to the marked points.

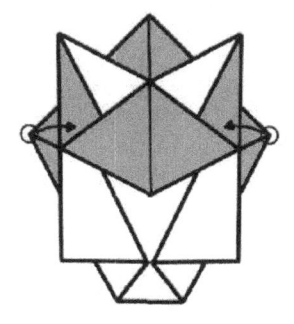

10 Fold inside.

241

11 Turn over.

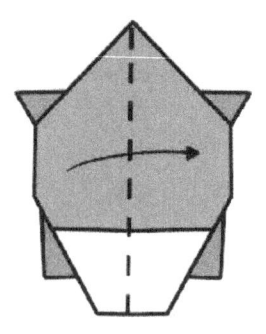

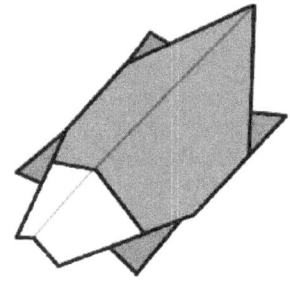

12 Fold in half.

13 Finished platypus!

Windmill

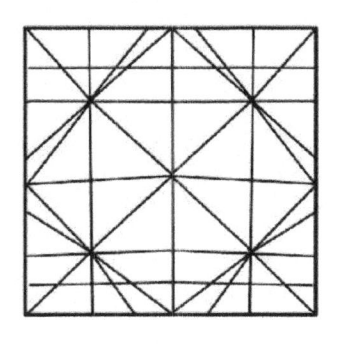

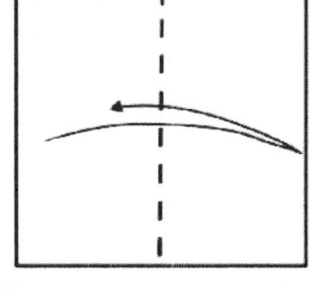

1. Start with the white side up.

2. Fold and unfold in half.

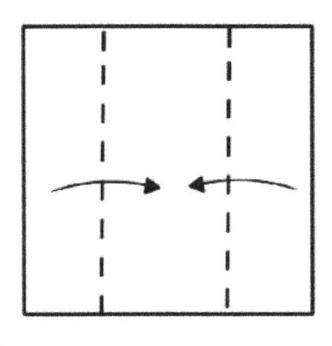

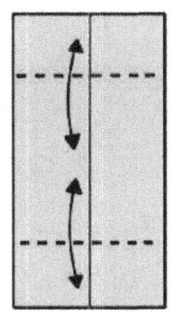

3. Fold to the center.

4. Fold and unfold in the dotted lines.

243

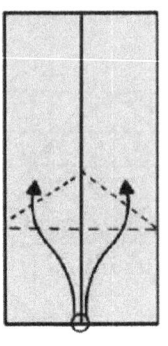

5. Open the layers and fold in the dotted lines.

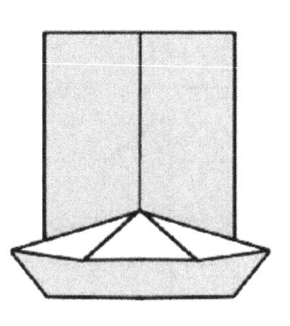

6. Squash fold.

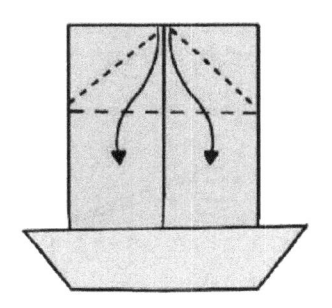

7. Repeat the steps 5 and 6.

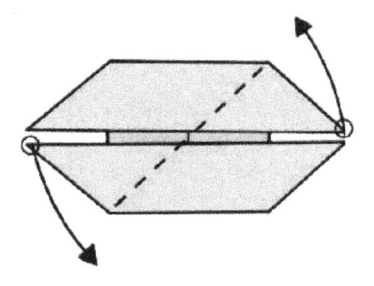

8. Fold to the marked points.

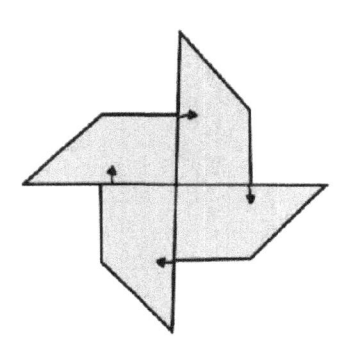

9. Open the pockets.

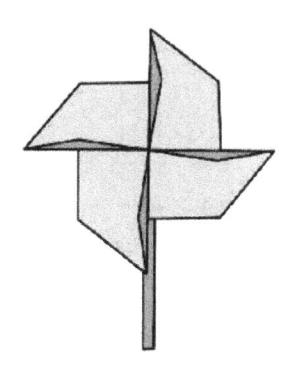

10. Finished windmill!

Pumpkin

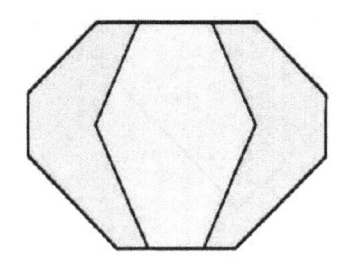

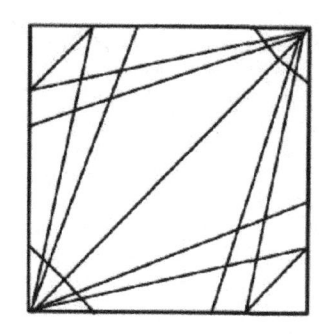

1. Start with the white side up.

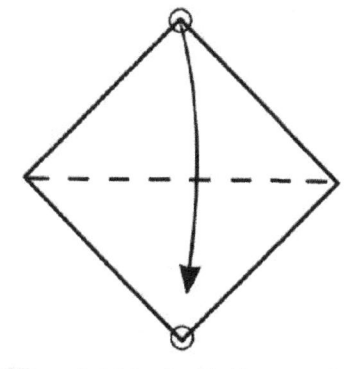

2. Fold in half diagonally.

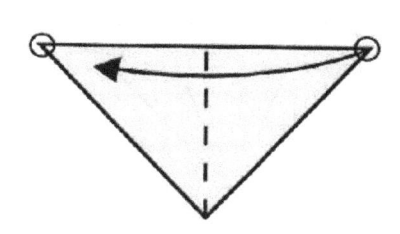

3. Fold the model to the marked point.

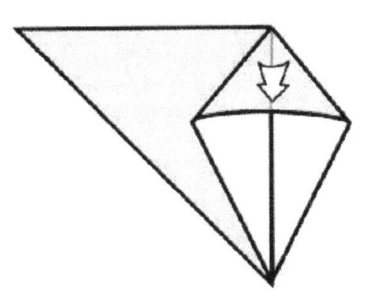

4. Squash fold the front layer.

245

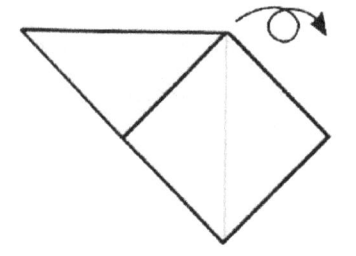

Turn the model over.

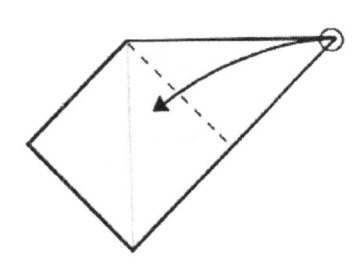

squash fold the other side.

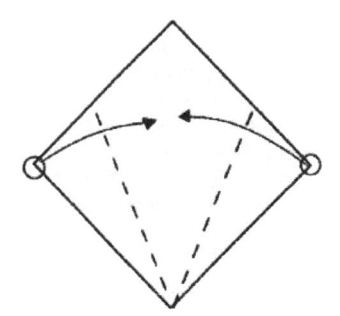

Fold backwards to the center.

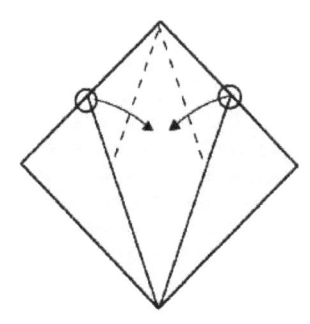

Fold backwards in the dotted lines.

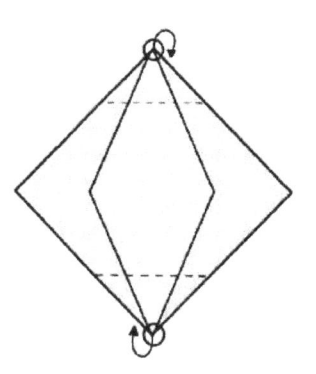

Fold back.

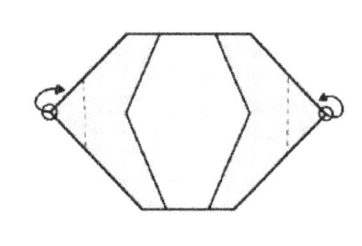

Fold back.

11 Finished pumpkin!

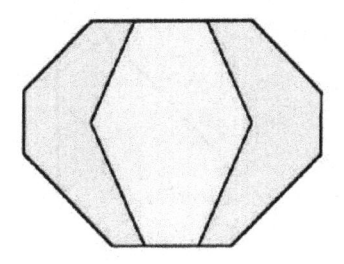

Chick

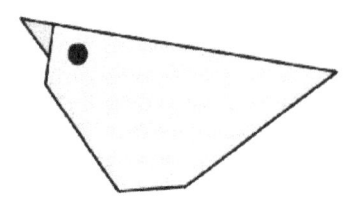

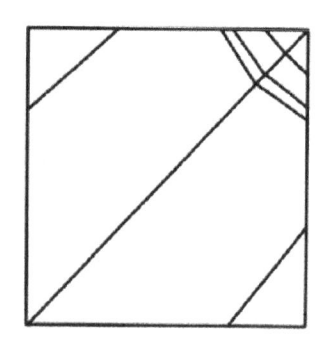

Start with the white side up.

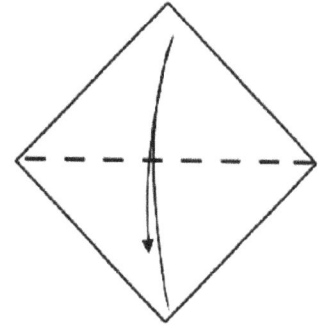

Fold and unfold in the half diagonally.

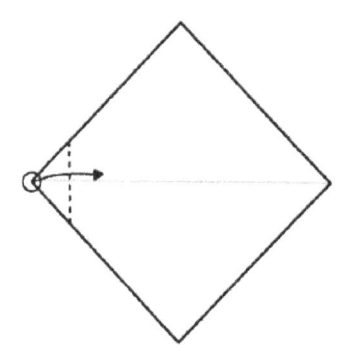

Fold in the dotted line.

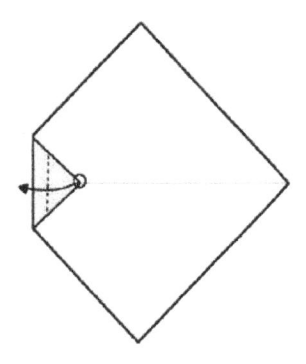

Fold the corner to the left.

248

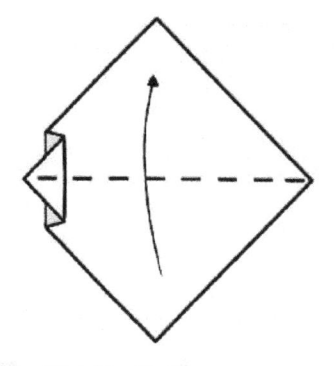

Fold in half.

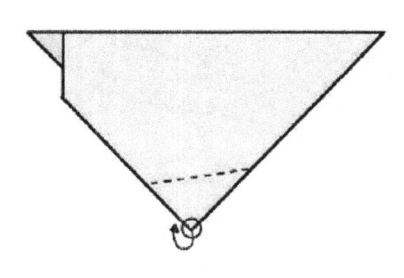

Fold inside in the dotted line.

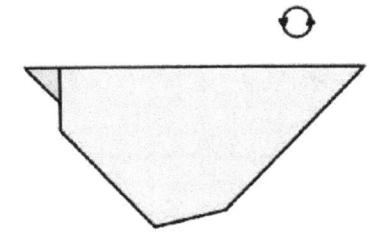

Rotate the model.

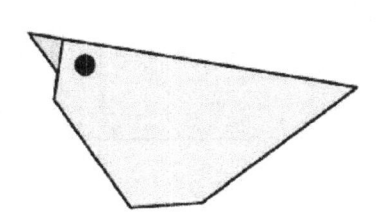

Finished chick.

Plane

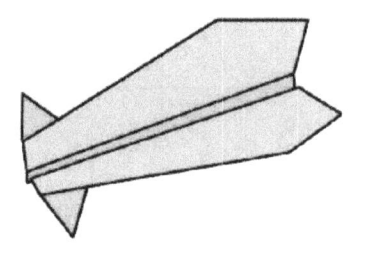

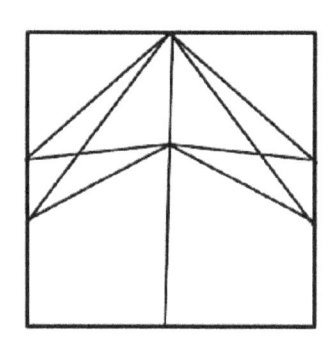

1. Start with the colored side up.
2. Fold in the dotted lines. 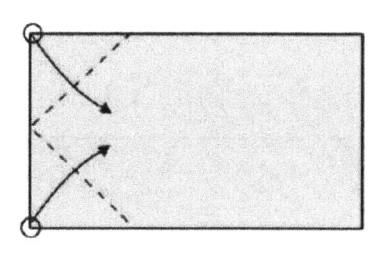
3. Turn over. 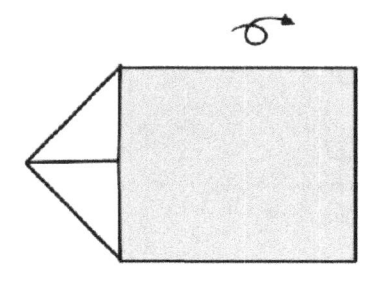
4. Fold to the center line. 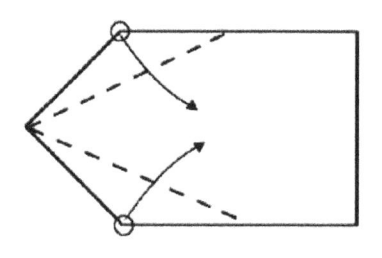

250

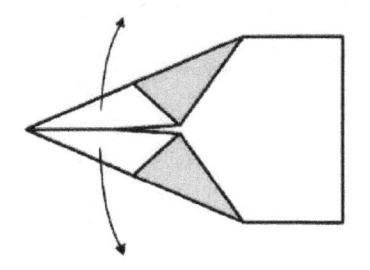

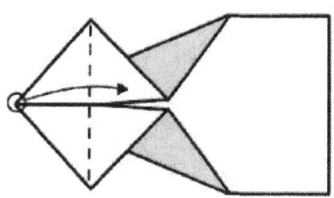

5 Fold back layers to the sides.

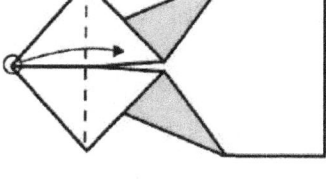

6 Fold to the right in the dotted line.

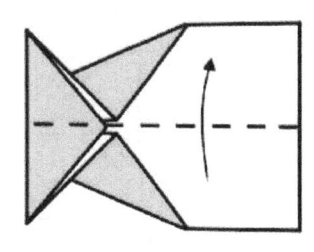

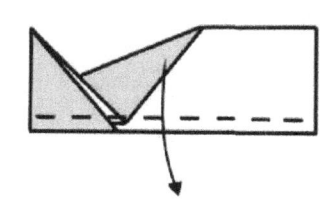

7 Fold in half.

8 Fold in the dotted lines.

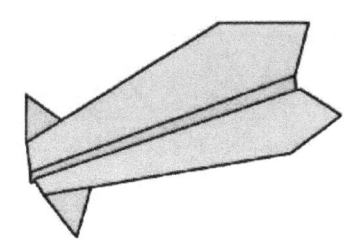

9 Finished plane!

251

Gibbon

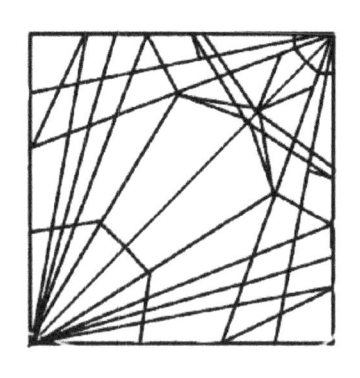

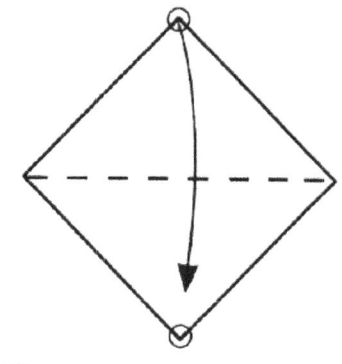

1. Start with the white side up.
2. Fold in the half diagonally.
3. Fold the model to the marked point. 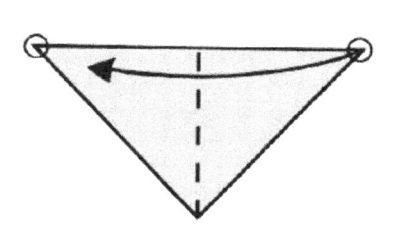 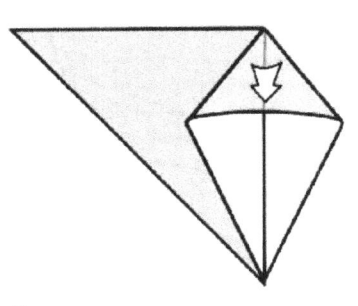
4. Squash fold the front layer.

5 Turn the model over.

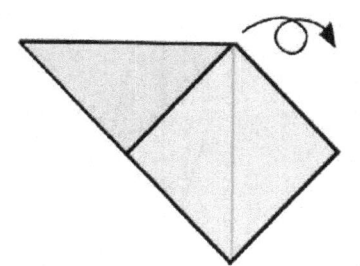

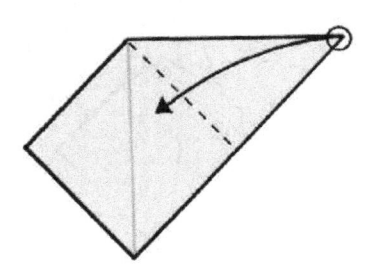

6 squash fold the other side.

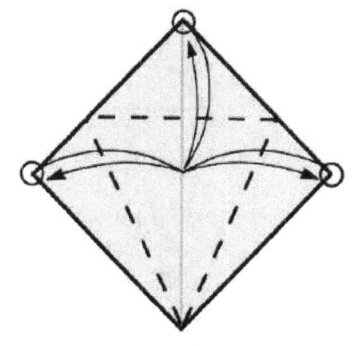

7 Fold and unfold the left, right and the top corners to the center.

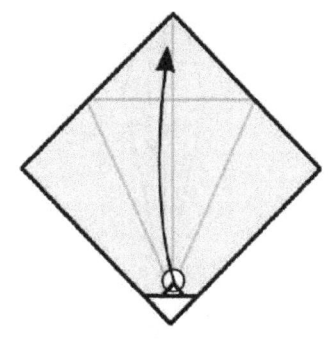

8 Lift the bottom corner up.

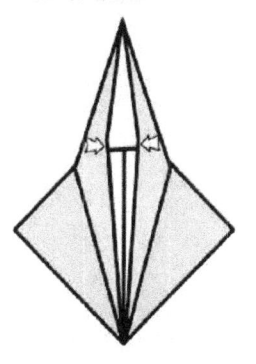

9 Squash fold the left and right sides.

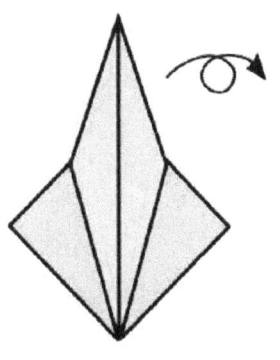

10 Turn the model over.

253

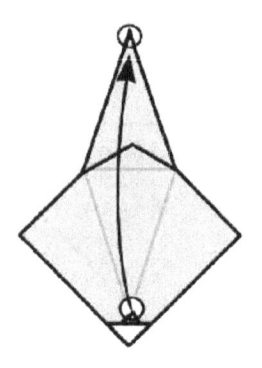

11 Lift the bottom corner up.

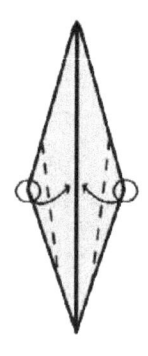

12 Fold the corners to the center.

13 Fold in the dotted line.

14 Fold inside in the dotted line.

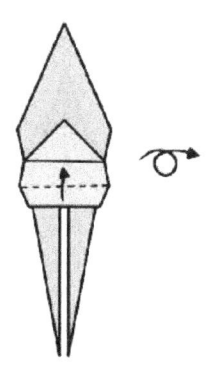

15 Fold back.

16 Step fold to form the ears.

17 Fold the hand down.

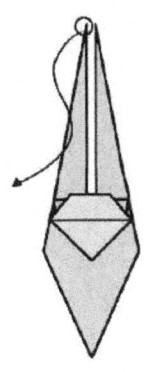

18 Fold to the marked points.

19 Fold the point back.

20 Finished Gibbon!

Merl

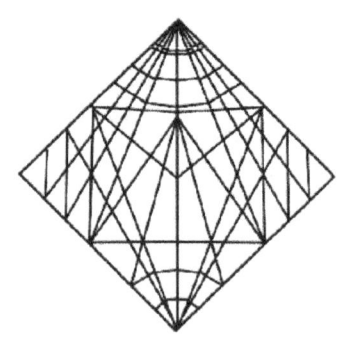

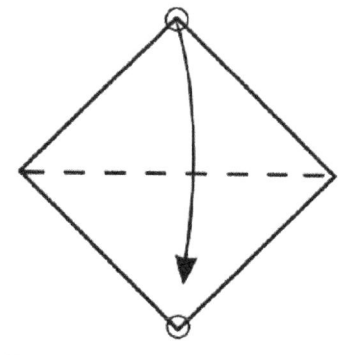

1. Start with the white side up.
2. Fold in half diagonally.
3. Fold the model to the marked point. 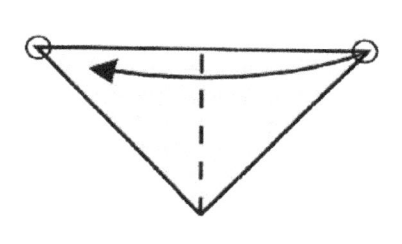 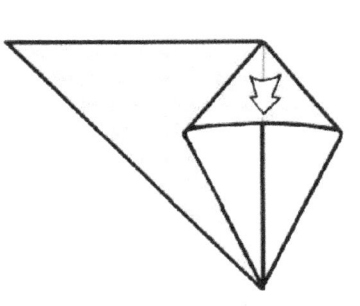
4. Squash fold the front layer.

5. Turn the model over.

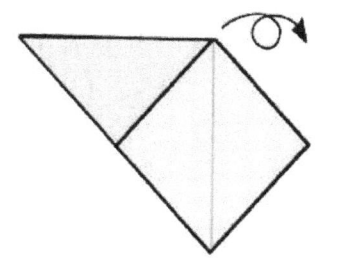

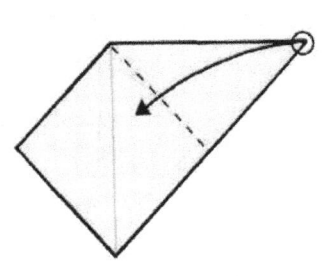

6. Squash fold the other side.

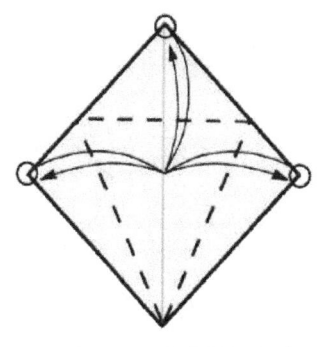

7. Fold and unfold the left, right and the top corners to the center.

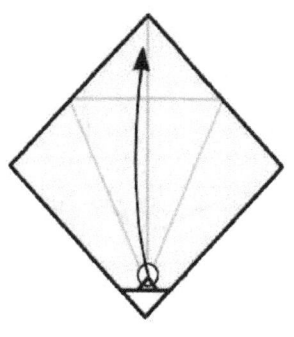

8. Lift the bottom corner up.

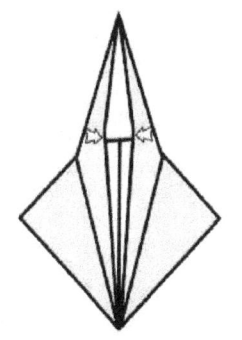

9. Squash fold the left and right sides.

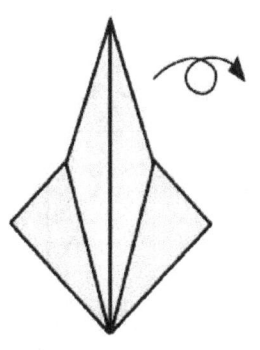

10. Turn the model over.

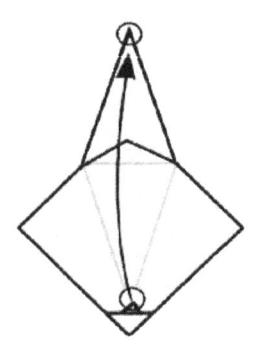

11 Lift the bottom corner up.

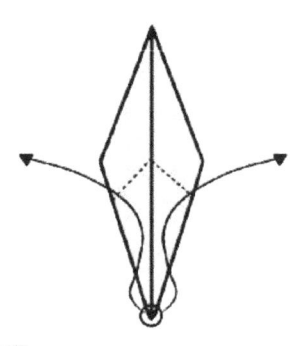

12 Fold to the marked points.

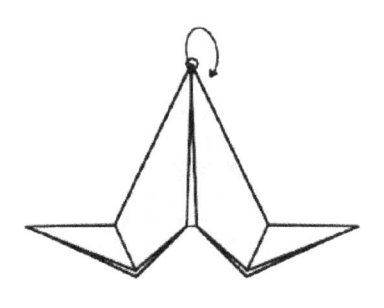

13 Fold Back.

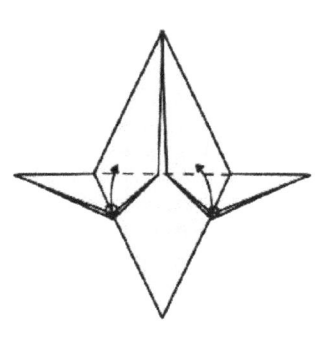

14 Fold up in the dotted lines.

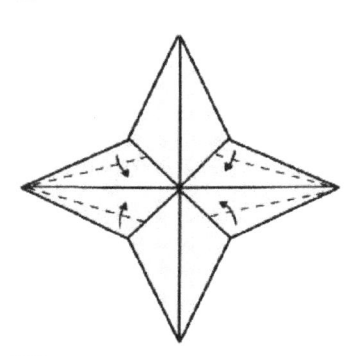

15 Fold inside.

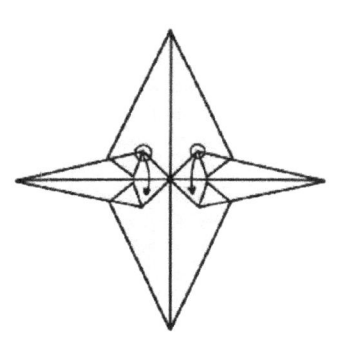

16 Fold down.

17 Fold in half.

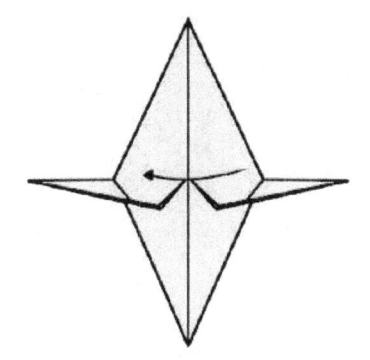

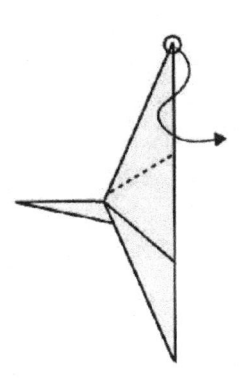

18 Do a pocket fold.

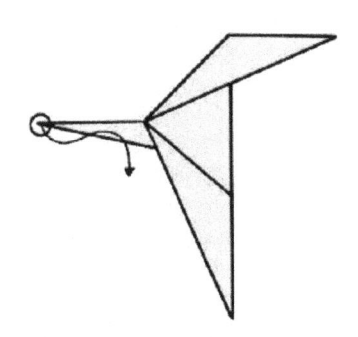

19 Pocket fold down.

20 Pocket fold to the left.

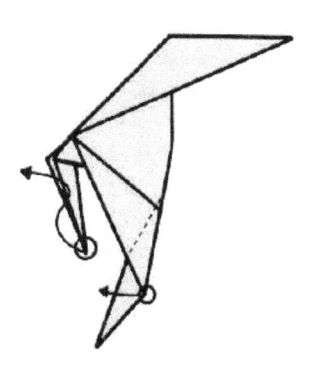

21 Pocket fold the leg and fold the tail to left.

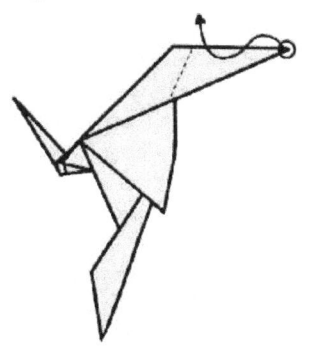

22 Pocket fold to form the head.

23 Do a step fold.

24 Rotate the model.

25 Finished sparrow.

Box

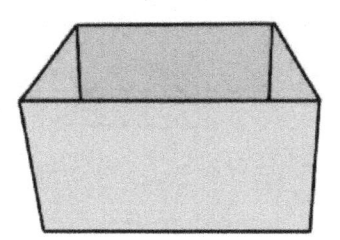

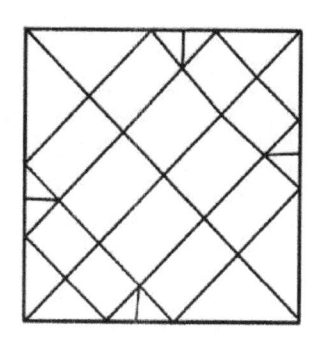

1. Start with the white side up.
2. Fold and unfold in the dotted lines. 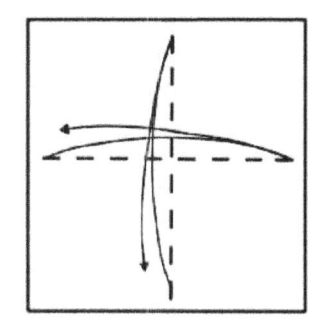
3. Fold to the center. 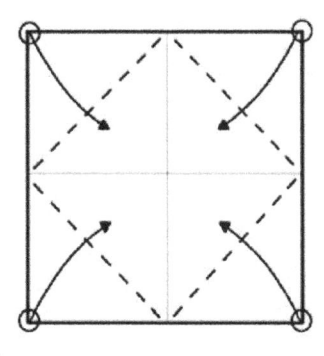
4. Fold and unfold in the dotted lines.

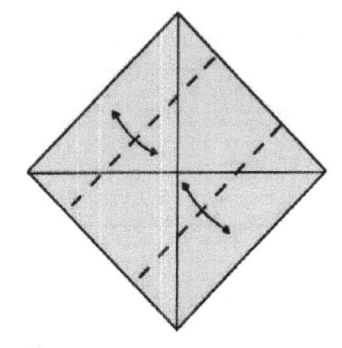

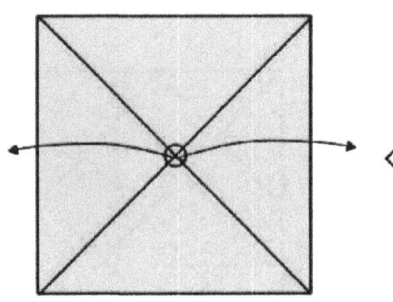

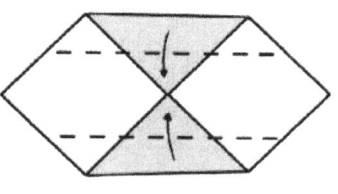

5. Unfold the right and left layers.

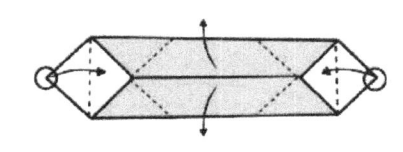

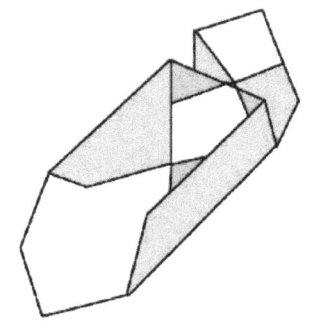

6. Fold inside.

7. Slightly open the folds and fold the right and left corners inside.

8. Flatten the folds.

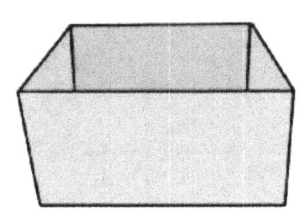

9. Finished box!

Do you need extra help?

Scan this QR code for video tutorials:

Note from the author

Thank you for purchasing this book!
I know you could have picked any number of books to read,
but you picked this book and for that I am extremely grateful.

If you enjoyed this book and found some benefit in reading this,
I'd like to hear from you and hope that you could take some time to
post a review on Amazon.

Your feedback and support will help this author to greatly improve his
writing craft for future projects and make this book even better.

Thank you!

Made in United States
North Haven, CT
19 July 2022